Degrees for Jobs

Employer Expectations of Higher Education

Judith Roizen and Mark Jepson

The Society for Research
into Higher Education
& NFER-NELSON

112432

The publishers acknowledge with thanks a most generous grant from the HIGHER
EDUCATION FOUNDATION towards the production of this book.

Published by SRHE & NFER-NELSON
At the University, Guildford, Surrey GU2 5XH

First published 1985
© The Higher Education Foundation

ISBN 1 85059 005 2
Code 8940 02 1

Typeset and Artwork by FD Graphics, Fleet, Hampshire.
Printed and bound by Billing & Sons Ltd., Worcester.

Contents

Preface

We would like to live in a society which distributes rewards equitably and in which all jobs are filled by the individuals who can do them best. We would also like a society in which the processes of education and recruitment are efficient and economical, and do not waste the resources of the nation or of employing organizations. We may well find that these values conflict; the management of those conflicts is the task of educational and manpower planning. However, educational policy and manpower planning have been bedevilled by the absence of adequate data about the relationship between schooling (at all levels) and work (of all kinds). Aggregate numbers have been juggled to suit the arguments of every camp – the vocationalists and the liberals; the dirigistes and the pluralists; the technologists and the humanists; the expansionists and the élitists. But the numbers record only those factors which can readily be counted, and those are neither the whole nor even the most important part of the story.

This book looks behind the figures in an attempt to uncover what employers really feel about graduates and their recruitment. In the employers' own words we can read, all too vividly, first how complex their requirements are, and then, in the world in which decisions have to be taken every day about who to hire and who not, how these requirements have to be simplified to judgements based on personal experience and intuition. We can see how there is an unavoidable conflict between the employers' need to be able to recruit economically and efficiently in a rapidly changing situation, the educational planners' need to know what kind of skills will be required ten years ahead, and the democrats' need to be assured that everybody has a roughly equal chance of getting the best job.

To plan effectively for the future stock and flow of educated manpower we must understand how employers perceive institutions of higher education, their courses and their graduates. These perceptions have rarely been rigorously investigated though many unsubstantiated assertions are made about them. As we argue here, traditional research on manpower needs has been relatively insensitive to internal stratification within the graduate labour market and has often failed to differentiate between types of courses and types of institutions. Employers often see sharp differences between institutions and courses even where they appear to be at similar levels and have similar names. Here we examine this issue and a number of others from the employers' perspective. We discover how the employers themselves define shortages of highly qualified manpower; we examine their strategies for recruitment, the value they place on work experience, the specific qualities which they seek in graduates.

Our work is intended to be a contribution to current debates on educational policy, to the study of social mobility generally, and to the theory and measurement of the transition from education to work. We hope that the use of the employers' own words as evidence (or 'data') will make their views accessible to parents, teachers and students, and enrich our understanding of the process by which graduates become employees. It is a far more complex, and at times irrational, process than we would like to believe.

This study is one of the main components of a programme of research into the expectations of higher education funded by the Department of Education and Science. As part of the programme, empirical studies were carried out with employers, careers advisers, students, and teaching and administrative staff in institutions of higher education. The programme research team involved a substantial number of people to whom we wish to express our thanks, including in particular John Furlong, John Kirkland, Chris Boys and Sheila Pugh.

In connection with the study reported in this book, we are particularly grateful to Sheila Pugh for her considerable administrative and nurturing efforts in co-ordinating the work of the interviewers and the secretarial staff who between them produced the data. The interviewers who translated the method into the evidence presented here were Lynne Alexander, John Harris, Margaret Harrop, Valerie Heyes, Nick May, Bev Lebatt, Harry Torrence and David Shapiro, and without them there could have been no study.

We want to acknowledge the special contribution of John Harris and Margaret Harrop. Both brought their own style of interviewing to the project based on long experience in different areas of senior management, in the private and public sector respectively. Their searching comments gave us the best test of the utility of this qualitative method in approaching a quantitative research problem. John Harris contributed a personal paper to the series based on his own analysis of the evidence in the light of his past experience and Margaret Harrop wrote a chapter in the original report. At the outset, we were also much helped by Harold and Pamela Silver's bibliographic and historical analysis which provided background against which to design the project. Of course, we are especially grateful to the very many employers who gave us their time and provided the rich evidence presented here. In particular we were helped in organizing their response by Maurice Roberts of the CBI, Peter Reay of Cadbury Schweppes and Keith Bell of Price Waterhouse, who contributed far more of their energy and advice than we could reasonably have expected.

The staff of the Committee of Vice-Chancellors and Principals helped us enormously in tracking down material difficult and time-consuming to locate. Typing long drafts, as well as the interviews themselves, was a difficult and tedious process, and among many who shared that burden we are especially grateful to Madeline Cohen of Textpertise, Sally Harris and Sheila Pugh. Finally, for their advice and support throughout the project we thank Martin Trow and Geoffrey Caston.

Judy Roizen
Mark Jepson

1 Introduction

This book reviews evidence that was gathered in a survey of employers' behaviour, perceptions and judgements in respect of the higher education system in England in the early 1980s. It is part of a larger programme of research that was known as the Expectations of Higher Education Project and worked to a broad brief first outlined by the Department of Education and Science.[1]

Reported here is that part of the research programme that focused on employers' attitudes to and expectations of the higher education system, on the experience employers have of the higher education system in the recruitment of graduates, and on their links with higher education institutions. Rather than attempt to assess the matter directly we have selected for discussion a number of specific, policy-related issues which provide 'windows' onto what employers expect of higher education. Expectation is an analytic concept in this study rather than a descriptive one. The Oxford English Dictionary defines *expectations* as 'the action of mentally looking for something to take place'. But most of the employers who participated in the study are actually involved with the higher education system through the recruitment of graduates and therefore are not quite so passive in their expectations as the dictionary would have them be. Expectations are reflected in both the attitudes and the consequent behaviour of employers. We have given particular attention to investigating unmet expectations, that is, expectations not met under the current system of informed student demand. So we include such issues as actual and perceived shortages of skilled manpower and assessment of the quality of the graduates recruited.

Our study is necessarily set apart from traditional manpower planning studies by its methods, its relative inattention to aggregate statistical data, and its relatively small sample of employers. Perhaps most important is the recognition that, although there is recurring public demand for accountability and forward planning, past attempts to link manpower to perceived national needs and requirements in, for example, the USA and the UK, have often resulted in statistical quagmires and in predictions which have been largely falsified within a few years. The general case for the desirability of manpower planning has been well articulated by Fulton, Gordon and Williams.[2] They see two important reasons for it:

The first is that higher education makes extremely heavy demands on society's resources and it is inefficient and inequitable to treat it simply as a luxury consumption good for a relatively small number of people. The second is that even in countries where higher education provision is based upon social demand, a very high proportion of the students do themselves consider that it has vocational implications for them. Unless appropriate jobs are likely to be available for students their social demand for higher education is itself based on a misapprehension.

However, a recognition of the desirability of manpower planning exists in a climate of opinion where it is no longer considered feasible. Recent reports by the Unit of Manpower Studies[3] and the House of Commons Select Committee[4] both begin by rejecting the feasibility of manpower planning. The UMS study concluded that it would be inappropriate to investigate anything more specific than very broad subject areas when studying the demand for and supply of new graduates. The Select Committee concluded that the proposal to link the output of higher education courses to any kind of manpower policy 'was quite impractical'.

Yet despite this lack of faith in manpower planning there is ample evidence of a concern with the relationship between higher education and employment. For example, the Confederation of British Industry (CBI) reported to the Select Committee that they wanted to see 'some movement in qualitative terms as well as numbers... from arts to certain vocationally orientated social sciences and from pure to applied research.' The Department of Industry wanted 'more emphasis... (to) be placed upon the supply of able engineering and technology graduates.' The Standing Conference of Employers of Graduates (SCOEG) in their evidence felt that there should be 'a stronger emphasis on encouraging course options that enable − or perhaps even compel − a greater mixture of subjects.' There are also frequent examples of individual employers criticizing the way in which higher education prepares young people for the world of work.

There is therefore no shortage of opinion on behalf of employers about their expectations of higher education but, as the Select Committee reported, there has been little consensus. More importantly, opinion and experience have not been recorded systematically nor have they been balanced with the views of other interested parties, such as students and providers.

While the brief for the whole programme of research was that it should inform the debate on 'national economic needs which higher education should aim to satisfy', the present study deals only indirectly with 'economic needs'. Included and analysed here is evidence from employers relating to their own economic requirements or demands and to a lesser extent their perceptions of other related economic needs. Economic 'needs', at a national level, are outside the scope of this study: they are something beyond the aggregate demand of employers and depend for a definition upon the prevalent social and political values given to resource allocation in a context where higher education is only one among many activities in which society wishes to invest.

It is particularly noteworthy that many employers in the climate of economic recession in which the study took place had to change both their expectations and their practice of graduate recruitment. A volatile economic climate precludes long-term forward planning of manpower requirements even within a single employing organization.

The initial planning of the study focused on graduate recruitment as being the most important interface between the higher education system and employing organizations. As Tarsh has argued, differential take-up of graduates into employment is a useful index 'of the value in the job market of different types of graduates.'[5] Traditional research on manpower needs has been relatively insensitive to internal stratification within the graduate labour market and has failed to differentiate between sorts of courses and between types of institutions.

Significant sources of variation in the social and academic characteristics of graduates have gone relatively unheeded in previous inquiries into the structure of the graduate labour market — characteristics such as type of institution attended, mode of study, extent of perceived vocationalism, social class background. It was felt that employers might well have different expectations of graduates they recruit from the major redbrick universities or from Oxbridge as compared with graduates from polytechnics or colleges of higher education, or that employers might consider students who have followed sandwich courses or highly vocationally oriented courses appropriate for certain sorts of career opportunities and inappropriate for others. On this view, the graduate labour market would be stratified in a number of different ways: stratifications which would in part be created by employers' experience of what sort of graduates are and have been most appropriate for the positions they have available, and in part by the overall supply of graduates. Employers would vary in the degree to which they could attract enough of the 'right sort' of graduates for their own needs. Some organizations would be over-subscribed and well able to be highly selective in their recruitment practices. Others might face considerable shortages of particular specialisms and therefore have to make up the deficit by recruiting graduates who were not their first choice candidates or make up the numbers with non-graduates. Thus, employers might have widely different 'expectations' of the higher education system because of their differing experiences of it.

A review by Silver[6] of the literature on expectations of higher education suggested that an important contribution to understanding employer expectations with respect to economic needs lay in describing the views and opinions of employers in the context of some of the contemporary debates on expectations. As an example, 'shortages' (of skilled manpower) is a concept often used in governmental inquiries, in academic papers, and by economists and others. However, little empirical work exists on how shortages are actually described by employers, how employers define shortages in their organization, what they believe accounts for shortages, the extent to which higher education has a role in the process, and how shortages might be overcome by graduate employment. This is also true of concepts like 'numeracy' and 'vocational'.

There are other more speculative questions important to our study: one being the identification of aspects of the social and economic context which produce appeals for institutional change in the interest of economic needs. The educational system is a 'soft' target in times of economic recession, social unrest or international embarrassment. Examples can be found in the speed with which the United States government moved to reform science education after Sputnik or in the introduction of Womens Studies options in higher education in the early seventies. We were interested in examining whether employers ascribed their problems to a failure in educational policy. Did failed expectations of the educational system play a part in explaining economic decline generally, or in any firm in particular?

Recent UK research suggests that educational issues may not be as important to many employers as they appear to be to educationalists and some departments of government. Reid, summarizing research on the employment of school leavers, argues that, although it is widely suggested that 'many employers are dissatisfied with educational and other standards of young recruits... (and), as a result of their dissatisfactions, employers are tending either to raise the level of the formal educational qualifications demanded or... disregard educational qualifications... altogether because of their unreliability as a guide to performance,' the evidence supports neither claim.[7] Most employers were, on the whole, satisfied with their recruits. Dissatisfactions that existed did not stem from educational qualifications, nor did the evidence show that educational qualifications were undervalued in cases where they were appropriate, for example, for technical jobs. Similarly, a recent report on the recruitment of managers to industry suggests that the issue of educational qualifications may be of limited concern to employers.

Educational qualifications did not figure among the twelve 'qualities' that were reported to be those sought in a job applicant. 'High intelligence' ranked tenth after such qualities as 'motivation' and 'good communicator'. (Educational qualifications were, however, routinely requested on application forms.) Additionally, the report shows that internal recruitment is most widely used to fill a vacancy (75% of companies) and that most companies (90%) rely on interviews to fill vacancies. Thus although educational qualifications may play an important part in recruitment to first jobs they do not appear to retain their value over time.[8]

A large number of commissions and committees have reviewed UK manpower needs and associated higher education policy. They have typically focused on single areas in the education and training of skilled manpower: for example, *The Enquiry into the Flow of Candidates into Science and Technology from Higher Education* (the 1968 Dainton Report)[9], *Engineering Our Future: Report of the Committee of Enquiry into the Engineering Profession* (the 1980 Finniston Report)[10] or the *Report of the Committee on Legal Education* (the 1971 Ormrod Report).[11]

One of the main conclusions of an early report, the 1946 Barlow Report,[12] was that, while there existed a sufficient pool of ability to justify an expansion of scientific training, and while the national requirements for scientific manpower could be defined, higher education was not producing enough highly qualified scientific manpower. Consequently, it recommended that:

> The immediate aim should be to double the present output, giving us roughly 5,000 newly qualified scientists per annum at the earliest possible moment. (Para 23)

Ten years later, the Zuckerman Report, *Scientific and Engineering Manpower in Great Britain*,[13] concluded that:

> The statements made by industrialists about their need for scientific manpower should be seen, at least for the next decade, as statements of intention; statements that without scientists and engineers, manufacturers cannot transform the character and also the scale of their operations. At the national level, the conclusion that over the next ten to fifteen years we should aim at an annual figure of graduations in pure and applied science of about 20,000 as compared with 10,000 today, is a statement of a minimum goal which needs to be achieved if the economy is to grow at an acceptable rate. If the universities and technical colleges can achieve more, so much the better. We are reluctant to believe that less could be accepted as a target. (Para 56)

In his role as chairman of the Committee on Scientific Manpower, Zuckerman produced another report, in 1959, which found that the number of scientists employed in Great Britain was about 173,000, representing an increase of just under one-fifth over the 1956 figure. The number of highly qualified scientists graduating each year had increased to 14,600 in 1958 with a projection of 18,500 graduating in 1961.[14]

The committee's biennial report of 1962[15] noted that:

> (We) were able to indicate for the first time that, although a shortage of scientific manpower was likely to continue for a long time in certain disciplines, the total supply of qualified manpower was beginning to approach the total of identifiable demand. (Para 46)

However, while the overall level of supply of highly qualified scientific manpower appeared to be approaching the level of demand for it,

> The relation between supply and demand differs greatly from one discipline to another. This has always been so, but in the conditions of extreme overall shortage which prevailed after the war, the first objective was to get near to an adequate total supply of scientific manpower. As we approach that first objective, analysis by discipline becomes increasingly important. (Para 47)

The 1968 Swann Report[16] and the 1966 Dainton Report[17] both argued for increasing emphasis upon a differentiated understanding of the nature of employer demands and the various types of highly qualified manpower which the economy needed.

The Committee of Enquiry into the Relationship Between University Courses in Chemistry and the Needs of Industry (1970)[18] reported that:

> Whatever the problems in the selection, education and employment of scientific manpower, short supply has not been shown to be one of them. What does emerge is the necessity for both university and industry at least partially to define their aims and needs with respect to chemists. Industry,

without a clear picture of the roles and relationships of its qualified manpower, is hardly in a position to transmit its needs to the universities. Only when the needs of industry are properly formulated will we be in a position to assess the responsiveness of the universities to them. As many of the chemists in this survey reminded us, the practice of chemistry takes place in society and the operations of the university and industry must, in the last resort, be assessed in terms of the needs of society.

Our study takes place in a context of economic recession which inevitably leads various sectors of the polity and economy to assess relative levels of responsibility for elements in the economic decline. Beyond the explicit questions raised in the Department of Education and Science brief is the question whether the higher education system is 'doing its part' to promote economic well-being — at least as perceived by employing organizations. A significant difference in the economic context of this as compared to previous inquiries is that the UK may be approaching a period in which shortages of highly qualified manpower are no longer a leading problem. This is certainly due, in part, to the effects of recession on the ability of employing organizations to afford to hire graduates, but it is also due to the ever increasing stock of highly qualified manpower — a stock which every graduating cohort augments. Additionally, the recession has not only affected employing organizations but has affected the willingness of government to maintain the same level of public expenditure on higher education. This, in turn, has affected perceptions of the value of higher education and access to it. Arguments for higher education are made increasingly in 'extrinsic' terms — the value to the economy in terms of productivity and international competitiveness. This can be contrasted with 'intrinsic' arguments — the value to the individual student. In economists' terms, the question is asked whether money should be invested in 'human capital' which may or may not be 'productive' in the future, and not whether education should be provided to all those 'consumers' capable of benefiting from it.

Recent work by the Unit of Manpower Studies (UMS) argues that 'the stock of economically active highly qualified people (those with first degree and equivalent qualifications) will grow by over one million between 1971 and 1986. Over the same period, there will be slower growth in the types of jobs which the more highly qualified held in 1971, which will mean that more and more of the highly qualified will have to seek work in new areas and in some cases modify their original employment aspirations.' In 1978, prior to the current economic recession, a UMS inquiry[19] argued, on the basis of the then current evidence:

There are now many indications that employers are adjusting to the increased availability of graduate labour. The army, the civil service, the clearing banks and other employers within industry and outside it are now seeking to emphasise the attractiveness to graduates of jobs which they might otherwise not have considered. It is also apparent that graduates have applied, and are continuing to apply, for jobs where employers are not actively seeking them. Increasing numbers are joining the civil service as executive officers and, although very few have as yet joined as clerical officers, this is a trend which could increase. Other employers such as the Coal Board and some insurance companies are receiving, and accepting, applications for an increasing stream of graduates for 'run-of-the-mill' jobs. As yet there is no hard information about possible changes in the content of jobs to align more closely with the abilities of the new incumbents.

The general availability of highly qualified manpower does not, of course, mean that there are not particular shortages, especially of those with technical and scientific training, or that there are not other inefficiencies seen by employers. Concern with shortages still pervades discussion both within higher education and among employers and must be central to this study. However, as we have said, and say again in Chapter 5, we may be at the beginning of a period of assessing manpower needs in which shortages are no longer the apparent or real educational and economic problem they were in the past. Mace[20] argued a decade ago on the subject of shortages of engineers:

> In addition, there is a need for a more precise terminology. 'Demand', 'need' and 'requirements' are used interchangeably, but actually mean very different things. To establish a 'shortage' it is necessary to specify whether it is with respect to some 'price' existing in the market, or with respect to some technological requirement in production. What precisely is meant by the term 'engineer' or 'scientists', or 'economist'? Only when precise meanings are attached to these terms, if this is possible, will it be meaningful to talk about 'shortage'. Too little work of this kind has been undertaken, and what has is usually ignored by those claiming that a 'shortage' of 'engineers' exists.

Employers, as we shall see, rarely describe their manpower problems with this level of precision.

THE PROJECT DESIGN AND METHODS
The areas of inquiry for this study were developed in a series of meetings with the Project Steering Committee, the Department of Education and Science, members of employers' organizations (for example, the CBI and SCOEG), careers advisors and the National Union of Students.

The most critical choice in defining an inquiry of this kind is in deciding on the balance between qualitative and quantitative aspects of the research method. Importantly, it is this which decides the precedents in which the research is to be located if a 'de novo' start is to be avoided. Typically, however, qualitative research concentrates on small and exploratory samples or sets of cases, sometimes investigating a single instance; while highly quantitative research is associated with rigorous survey sampling, usually with large numbers, and tends to look at populations. Qualitative research is often concerned with the development or revision of concepts; quantitative research depends upon some prior agreement about the appropriateness of concepts and behaviour as perceived by the individual respondents. Thus the respondent typically has some measure of control over the research process. 'Data ... are qualitative in the sense of recording actors' meanings,

definitions of the situation, frames of reference, understandings, perceptions....' Clearly, as Martin Bulmer argues, the research design also inevitably
reflects 'The investigator's general sociological orientation; ... the richness of
the existing literature... the nature of the phenomena being studied... not all
phenomena lend themselves to intensive study by means of drawing out
members' own categories.'[21] The present inquiry is neither clearly qualitative
nor quantitative. It calls for a highly qualitative interviewing technique but
also a well defined sample (if not a statistical survey). What does distinguish it
from quantitative research is its *primary aim*, which is not in the first instance
aggregation and generalization, but particularization. What is gathered and
analysed is evidence which shows the range and types of instances of
arguments, analysis and conceptual variation in employers' perceptions,
opinions and behaviour in respect of higher education.

Our early review of employer surveys and our discussions with informants
from employing organizations suggested that quantitative surveys had had
low participation rates. In part these low rates had often been due to requests
for information that firms did not keep. Also, firms did not want to be tied to
what were felt to be the stereotypic response categories of many quantitative
surveys. Further, we wanted to interview senior personnel, and they
expected a full hearing on problems related to their organizations as well as
apparently wanting a measure of control over the form of the interview.
There were practical difficulties in developing a questionnaire suitable for
quantitative analysis. Keeping in mind the diversity of jobs within an
employing organization and differences in type of the organizations
themselves, as well as the differences in perceptions of higher education
from different jobs within an employing organization, the initial closed
ended questionnaire was unmanageable. Testing our early questionnaires
on employers also suggested that questions could not be asked in a set order.
Senior managers and recruiters are themselves skilled interviewers, often
with well articulated views of the relationship between the labour market and
higher education. Tenacity on the part of interviewers in trying to pursue
particular lines of questioning was not sufficient to alter the course of some
of the early interviews.

The task was to represent diverse employer perceptions and arguments
about higher education to several audiences: government, the academic
community, employers and employers' organizations. As part of our
negotiations for interviewer access we agreed with employers and their
representative organizations a method more similar to gathering individual
evidence for a parliamentary committee than to testing a sociological theory.
Some employers were not entirely comfortable, we discovered, about
participating in an academic inquiry. What might be seen as a lack of trust
was overcome by designing a study that met the needs and demands of the
employers and their representatives by including personal interviews rather
than questionnaires; an agreement to rely heavily on analysis of the
employers' own words; and particularly strict guarantees of confidentiality
and anonymity. However, since the study was above all intended to inform
policy debates in higher education the sample of firms had to be rigorous.
An intensive exploratory study of a few firms would not have met the needs
of the funding agency, nor have contributed enough to policy debates.
Further, the contentious nature of some of the question areas, for example

those dealing with employers' perceptions of different types of institutions or of the appropriate balance of natural and social sciences subjects in higher education, meant finding a means of rigorously indexing and retrieving evidence from lengthy interviews.

Because of the elusive nature of much of the material we were after and because we were interested in unpacking the meanings of concepts in the debates on employers' expectations of higher education, we chose a method which depends on 'oblique' questioning and informed probing and inference. What we wanted were the words and arguments that employers and representatives of employing organizations use to describe higher education, their experience and expectations of it. This reliance on words is cumbersome and – at times – somewhat inarticulate. However, it gave us access to types of information which are elusive in other forms of inquiry. As the evidence will show, answers to particular questions or discussions of particular issues do not usually yield a simple, one-dimensional response. What is offered is, in many cases, tentative, bound into a particular economic, social, and organizational context. Moreover, the data do not easily yield to a form of analysis such as 'employers want better careers advice' or '80% of employers want x and 30% want y'. The evidence collected is made up of highly complex pieces of analysis by the employers, who often include a number of arguments, interspersed with their own anecdotes and analytic material. We often analyse *their analyses* of complex questions.

As we have argued above, a good deal of the research and reporting on the stock and flow of highly educated manpower has failed to explain empirically the *concepts* which are essential to the analyses given: for example, concepts such as 'shortages' or even 'a degree'. This study focuses on the meaning to employers of some of these concepts, both by a close empirical investigation of their *uses* in arguments and by direct questions. (In some cases we were also interested in the absence of use of a concept: for example, of 'vocational').

The main focus of this study is not theoretical. We are not in the first instance aiming to test hypotheses against the evidence. Rather we are trying to develop the meaning and empirical content of concepts useful to a number of theoretical perspectives. As Bulmer has argued: 'Concepts in themselves are not theories. They are categories for the organization of ideas and observations. In order to form an explanatory theory, concepts must be interrelated. But concepts do act as a means of storing observations of phenomena which may at a future time be used in theory.... Concepts then mediate between theory and data. They form an essential bridge, but one which is difficult to construct and maintain.'[22] We begin with concepts used in previous inquiries and seek to unpack their different meanings and uses. This does not mean that we have proceeded without an eye on many theoretical questions. For example, analysis of the graduate labour market over the past decade has relied on several theories – one, in particular, looks at higher education as a screening or filtering process, while another looks at education as essential to the development of human capital. Both seek to explain the positive correlation between educational achievement and earnings. Both theories depend, in part, on concepts about which very little is known empirically, for example, shortages, and the value of a degree.

Alternatively, social stratification theory and its correlative empirical modelling depends, in part, on a clear articulation of the transition from school to higher education and higher education to work. Only relatively recently have models of this process begun to account for status differentials among higher education institutions. In respect of these theories, little is known empirically about employers' perceptions of institutions and courses and their differential recruitment of graduates as a result of differences in perception.

Most research on the stock and flow of educational manpower into employment is firmly grounded in a quantitative tradition of research and reporting. Therefore, we have had to look to areas of inquiry which have a more well developed qualitative tradition — such as research on schools. We relied in large part on research by the late Lawrence Stenhouse and colleagues at the University of East Anglia. We concentrated on a study of cases — each employing organization making up a single case.

For each organization a 'case record' was developed. From such records the individual pieces of evidence were selected for presentation. The case record created by the interviewers included: transcripts or partial transcripts of interviews; annual reports; published descriptions of the firm; and newspaper articles covering the period of the research. In addition, each interview included contextual descriptive material on the employing organization, on the mode of recruiting graduates, on the effects of the economic recession on the firm, etc. Although not all of this material is included in the analysis presented, it formed the analytic framework used to select and interpret the evidence. One important advantage of a study of cases is that the richness of the material facilitates multiple interpretations by allowing the reader to use his own experiences to evaluate the data. The research serves multiple audiences.

Writing for multiple audiences — employers, educators, careers advisors, students and parents — inevitably affects research design. As Stenhouse argues,[23] this particular research methodology tries to capture 'the texture of reality which makes judgement possible for an audience.' The methods employed here make the same attempt. Both involve a conception of research which moves away from research *on* (for example, teachers and employers) to research *with* (teachers and employers).

Contrasting quantitative, typically survey, research with the illuminative tradition, Stenhouse argues:

> We may sum up the situation by saying that work in the statistical paradigm offers to do better than professional judgement in judging what best to do, and that in overriding professional judgement it fails to strengthen it. It appeals to research judgement: if the design and conduct of my research is correct, then my results must be correct. If you think they are wrong, then fault the design and conduct *of the research*....
>
> The important point about the illuminative tradition is that it broke away from this and aimed to appeal to, and hence to strengthen, professional judgement.... In particular, there is a need to capture in the presentation of the research the texture of reality which makes judgement possible for an audience.

We have further borrowed from this tradition the crucial 'distinction' between 'data' and 'evidence':[24]

> The alternative style of interviewing which is my concern here has as its
> objective to elicit, not data, but evidence. When we interview for data, we
> attempt to gather information whose reliability and status is defined by
> the process of data gathering. When we interview for evidence our aim is
> to gather information whose reliability and status is left problematic and
> has to be established by critical comparison and scrutiny. Meaning is
> ascribed to information by critical interpretation: its reliability or status is
> assessed by critical verification. The process of critical verification and
> interpretation is one familiar to the historian.
>   The objective of the interviewer who is gathering evidence must be to
> evoke extensive and naturally expressed information because rich texture
> and contextualization is necessary if an adequate critique is to be
> mounted. Moreover, vivid natural discourse may be needed to support
> communication with the reader to whom the researcher appeals for
> verification of his own judgements by presenting evidence. The reportage
> of research in this tradition is not a presentation of results, but of
> interpretation accessible to reflection or discussion.'

Throughout this study the term 'evidence' is used to suggest the problematic
status of transcription from interviews. Each transcription is a single opinion
or perception which gains weight from its consistency with other pieces of
evidence or gains utility in allowing the analyst to further the empirical
differentiation of key concepts.

The problem is reducibility and choice. With respect to reducibility it is a
matter of retaining the life and texture of the original source. The
transcripts often are ambiguous on a problem area, sometimes inconsistent,
sometimes inarticulate. Almost always an argument is multi-dimensional.
Over-refinement of the evidence presents an artificial clarity of view. As
Wild argues:[25]

> What we must avoid is the error of tidying. The enemy of understanding
> is the tendency of many of us to equate rigour with orderliness.

As to choice, the same principles have not applied in all chapters or within a
single chapter. On the issue of employer perceptions of public sector
institutions, the excerpts from the interviews are quite comprehensive. On
the other hand, in analysing the dimensions of shortages, single examples
have been used without regard to frequency.

The sample of employing organizations is large for qualitative research,
and modest by the standards of most manpower surveys. One hundred and
thirty-nine organizations participated. These include the civil service, one of
the armed forces, several local authorities, nationalized industries, and a
large number of the largest public sector employers. The sample is rigorous,
although not a statistical survey. Organizations were chosen, from available
lists, with regard to size, economic sector, and location. The sample is
described in Chapter 2 and Appendix A. The problem set used in the
interviews is included in Appendix B. The full description of research
methodology is found in the original report.

A GUIDE TO THE READER

In preparing the study we have had to condense many thousands of pages of interview transcript and evidence. Our condensation of the material leaves the reader with the opportunity to analyse the excerpted evidence for himself. The reader needs to be prepared for the volume of words, which, it must be kept in mind, are the 'evidence', as tables and statistics might be in reports of another kind. Our purpose is not to argue what we 'thought' employers said but to organize and present for review what they did indeed say. Our analysis of question areas is for the most part presented separately from the quoted material and the last chapter is entirely for analysis of the evidence and some of its policy implications. But we invite readers to study the employers' own words, relate them to their experience, and draw their own conclusions.

The descriptions of firms (for example, 'large manufacturing firm which recruits few graduates') are given to put excerpts in context. It is important that the reader keep in mind that the material quoted was selected for a variety of reasons – because it was well articulated, or representative, or was the only expression of an important dimension of a problem. Therefore it would be inappropriate to link statements causally. For example, it would be wrong to conclude from the interviews that firms believe that the answer to shortages of qualified engineers is to institute better careers advice simply because some firms did speak of the two problems in the same breath. Evidence which was not included here may well have combined these dimensions in a different way. In an effort to avoid such misapprehensions we have included a number of full and lengthy statements in response to some questions. It is important to see what variety of relations between different dimensions employers see for themselves, and not to attribute to them a spurious simplicity.

For ease of writing we use a number of terms interchangeably to denote employing organizations; these include 'employer', 'firm' and 'employer's representative'. The original report,[26] on which this work is based, includes a full discussion of the research methods (of which only the section on the sample of employers is reproduced here), separate chapters on accounting and numeracy, and a great deal more of the evidence itself.

The chapters in this volume are relatively self-contained, presenting evidence on particular problem areas. Chapter 2 looks at employer strategies for graduate recruitment; Chapter 3 begins the discussion of the value of a degree for employers – and concentrates on the qualities employers associate with hiring a graduate; Chapter 4 looks at another aspect of how degrees are valued – by their institution of origin; Chapter 5 is devoted to the evidence on shortages; Chapter 6 explores employers' general expectations of the higher education system; Chapter 7 is a review and analysis.

2 Recruitment

A principal theme of the debate surrounding the relationship between higher education and employment lies in the varying 'demands', 'needs' and 'wants' expressed by employers, and in the various ways in which these are translated by higher education institutions. In the course of this investigation, we discovered how recruitment policies and selection criteria are the organizational expressions of the views taken by employers of higher education. Of the many links between higher education institutions and employing organizations, the most sustained is the actual recruitment exercise. Decisions taken in recruitment reflect employer expectations and employer values about higher education more clearly than anything else.

While a great deal is known about the transition from school to work, surprisingly little is known about the micro-processes of graduate recruitment: by which we mean the organization of recruitment within firms; the elements in the process of recruitment (eg number of interviews an applicant is given; basic personal information collected); the level within the firm and the training of those who screen applicants for jobs. In this chapter we look at four aspects of graduate recruitment : first, its organization; second, the use of sponsorship and sandwich places, both of which are important recruitment strategies; third, its procedures; and fourth, the effects upon it of economic recession.

The general debate about the relationship between higher education and employment, and the more specific one about the movement of graduates out of higher education into employment need to be grounded in an acquaintance with some of the characteristics of British commerce and industry and with those of the higher education system.

As estimated in the 1976 census of employment there are over one million employing units in the UK.[1] These range in size from those employing one member of staff to those employing over 5,000, with the majority employing under ten. Of the nearly twenty-two million employees included in the census, nearly ten million were in organizations with less than 200 staff. There is, of course, considerable variation in size of organization within and between economic sectors.[2] For example, in the oil, chemical and allied industries group about 40% of employees are in organizations with more than 1,000 staff and only 2% in organizations with less than ten, while in banking and insurance about 35% of employees work in organizations with less than twenty-five staff, and 8% in organizations with over 1,000.

Only a relatively small proportion of these units employ a substantial number of men and women with post-secondary qualifications. Employing organizations vary substantially in the number of graduates they recruit each year and the proportion of graduates in their work force. Few firms know the number and proportions of graduates they employ. Employing organizations which recruit graduates range in size from the civil service to individual firms with only a handful of staff. They cover a wide range of industries, services and commercial interests in both the public and private sectors. There is no common list of them. Two important contributory lists are the membership of the Confederation of British Industry (CBI) and of the Standing Conference of Employers of Graduates (SCOEG). Of the first, a list of some 5,000 firms, an unknown proportion recruit graduates; the second includes 400 of the largest graduate recruiters, but is self-selected from an unknown base number of such firms. The process of graduate recruitment often varies according to the structure of the firm. Some leave graduate recruitment in the hands of the central office; others have the central office recruiting a handful of the firm's graduates, but diverse subsidiaries recruiting the majority.

Appendix A shows how the sample of firms was drawn. Included in our early selection were some holding companies, some multinational corporations, and some companies which had separate senior recruiters in their various divisions. Interviews were obtained with recruiting units which had been defined as such by a representative of each employing organization : in some cases we selected independent subsidiaries, in some, separate divisions of one organization. As we shall see, many organizations which are taken to be single enterprises for some formal purposes may operate any number of separate and discrete recruitment drives. Conversely, a single recruitment exercise may cover a number of otherwise separate employing organizations. For the purposes of this study, we have in most cases used the character of recruitment to define the organization. The number of interviews conducted in each one varied and was negotiated as a function of the individual recruitment structure. Some very large corporations with decentralized recruitment had a single personnel director who spoke for the firm, while some smaller firms felt that three or four interviews were nevertheless needed to cover all their relationships with higher education. In almost all cases the senior recruiter for a firm was also one of the two or three individuals which an organization authorized to speak for it on issues related to higher education.

We assumed that employing organizations who differed in their relationship to the graduate labour market would also differ in their experiences and expectations of the higher education system. The sample was therefore stratified according to criteria based on the recruitment of graduates. By spreading the interviews across a fairly large number of organizations which varied in relationship to the graduate labour market, we felt we would capture a significant (although statistically unknown) part of the variation in 'expectations' if it existed in the larger population.

This sample selection process, as can be seen from Appendix A, gave us eighty organizations regularly recruiting graduates, fifteen small firms, twelve large organizations not regularly recruiting graduates, sixteen organizations specially selected from regions away from the south-east of

England, ten 'arts' employers, and six small professional practices. This was close to our target of 150, since it included 'multiples' such as the civil service. The employing organizations which were finally selected make up a substantial proportion of the larger regular recruiters of graduates.

According to information supplied by the SCOEG, the maximum number of graduates recruited by any individual employing organization in its last annual round of recruitment was just over 320. Organizations included in the present study ranged from those recruiting no graduates to those recruiting over 300. As well as in size, there was considerable variation in current recruitment experience. We included employers who had discontinued graduate recruitment the previous year, employers who had increased it, and those who had held it constant. Also included were some who had just entered the market for the recruitment of graduates, and some who had decided to concentrate their recruitment efforts on graduates with some work experience.

Unfortunately for our purposes, the term 'graduate' does not have a common meaning across employing organizations. That used by the Universities Statistical Record in the 'First Destination' statistics,[3] denotes all first degree students graduating in a particular cohort. Employers, however, use many other definitions. Some use 'graduate' to mean any person with a Bachelors or postgraduate degree; others to mean only those with university degrees. And, indeed, some have no clear conception at all of what a 'graduate' is.

As the evidence below will show, employers are no more precise about the types of jobs for which graduates are recruited. Any given job may be defined by its function, location in the firm, training requirements, salary level, or career trajectory. Differences in future prospects will often be reflected in the effort spent on recruitment. Often employers are most concerned with their recruitment exercise for 'top management' or accelerated management. This is not always clear from the name of the job. Descriptions of first job assignments, some of which refer to the same job function, include:

production planning	management consultancy
marketing	purchasing
manufacturing	research
administration	personnel
engineering	retail management
sales	consultants
management services	overseas division
finance	design
site management	

Alternatively, the job name might be in terms of a specific role which the graduate recruit will take on. For example:

accountancy trainee	analysis officer
trainee administrator	process engineer
development engineer	social worker
systems programme	data processor
actuarial worker	architectural assistant

Both types of description are vague. They reveal little about the level of the appointment within the organization, or its long-term prospects, or what the job actually entails. The difficulties of classifying the jobs for which graduates are recruited are illustrated in the following extracts.

A footwear manufacturer and retailer recruiting a large number of graduates each year:

> I'm going to be talking about what we call our top management recruitment programme... as opposed to what you might call 'the first bounce' recruitment of graduates... totalling three dozen graduates each year.... The programme I'm talking about sets out to recruit around 12 top quality graduates each year.

A spokesman for a manufacturing and retailing organization which is a large recruiter of graduates:

> ... What we call the fast track opportunity and we're expecting people coming in on this track ... (to be exposed) ... much more rapidly to the more senior management almost from the start. We see quick promotion and development into management status, and take up to four per year on that basis....

The chief recruiter for a small publishing firm recruiting small numbers of graduates each year:

> (There)... tend to be a lot of graduates in publishing right down to the lowest level, there are few ways in which graduates can get into publishing and they take whatever jobs are going. Secretaries here are graduates and this is the way in which they get a 'foot in the door' and progress in the firm, applying for other jobs.

A spokesman for a large chain of food retailers which is a very large recruiter of graduates:

> This year we'll probably recruit about 135.... The bulk of (those) we recruit − about 100 ... are on an accelerated retail management training scheme which lasts approximately six months.

However, a recruiter for a small public sector organization made the case that he had:

> absolutely no figures.... It's just not something we are interested in as a qualification. (Q: Have you recruited any graduates this year?) Not graduates as such, I wouldn't really know, we don't really sift people like that.... We employ people for what they are in an organization like this, the fact that someone's a graduate doesn't help them at all, they would start at the same point as anyone else coming here with no experience.

A senior partner in a medium-sized firm of solicitors which is a medium-sized recruiter of graduates took on:

26 or 27 (each year) ... but we also took on a few assistant solicitors in 1981 who may or may not have been graduates; once a solicitor we don't really care much if they were graduates.

What do employers expect when they recruit a 'graduate'? This varied from expecting the graduate to progress quickly through the corporate structure, to expecting him or her to work competently at a fairly low level job (for example as a secretary). The definition of a graduate's new job may therefore be in terms of the substantive nature of the post, and/or the expectations which the employer has of an individual graduate with respect to promotion prospects. Referring back to two of the examples quoted above, one organization which recruited both 'fast track' and 'normal' graduates put both types in general trainee management positions within their manufacturing, retail or marketing functions, while another had different expectations of the two types, which were reflected in the different names for the posts to be held : 'senior management trainee' and 'general management' respectively.

Mapping the movement of graduates into jobs, while seemingly straight-forward, is not so in practice. There are over 80,000 new graduates each year from higher education institutions in the UK. They will have followed over 160 different types of course in a wide variety of combinations of subject area and modes of delivery. They will move into thousands of jobs within and outside the UK. In this chapter and the two which follow we outline some of the conceptual issues useful in analysing their movement into jobs, mindful that our sample of employing organizations and graduate recruits makes up a small proportion of all relationships between employers and graduates.

ORGANIZATIONAL STRATEGIES FOR GRADUATE RECRUITMENT

Employers adopt a wide variety of strategies for graduate recruitment in order to meet their requirements. We outline three of them here; each of which could be subdivided and further analysed to take account of the economic, personnel and other characteristics of the organization. Although there are some recurrent regularities (eg smaller firms tend to have centralized recruitment), we did not find any one simple set of relationships between the type of recruitment strategy and the structure of the firm, its economic sector, the size of firm or its recruitment intake.

Perhaps the simplest recruitment pattern occurs in those organizations which conduct *centralized recruitment*.

A small electronics firm which has recruited graduates only sporadically in the past:

The firm is divided into two different sections, sales and circuit boards. The recruitment of graduates is undertaken by the managing director.

A computer equipment manufacturer which is a small recruiter of graduates:

I would personally interview anybody with a job in mind. In fact it's got to the point where the Labour Act (the Employment Protection Act) makes it so difficult to get rid of these monsters once you've got them, that I won't allow anyone in the company to hire anybody without me seeing them.... Even the cleaning lady now, I want to see her face.

A small firm of accountants which is a medium-sized recruiter of graduates:

One of the partners is in charge of that (the recruitment of graduates) ... bears the brunt of the administration, who we see and interview, and there's a panel of five other partners who sit with him.... We make up our minds and decide who we will take.

A merchant bank which is a medium-sized recruiter of graduates operates:

... a centralized system of recruitment, as all graduates will work at one particular location. All 'second interview' applicants are interviewed there, with the directors of the company taking the final decision.

A firm of solicitors recruiting small numbers of graduates annually has:

... a committee of three partners to organize most graduate recruitment, sift applications, select candidates for interviews, conduct the interviews and make job offers.

The representative for a holding company recruiting small numbers of graduates each year described his organization's recruitment policy:

(I) ... and a training officer, which covers school-leaver intake and graduates.... From the milk-round we select people for a final group selection, 24 to 36 hour selection involving interviews, tests and group exercises.

A senior partner in a medium-sized firm of solicitors:

I organize the recruitment of qualified staff. There is a committee which is responsible for this. I am the secretary of the committee if you like, but there are five partners involved.

A spokesman for a firm of traders which is a medium-sized recruiter of graduates:

Four of us ... scrutinize each application and we score: 0 − 4 not worth seeing; 5 − 7 see if possible; 8 − 10 must be seen.... Having got our list of (those) we want to see from the applications, we then try to see as many as possible at the universities.... I visit all the universities and am accompanied by one of the scrutineers. Scrutineer 'A' will go to Cambridge, Scrutineer 'B' will go to Oxford and 'C' will go with me to Durham.

In this centralized model of recruitment, the employer's expectations are expressed by an individual or a small group with sole responsibility for it; the same individual or group also decides how to organize the process of graduate recruitment. Such a style is typically found among the small recruiters of graduates or among some large recruiters who recruit all their graduates into similar types of job function. This uncomplicated process allows for a relatively easy relationship between the expectations of the employing organization and the processes of recruitment set up to realize them.

In contrast, some organizations conduct *decentralized recruitment*. In this case both the definition of corporate expectations and the recruitment strategies adopted to achieve them are defined by a number of individuals and/or groups who operate independently but under the auspices of the overall organization.

> ... each of the main departments — accounts management, media and creativity — carry out their own recruiting, both for new graduates and also graduates from other organizations.

The representative for a large business machine manufacturer which is a very large recruiter of graduates:

> We recruit on a decentralized basis. We are a world-wide corporation (we have different divisions all over the world) any one of which may happen to be in the UK ... (therefore) ... each division recruits to its own needs.

The senior recruiter for a very large international building manufacturer which is a medium-sized recruiter of graduates:

> We realize... (that for a) ... structurally autonomous subsidiary there's no way we can set out principles, so we do allow them fairly easy means and methods of choosing how they get in these graduates.

In one large accountancy firm:

> Each regional office was basically responsible for its own recruitment.

A large, diversified manufacturer of paper-based products recruiting small numbers of graduates each year:

> First of all, we are ... one of five main operating divisions of the parent company, (company name). Each of those five operating divisions has considerable autonomy in every aspect of its work, including, since 1975, the first stage of graduate recruitment which is done then autonomously by each division. Prior to 1975 it was carried out centrally by (the parent company) but that has now been changed.

A spokesman for a large manufacturer in the motor industry which recruited only a small number of graduates in the previous year:

> It is perhaps worth noting that for the rest of (the parent company) graduate recruitment is decentralized.... We have a history of being a fairly large graduate recruiter for the size of the plant, and since the merger with (the parent company) we are still autonomous.

A director of a medium-sized precision engineering firm:

> Now, each of those divisions (within the group) has a presence in the UK, but apart from saying hello to them in one or two regions of personnel, we really operate autonomously.

Employing organizations who adopt this approach tend to have large corporate structures, and/or have a differentiated corporate structure by region, practice, or division; or operate on the basis of holding/parent companies and subsidiaries, and/or recruit large numbers of graduates, and/or recruit graduates into a number of different types of job. There is usually no clear statement available from the parent employing organization of its total overall recruitment expectations, or of the strategies it adopts for realizing them. These issues are dealt with by autonomous groups within the corporate structure; and there may therefore exist conflicting and contradictory expectations and recruitment strategies within one 'employing organization'. The expectations of such organizations cannot be articulated by any single individual with 'overall responsibility' for the recruitment process. In contrast to the centralized model, decentralized strategies involve a number of individuals making separate recruitment decisions. A number of people are responsible for an organization's relationship with higher education and they may well have contradictory or incompatible perspectives. However, organizing recruitment in this way does allow individuals 'nearer the coal face' to decide which graduates will best satisfy their working expectations.

Between these two extremes of centralization and decentralization there are many examples of what might be described as *federal recruitment*, in which overall responsibility lies with an individual or small group at the centre of the organization while particular aspects of the exercise are conducted by others within the organization. Usually this type of recruitment takes place in organizations which aim to allow individual operating groups the opportunity to express their requirements for graduates, while at the same time to provide a degree of participation by those at the 'head' of the organization. Inevitably, a fairly complex organizational structure is required to accommodate this system, as the following extract illustrates.

A senior representative for a very large consumer products manufacturer which is a large recruiter of graduates:

> Graduate recruitment in each country is the responsibility of the national management of that country. The only role of the central international personnel division — which this is — is to set certain targets and standards that will say, 'you need a certain number of graduates who at the time of recruitment are thought to have the potential to get to a certain stage....' The role of the central recruitment departments is twofold. There is one department which is really attached to the research division which has been recruiting for the two major laboratories in the UK. That is primarily done by the laboratories themselves with co-ordination from the research division centre. What the national personnel department concentrated on was two jobs really. One on behalf of the companies in the UK recruiting something like 60 to 70 graduates a year.... In addition

to act as a sort of service while doing that job for recruiting other graduates that the companies will more or less say... 'while you are it, could you find a mechanical engineer or an historian or whatever.' It doesn't necessarily have to be at the same level.... So we don't have streams à la old style civil service if you like.... But at the time of entry we are taking in two streams. The quality of the streams would overlap for the national personnel department and the quality of the people coming into research would also be two overlapping levels. We would take in research: primarily PhDs coming into a job direct where they could deliver immediately at research level... that might be 15 a year. We would be taking in a further 40 or 50 maybe going in as assistant managers at the equivalent of the lower level intake.... We recruit at two levels through the national personnel department, the bottom level there is just another way of getting in the companies' recruiting themselves − if you like we are competing with that group. And the research group also taking in at two levels but both in research division and in the companies, once someone has joined, how they get on depends on the appraisal system.... The selection boards − the make up on the event would be to have five candidates along with two selectors who would be lay selectors, senior managers, that is, people of the level of the higher end of the scale for which these people would be selected, and hopefully people who would be a reasonable model because it is a two-way selection process and you don't want to turn out every dumb dumb as a selector or they will go some place else. Two selectors and one person acting as what we call President. The selectors would be almost always from the operating companies, virtually never personnel specialists, unless we were specifically looking for personnel candidates. The President would either be the head of recruitment at the time ... or the national personnel manager or one of the other boss men of the national personnel department.... But generally it would be the head of department for 50% and the other 50% would be split between this group of people.

Characteristically, a federal system of recruitment attempts to get the best of both worlds − centralized and decentralized. On the one hand, staff at the 'head' of an organization are able to participate in any co-ordinate recruitment activities, while on the other, the expectations of those most likely to work with the graduates recruited find some expression. As with the decentralized system, it is implied that such organizations have multiple expectations of graduate recruits.

A very large producer of industrial equipment:

Yes, I'm responsible, my job title is 'Recruitment Officer'..... In the present organization as we stand now in 1982 ... I'm responsible for the co-ordination, the actual recruitment is done by the unit who is going to employ the graduate, but I set up and make the arrangements.

The senior recruiter for a medium-sized pharmaceutical group which is a large recruiter of graduates:

Because of the divisional nature of the business, we handle graduate recruitment centrally, for ease of administration. As personnel services manager, I have a graduate officer and a graduate recruitment assistant whose main task is setting up the whole graduate recruitment exercise. I hasten to add that we don't make judgements on the suitability of graduates, that is not a thing we're capable of doing, but we act as contact for the graduate.... (It is) highly complicated because one discipline may be of interest to several parts of our organization, so that if you are a chemist, you may be of interest to our marketing people/production chemists/research projects in that division. The papers either have to be sent in three directions at the same time or right the way around the park.

A representative for a large nationalized firm which recruits large numbers of graduates annually:

> We organize our recruitment in a way a little differently from many companies, in that we operate a milk-round, but not in the sense that most companies do. We have a particular line manager who is responsible for each campus in the country, so that every campus will have at least one or two managers who are allocated to that campus ... and they, as a part time voluntary responsibility, do the recruitment on our behalf.... They've been given precise specifications by us, they've been given standard interviewing training techniques by us, and they attend regular training workshops to make sure that they're working to, as near as possible, a common standard.

The managing director of a manufacturing and retailing footwear firm:

> I work for the holding company. The actual recruitment individually is by the subsidiary, the manufacturing wholesale company and by the retail company, but the holding company has a watching brief over all management. We have a co-ordinating role at the centre and there is some central thinking in the management and development programme.

A spokesman for a large computer systems consultancy which is a large recruiter of graduates:

> I'm responsible... for ensuring that we get enough applicants for the vacancies.... It's centralized for both training and experienced staff in the sense that there is someone in the personnel department who issues offers and places ads,... but decentralized to the extent that interviews will be conducted by someone from the operating units.

In the same vein, the personnel officer for a local authority noted:

> We are concerned centrally with establishing broad policy guidelines. If a department says to us, I don't believe in recruiting graduates, that would be contrary to the organization's policy which has to be thrashed out in departments. Equally, if departments say in view of the current labour situation 'we'll recruit graduates very much more extensively'... we would say that's not in accordance with (the organization's) policy either. The

broader approach to graduate recruitment therefore is that we encourage departments to recruit graduates ... for all the professions involved in local government work, which spans a very wide field.

A representative of a medium-sized computer manufacturer which, last year, recruited few graduates:

> The total task of graduate recruitment is split between the divisions. Each have their own personnel departments.... We have an advice and counselling role, controlling standards, introducing selection tests and monitoring the ways divisions set up selective days. We impose a company-wide standard.

A recruiter for a diversified manufacturing group which is now a small recruiter of graduates:

> Up to three years ago we had a central budget and recruited graduates centrally ... (both) ... first job graduates and straight from university.... Three years ago we devolved the responsibility of a number of aspects of personnel management to the operating group. Each has a group personnel manager. It is still convenient to operate from here (headquarters) because people would have heard of (us) in DOG, GO, etc., but wouldn't necessarily have heard of some of our subsidiaries. We continue to advertise (under the group name) and when people apply saying I'm interested in transport, distribution, they are referred to the appropriate section.'

A senior partner in a large accountancy firm which is a medium-sized recruiter of graduates:

> We have a national recruitment partner ... who is my boss. We then have a recruitment partner for each office, who is very part time as a recruitment partner, but he is given that title as a focal point for recruitment into head office.

According to the representative of a holding company for a variety of manufacturing firms:

> There is a central, (company) face who deals with the undergraduate sponsored schemes which are central and the placements of graduates following the university tour which (we) conduct every year.... If someone wants to have a co-ordinated view of what's happening over the group, I am the contact. If someone wishes to ask questions on graduate activities of a specific company, they would be directed to that company.

While for a spokesman in an electronics engineering firm:

> My personal role is to have correspondence and discussion with general managers of these companies to establish what our needs are for the following year and to collate that information, and to present it to the

manpower panel of the company which is made up of the main board of directors so they say, we should concentrate on (particular) disciplines, engineering or whatever. Having established what we are in the market for, I sit down with the education officer and work out a programme and from there he takes over and I have a supervising role. He establishes the milk-round, gets involved with other people in the first category, final selection is done by the operating people.

Recruitment in a large photographic equipment firm which is a medium-sized recruiter is:

> ... decentralized to a great extent. There is a general, overall sort of view of what the needs are for the future. I try and get a feeling for that view.... I go backwards and forwards with central management on what the overall need is, but when you get down to it, it's really the divisions that decide how many they can take within the number they're supposed to have on their staff.

Included in this 'federal' group of recruiting strategies are styles which are more typical of decentralization, and others which are closer to centralization. The central responsible agent may just have a watching brief, and be quite passive in actual recruitment, or he may exercise a more active role in co-ordinating recruitment, sometimes with involvement in interviewing and selection decisions. Specifically, central recruitment agents may be responsible for (i) the general policy statements about the organization's expectations from recruitment, with others undertaking the actual recruitment; or (ii) the elaboration of general policy, with some minimal role in actual recruitment; or (iii) the elaboration of general policy with a major role in recruitment, leaving only the actual hiring to others.

Not all organizations run a separate graduate recruitment exercise: a number recruit individuals regardless of whether they are graduates or not.

A local authority which is a medium-sized recruiter of graduates:

> (we) don't try to pick out the graduate factor ... when we advertise for social workers and when we appoint them, we're really looking to make sure they have their CQSW (Certificate of Qualification in Social Work).... We don't go out of our way to recruit graduates as such.

For a large manufacturer and retailer of toiletries which recruits few graduates:

> The graduate recruitment is organized as part of my job of (general) recruitment. We don't have a separate graduate recruitment officer; it's seen as an overall manpower plan.

When reflecting on his experience, a recruiter for a diversified manufacturing group said:

> I was not looking for a graduate, just someone I thought could fill the position ... (one) was in computer science, it just happened graduates

applied.... I was interested in their technical background rather than their degrees. Their degrees only helped.

One large employer of arts graduates:

> ... there existed no particular policy for or against recruiting graduates, and that graduates 'discovered (the organization)' rather than the other way round. Thus when conducting recruitment, the organization were 'looking for a certain type of person' rather than any kind of qualification.

These different patterns are not fortuitous; they reflect the ways in which organizations feel they are best able to meet their needs for graduates. Diverse strategies used by organizations differentially placed in the recruitment market reflect different organizational requirements. Recruitment strategies are developed and changed according to changes in organizational expectations and requirements over time. Within each organization expectations and requirements are determined by varying numbers of people; similarly varying numbers are involved in the actual process of recruitment. As we have noted, this is by no means strongly correlated with the size of the organization or with the industrial or commercial sector. The question is clearly raised: 'Who speaks for an employing organization on issues related to higher education?' In some firms, even some very large ones, one or two individuals can reasonably do so; in others, interviews with dozens of staff would be required to obtain a full range of fact and opinion. For this study, employing organizations nominated one or two individuals, who were usually directly involved in recruitment and relatively senior, to speak for them. However, the degree to which they actually represent the perceptions of their colleagues is an unknown which raises a thorny problem for policy-related research of this kind.

THE RECRUITMENT PROCESS

Organizations have different operational 'theories' for the proper management of the recruitment exercise – reflected, for example, in the degree to which the personnel office rather than the relevant departments and divisions control recruitment. Organizations differ in the importance (and resources) they give to face to face contact with graduates; in the importance they put on the initial 'paper sort' of applicants; in the seniority of the firm's interviewers; indeed, over which questions they ask applicants in their, generally confidential, interview schedules. What the following excerpts demonstrate is the complexity of the recruitment exercise for many organizations and the cost in time and money of having to reduce hundreds of applications to a few new graduate recruits.

A footwear manufacturer and retailer:

> In an average year, we will get something like 650 to 700 applications ... but out of that lot, we will have milk-round interviews of anywhere between 250 and 300 (depending on what we do on paper pre-selection), and out of that lot we invite 85 to 90 down to the company location for second interview, and out of that lot we hope to recruit up to 12 of what we hope are top quality graduates.

In one large public corporation:

> ... candidates apply for particular fields, but, at first interview they are assessed by the staff and, if found suitable, put forward for a second interview in a field which is not necessarily the one which they first chose (for example, someone who applied for research might be put forward for engineering or vice versa). The first interview is largely technical, to assess their knowledge as well as their personality. The second interview is with a senior manager from the particular area, accompanied by a member of the training section.

A very large diversified organization:

> operated the milk-round centrally. The department decides what they want and we organize them.... The second interview stage is done by these areas. They decide what they want, ... we collate the bits (of information) so we know what exercise to mount.... Whenever possible, we like the line managers to go out (on the milk-round) and give them a first interview and the information they require. The recommendations are then made about who should be passed on to whom, or rejected. The departments then call these people for second interviews and they take decisions, the line management directly take the decision and we co-ordinate the joint decisions... *they* decide.

For another large public corporation:

> The preliminary stages, ie paper sift and first interviews, are conducted by the personnel department, with the second interview undertaken by the departments concerned, along with offering jobs.

A very large nationalized industry which is a very large graduate recruiter:

> (We) have a particular line manager who is responsible for every campus in the country, so that every campus will have at least one or two managers to that campus... and they, as a part time responsibility do the recruitment on our behalf.... We call these guys 'Liaison Officers'.... We have about 80 liaison officers and each of them have their own personal relationships and it's a very good system for making the diffused message. The problems at the end of the day are obviously standardization and, at the end of the day we have to centralize it, and we reach a central selective process as a second stage.... There would be a 24 hour selective process at one of our management training centres, where they would undertake aptitude ability tests in numerical, verbal, special skills.... The computer programmers will have had an aptitude test previously but different tests from what normal candidates would take and that would be a prerequisite that they would achieve a certain standard before we interview them.

Another very large nationalized industry:

> At the moment, because of the sheer numbers currently, we are tending

to adopt a paper sift method first, and interview everybody who passes that. We do a preliminary test session after that paper.... The thing which decides whether or not we accept is the final selection board which can be held in the regional headquarters or here.... What he's (the trained assessor) looking for is the bloke who will sell himself in 15 minutes (in the first interview).... What we're looking for here is the high flier. You can identify the high flier in 15 minutes,... he's got 15 minutes to sell himself.

A local authority representative, however, said:

All recruitment is done through personnel. (For example if 'engineering' decides it wants someone, first it goes through monitoring). Once that's agreed, then we contact the universities.... We (personnel) scrutinize the applicants and they come back. The applications then go back to personnel to make sure that no-one has been left out.

A senior recruiter for a large manufacturer of toiletries:

The nature of the first interview is fairly short... and I use that visit as a conversation, speaking and getting a feel for how mature he is, how certain they are of what they want to do, why they feel the organization will play a role in their career. I whittle down on that basis and I'm pleased to say, by the time I (personnel director) get a short list of 12 people for six vacancies.... If I've done my job properly, all of these people will do what we want them to do and do it with a fairly similar degree of success.... When those 12 people come along for interviews with senior management a lot of the consideration is ... the chemistry of that person and do their ambitions fit in,... do the various aspects of their personality fit within the aspects of the company.

A manufacturer of electrical domestic appliances:

We're fairly bad at selection, in that there are about four people getting involved in milk-round; the training manager, resources manager, the factory training manager and training officer and the employment officer, and all go off and do preliminary interviewing. It was more than useless because people didn't report back in concise order. There was a little bit on the application form saying 'good appearance' or something then, from a fairly sketchy or non-existent report (although some were very good) we decide on about 10 people to come here for interviews or a second interview. They see me again (or perhaps for the first time) and the manager of the department concerned. What goes on from there depends on the department.

A spokesman for a very large banking organization which is a large recruiter of graduates:

I and a colleague will do the first interviews. On our recommendation, a second interview would be recommended for the student in one of three specialist areas, and they will conduct their own interview sessions. I only return to those interviews to tie up the various formalities.... Last year approximately 3,000 (applied).... We gave first interviews to 1,200, second interviews to about 260 (probably one in four or five will get a second interview). Job offers are something in the order of 100.

The senior recruiter for a manufacturer and distributor of food products which is a large recruiter of graduates said:

> I (the personnel director) am responsible for interviewing all the pre-selections. As regards initial interviews, I co-ordinate that and... get the divisional personnel managers with a fair degree of interviewing experience to interview with me.... Coming into the final selection programme, each is run ... by a particular division. I help organize that and ... try to keep fairly well out of the actual decision-making process.... The Managing Director then makes a decision based on that.... The research and management division have their own day long sessions, but we believe in having a commitment from the senior management ... so it's their decision; if they want that individual they take that individual.

A small international trading firm include on their milk-round:

> Oxbridge, Durham and London ... we also get a lot of applications from the universities and we invite them to London. We set aside two days in London for applicants from universities not invited.... After the first interviews at universities, we send them abroad with the President of the company and top merchants. I enjoy speaking to graduates.... The top management in (name of city abroad) can see themselves the type of person who is coming through this year and they always want to see them.

The potential graduate recruit thus typically moves through a number of recruitment stages before being accepted into an organization. Typically this process might consist of (i) a paper pre-selection process; (ii) first stage interviews, often on a company milk-round; (iii) second stage interviews; (iv) job offers. During this process, different groups and individuals within an organization take responsibility for different stages in a graduate's recruitment. A number of different patterns are evident:

a The central personnel division undertakes stages (i) and (ii) above, with stages (iii) and (iv) being undertaken by the particular divisions/units/functions, etc. who will employ the graduates. Personnel division undertakes responsibility for weeding out applicants who are seen to be 'unsuitable' for the company, with the divisions being allowed to evaluate more technical competence.

b The divisions/units/functions undertake stages (i) and (ii) above and personnel stage (iii), with the final job offers being made by the divisions/units/functions.

c Personnel undertakes an enabling role in which they co-ordinate the recruitment activity but allow the particular divisions/units/functions to conduct their own recruitment strategy.

d Personnel undertakes all stages of the recruitment process, with the demands for new graduates expressed to them by the particular divisions/units/functions.

Indeed, for some positions the general recruitment procedures do not apply, as in some cases a 'mini recruitment' process is organized. The following give examples of such small scale operations, which in the aggregate result in the recruitment of many graduates.

A manufacturing and retailing firm representative argued that for the large number of graduates they recruit annually:

> We make it known that the 'fast track' is available, so any graduate who feels that they are outstanding for one reason or another (which may be the quality of that degree, personality, or just that they are a dunkhead or whatever).... If we consider that this person has something which makes him stand out head and shoulders (and we mean that) above the normal run we expose them to a little more than the normal interview process, which means working on a little project, making a presentation to us of a particular theme, being interviewed by a much higher level panel of general managers.

For a very large chemicals manufacturer which is a very large recruiter of graduates:

> ... (the general process) applies in all disciplines, except, interestingly enough, the biological sciences and the reasons for that is that there are relatively few parts of the organization recruiting in those fields, and they have established their own links with particular departments at university and don't meet the central bureaucracy....

A large diversified manufacturer of paper-based products:

> There is only one exception (to the general recruitment policy)... is the (corporate) accountancy training scheme, and that is run by the corporation, but for the purposes of convenience,... is a corporation scheme and not a group scheme.

A medium-sized manufacturing firm's representative:

> Yes (I am responsible for graduate recruitment) but our Hull office takes on one or two per year; not every year and they recruit their own. It's an insignificant part of our recruitment really.

To some extent the variation in the organization of recruitment depends upon the types of jobs which are to be filled. Those organizations which are mostly recruiting into scientific, specialist or technical roles tend to be characterized by the personnel department taking an enabling role, which allows the departments to devise their own most appropriate selection techniques. Organizations recruiting more for generalist roles, however, leave more to their personnel departments.

Further, the background and seniority of individuals who have responsibility during particular phases of recruitment may well be different as between otherwise similar federal or decentralized organizational structures. This is true also for different parts of the organization. For example, central personnel functions in particular federal systems may undertake either initial screening of applicants, first stage (milk-round) interviewing, second stage interviewing, the offers of jobs, or merely provide an administrative service for the rest of the organization. When discussing the organization of recruitment, then, we must consider *both* the form of the allocation of responsibility for recruitment and how the form is fleshed out by particular staffing arrangements. Consequently, we must take account of who takes which decisions when considering how employers' expectations for graduates are expressed in their recruitment strategies.

Our description of recruitment practices should be treated with some caution. We have not attempted to codify strategies and processes. Instead we have tried to show some variation in the organization of recruitment; variation in the number of individuals involved; and something of the difficulty of finding the appropriate spokesmen on educational issues.

SPONSORSHIP AND SANDWICH COURSES

Both sponsorship and the taking up of sandwich students augment the recruitment exercise in many organizations. They are alternative strategies for identifying potential manpower. In this section, we review the evidence on sponsorship and sandwich education and their contribution to recruitment.

John Harris, a retired senior recruiter for Shell Corporation, writes in a paper contributory to the Expectations of Higher Education Project:[4]

> The subject of sandwich education is itself a minefield of possible misunderstandings. There are two basic types of sandwich course: 'thin sandwich' means courses where two or more periods, usually of six months each, working for an employer, are interspersed in three years of academic study. Usually, but not always, students go from secondary school to the academic institution first but sometimes go to the employer and begin academic study six months later. The whole course occupies four or five years. A 'thick sandwich' course is the arrangement of one or perhaps two periods, usually of 12 months each, fitted either before, during or after a three-year academic course. Industry-based students are usually expected to work with their employer in all industrial periods. College-based students may work with different employers in each industrial period. The word 'sandwich' is not generally used to mean the one year's employment that many people seek between leaving school and going to university or polytechnic, nor is it used for the traditional nine months after taking 'Oxbridge entrance'. It is not usual to refer to the new enhanced courses as 'sandwich courses'. A few employers had got so used to the old pre-1956 system when sandwich students were people aiming for Higher National Diplomas, that they still tended to use the word to distinguish that level of education from degree level.
>
> The works 'sponsor' and 'sponsorship' also cause problems. One oil company 'sponsors' students, ie it takes them on to its payroll at 18+ and pays them through three or more years' study at rather more than a

standard LEA grant. A firm of civil engineers 'sponsors', ie pays students for six-month periods of employment between periods of study during which latter they fend entirely for themselves financially. A big technological firm sometimes encounters a student on a vacation course and 'sponsors', ie pays him a sweetener to maintain mutual interest until he gets his degree. A nationalized industry 'sponsors' those who have been employed since the age of 16, then qualify for and enter higher education on paid leave.

While many sponsored students are on sandwich courses, most sandwich students are not sponsored. Employers often mix and sometimes confuse their comments on the two programmes. It is, therefore, difficult in some interviews to disaggregate the different comments. In some firms experience of sandwich education and sponsorship would itself take the full interview, others would have no clearly articulated views.

Among the employers included in this study, most sponsorship was arranged by firms recruiting into engineering jobs.

A small firm of engineers:

> We have tried to breed our own graduates who in the main are timber technologists or BTechs. We prefer to take sandwich course (students) where we can sponsor them, preferably six months in industry and six months at university. They get time to know us and vice versa. By the time they have graduated, they know where they want to work and we can assess if we want them.

While a large diversified industrial organization felt:

> We have got to get the better academic standard of engineers, so we go for university applicants. We don't see the recruitment area in ready-made graduates. We think there is a big void there. Consequently we would rather recruit the sponsored type — we take the A-level standard with a university place, a BSc standard of degree with mechanical bias on production side and we feel that with four-year sandwich courses, six months academic in-training, by the time the boy is 22 (having) completed his degree he's reacting all the time to our requirements whereas if we recruit a ready bade BSc from university, more often than not we find they have frittered away four years. We find (sponsored students) have a better potential, the student identifies himself with the company, he makes friends, we take him away from university, put him in work and then back again.

A holding company for a variety of manufacturing firms, which is a very large recruiter of graduates:

> We have in the order of 25 to 30 each year who are sponsored from day one. Obviously, if people on that route leave for whatever reason, we will be seeking to top up, and the main mechanism by which we do that is by taking an individual on a single industrial placement so that they can have a look at (the company) and we can have a look at them. We may then

continue after that in offering sponsorship. For example, in the undergraduates who finished their sponsorship in 1981, seven of the individuals we subsequently took on were a part of the group by that route. For 1982 we anticipate offering five or at the most six industrial placements because we've not had graduates dropping out of our sponsorship scheme.

A very large manufacturer of industrial products:

We only sponsor on enhanced (engineering) courses, at Brunel and Imperial College. We take it a stage further in that we are trying to get our line managers affiliated to specific universities who run enhanced courses with a view not only to ultimately recruiting the best graduates, but also of making tutorial input to the running of enhanced courses in, say, industrial relations sessions and the management project.

An electronic engineering firm's representative:

If you go back three years, the employment situation isn't what it is today. We were competing with other companies, where (the company) was not a household name. We've always been beaten to the post by other companies so we decided to increase our recruitment opportunities with sponsorship of this sort.

A director of a very large engineering contracting firm:

The reason for doing (sponsorship) is from a recruitment point of view, as much as anything else. We find that a year's practical training where they can see us and our industry, we can see them and actually see what sort of work they're capable of, albeit at a very junior level, they've only got two years' experience behind them, they can still make quite a major contribution ... and we can see them at work over a year and test them out in various situations, it makes our recruitment at the end of the day a whole lot less subjective, as compared to two interviews at the end of the milk-round, and of course the graduate training is that much shorter at the end of the day. Over a four year period they would come to us for approximately two to two and a half months during that first summer vacation and then they would really be with us for perhaps as much as 18 months over the industrial training year in the third year because we would take them for the summer vacations either side of that as well, so it's perfectly possible for a student really just to come as a graduate to do his objective training at the end.... (Q: So economically, it's worth your while?) Oh yes.

A personnel director of a large manufacturer of electrical domestic appliances explained:

Yes, we engage in sponsorship. This year we have undergraduates in Ealing, Bradford, Bath, I think that's it – three institutions. It's declined... in the main beause of the employment structure of the company and the economic situation. We have certainly been reducing numbers for about three years. That and the fortunes of the company are affecting graduate intake and undergraduate sponsorship.

A spokesman for a manufacturer in the motor industry:

We sponsor undergraduates and the figures we've been using over the last two years, including this year, are six undergraduate engineers for sponsorship. Two years previous to that we took 10. Each of those years we had something like over 400 people chasing those sponsorships and some very good people. We take them on at 18 − one or two might have done a technical diploma at college, but the vast majority are ex-A level and grammar school. They mostly go to the university of their own choice. In practice, that limits it to 10 to 12 universities, but they do go of their own choice and we tend to restrict it in England or Wales because of the difference in the educational system in Scotland, and the necessity of that to involve four years sponsorship as opposed to three.... We insist that all undergraduates spend some time in industry before going to university ... because we want the undergraduate to go to university as an employee of this company. Although we use the word sponsorship in a loose fashion, as far as we're concerned it's not sponsorship in the sense that the individual is freed. He's not contracted to us in any way formally but he goes as an employee of (the company).

A senior spokesman for a large consumer product manufacturer:

Some of the companies will do a little bit of sponsorship on individual courses, we have been involved for the last three or four years in sponsoring just a few engineering students on these enhanced engineering courses and what we have done to try and contain the work involved in it is to just sponsor people at a limited number of institutions. We've stuck to Imperial, Birmingham, UMIST, Oxford and Cambridge and even then it becomes an enormous amount of work. You end up with certainly four figures of applications for the sponsorships and before you know where you are you have almost got a recruitment department for sponsorships. Quite an issue.

'Sponsorship' evokes a number of issues when raised with employers. In some firms there are clearly problems in determining the need for it, involving, as it does, projections of future recruitment. Firms have to assess their relative position in the sometimes competitive graduate market, while trying to predict their future growth and the effects of the economy. However, many employers undoubtedly see specific advantages in sponsoring students − perhaps the most commonly perceived being that of work experience prior to graduation. Employers see sponsorship as producing more competent graduates, balancing the theoretical slant of their studies by 'keeping their feet on the ground'. It also has a selection function. Having been able to see undergraduates performing in a 'work' situation, employers may be able to evaluate more fully their competences as recruits. Among other advantages mentioned are that employers wish to retain particularly able staff who joined the organization straight from school, and may sponsor them in the hope of keeping them. Or employers may identify problems and scarcities in the recruitment of certain types of graduates, and decide to 'pre-recruit' at eighteen and sponsor the students on particular courses, thus pre-empting the shortages which may be anticipated at graduation.

Attitudes towards sandwich courses were more varied, in part reflecting the uncertainty employers feel about returns on their investment. Most employers were positive about such courses, however, and saw them as potentially beneficial for their own organizations.

A spokesman for a pharmaceutical group:

> (Sandwich courses) are very popular. We have to limit them for financial reasons but − I think we get more requests for these than we're able to fulfil − around 20 to 25. Again they'll be a mixture of disciplines − chemists, pharmacologists from Chelsea, two from Loughborough in medicinal chemistry and require a sandwich period in industry. Quite a number of these going on.

A large technical recruiter said:

> Our gain is in the sandwich courses because I do think it's very useful in giving them some idea of what they want to do after graduation. I cannot think of any instance where any sandwich student has failed.

A spokesman for a food retailing chain:

> They have a better ability to relate to other people, to manage other people and they have a better appreciation of what the world of work is like, so in the first place if they come to us they will have been able to analyse whether they're the right person for the job better than those who haven't had the experience of the world of work and when they do start they have better expectations because their previous naive expectations have already been altered by the experience of work, which many of the graduates, even those with some vacation work experience, will still have extremely naive understanding of what the world of work is all about.
>
> (Q: So you would quite like to see more sandwich courses?) Yes, I think so. I must admit that we like to go back a little bit. Some of the sandwich courses that used to be run were equally remote. The emphasis was very much on the academic side and the weighting given to the industrial/ commercial experience seemed to be out of balance in terms of the final award of the degree. I think that's coming back into some kind of balance as far as the weighting is concerned. But yes, this exposure to the commercial world I think is valuable, as long as that period of training, and this is our responsibility, I think, is structured. Certainly we have what six, seven industrial placement students with us on the retail side at the moment and we've given them the formal work training programme that we give to our graduate trainees. That seems to form a framework in which they can both learn about the business and also contribute something to the business ... our statistics have shown that if someone stays with us for six months then they stay indefinitely. So if we can retain

them for six months, and obviously as an industrial student, they will be with us for the whole year or at least for six months, then hopefully the likelihood is that they will want to come back and what we could offer them is the opportunity to come in as an assistant manager with perhaps a two-week refresher course so that they would be on an even faster track then than a graduate coming in from outside.

A large manufacturer of computer equipment:

> In the year... we made offers to 137 industrial trainees... six to 12 months. A similar number in development labs, manufacturing plants, etc. Probably 250 industrial trainees. (Q: Sponsorship?) No, if it's difficult to select at 21, how much more difficult to select at 18. There's no need for us to sponsor. We get queues at our door. We do take a lot of college-based students.

A large pharmaceutical company said of college-based students:

> We always have 12 to 16 kicking around the place, yes. Sometimes they will join us; it occasionally happens. (Q: Sponsors?) We used to but have given it up. If I recruit a sandwich course graduate, I will pay him/her more than a three-year straight Honours degree graduate. We would probably pay him more than the Oxford graduate who's done four years, probably. We would probably pay them about the same as the person who's been with us for one year.

A nationalized industry:

> (Q: College-based students?) Yes, we do indeed. The numbers are fairly sizeable. We do it because we feel we ought to do it and also because it's a helpful way of keeping in contact with individual departments.... With the cuts, we've been suffering, it might be that the opportunities will diminish but we would not like to extinguish them.... (Q: Sponsorship?) Several ways and it's a complex pattern. It is a very large exercise.... The thing that has done most to get bright lads across into engineering is sponsorships.

A large motor manufacturer which is a small graduate recruiter:

> (Q: College-based?) I would be planning on 12 out of 15 each year. (Q: Sponsorship?) 192 engineering students in the pipeline − 50 per year average... our preference for thin sandwich concentrated on a small number of universities. Add 58 business students. My instinctive feel is that in a large organization, finding your way is the biggest single factor in the transition from HE to employment. Where students (ie sandwich) have three and a half to four years' advantage head start.

A small manufacturer, sub-section of a large organization:

> (Q: College-based students?) It is a policy to do so. In practice, placing

would be a factory matter. We would encourage it. Sponsorship has been going for many years, annual intake would be around 100. We can cope with 131 thin sandwiches, etc. If they are going on a three-year degree course, I think our company will always insist that they do a pre-university year. There are all kinds of variations. I would say that increasingly the polytechnics are being shunned. We are inundated with applications for sponsorship and therefore we tend to go for the guys who have got five As at O level.

A number of employers were less enthusiastic. The reasons were chiefly related to resources of time and the effects of 'de-manning'. A few felt that sandwich students did not offer sufficient continuity and some thought they were not among the best students academically.

These arguments are usefully summarized by a personnel director for a large engineering firm:

> From an ideal point of view, we would welcome sandwich degree students but we have to take into account that, if we promoted that view strongly, universities/polys would quite rightly demand that we take people onto industrial training periods and we just haven't got the places. We would fall down on that commitment. Second, (I have to be guarded here) generally speaking the top of the first division universities − as far as civil engineers are concerned − are running three-year full-time degree courses. Now that means that they will attract the cream − we are looking for the cream − and if we only looked in the area of sandwich degrees we would miss out some very valuable people.

So sandwich courses are a mixed blessing in the eyes of many employers. They satisfy the need for work experience in undergraduate education but they create the problem for employers of providing that experience. Sandwich courses are not generally provided by the elite institutions and consequently are not perceived as attracting the best students. Further, the short period of the industrial placement is seen by some employers to disrupt work organization. The recession has exacerbated the problem. In the period which has seen substantial laying off of staff, it is difficult to use alternative sources of labour, even in the interests of education.[5]

All sandwich and sponsored students are *potential* graduate recruits. In part, then, attitudes towards sandwich programmes will depend on the effectiveness of other patterns of recruitment. Although sandwich courses provide students with the work experience employers apparently favour, sponsorship is the more important strategy used to maintain continuity in recruitment. Sponsorship was seen as particularly important in firms which had undergone some decline in the market and feared loss of competitive advantage for highly trained graduates.

THE EFFECTS OF THE ECONOMIC RECESSION UPON GRADUATE RECRUITMENT

Our interviews with employers were undertaken during the dreary months of the economic downturn of 1981-82. The gloomy atmosphere was reflected daily in the newspapers in stories on the numbers of jobs 'lost'.

Indeed, several firms that had been contacted to participate in the study had closed, and several felt their position to be too precarious to make statements about their experiences in the labour market. The only positive result of this was the opportunity given to discuss with employers their recruitment strategies in the light of changes in the economy.

A spokesman for a large engineering contracting firm recruiting small numbers of graduates each year:

> We base our judgement to some extent upon future job opportunities after training, but also we have to take into account the actual training opportunities for particular graduates at a particular time. We like to base our training scheme on actual work that is going through the company... and clearly when our work load is low the actual work is low... so it (graduate recruitment) is half what it was.

This was echoed in one of the nationalized industries:

> And of course, as you'd expect, our (forward management planning) has gone astray at the moment because the wastage factors we've built in don't apply because people aren't moving so much.

While according to one small manufacturer:

> We have 75 (employees) now, we had 125. Of those 50 people who were laid off, probably 25 were directly due to the recession.... It's very hard to justify hiring new people when you're firing them at the same time.

For some organizations, their own worsening economic performance and its influence upon the organizational manpower structure had compounded the difficulties of recruiting new graduates: a deteriorating economic performance tends to make new graduate recruitment particularly difficult if existing staff are being made redundant at the same time. Moreover, even if there is no absolute decline in the numbers employed by an organization, the perceived decreasing mobility amongst employees carries with it implications for new recruitment. Employers have argued that it impairs their capacity to recruit new graduates. In the past, graduates may have been recruited on the assumption that a number of them would leave. As the retention rate increases, however, organizations will have more graduates after two or three years than they had expected. Not only does this imply a disruption of forward planning, but also that current recruitment in such organizations is being shaped by the characteristics of the present manpower structure.

An increase in the retention rate amongst existing employed graduates is one result of changing economic fortunes. There are others – including initiating a smaller milk-round.

A spokesman for a large accountancy firm:

> They had decreased the numbers hired by that organization partly because of poor estimates of their labour requirements but also because the recession had made them 'have to be more efficient to the use of labour'.

A medium-sized retailer of dairy products which is a medium-sized recruiter of graduates:

> This year we're not recruiting them (graduates), but last year we were looking for two and got one, but the decision this year has been that we'll manage with what we've got.

A small chemical engineering firm which is a sporadic recruiter of graduates:

> We haven't needed to recruit graduates at this time.... As it happens, we've been going through a period of consolidation. I haven't needed to recruit graduates, and haven't been in that market for two or three years.

The senior recruiter for a subsidiary of a large electronics firm:

> Yes, there are two major changes ... (we are) ... far more selective with our preselection processes. We now look for those disciplines which are more relevant; for higher degrees, with more specialized options ... (and secondly) ... we have become a lot more cost-effective. We now look for the places with the best courses and where we'll get a decent response from the students.

A large media organization, according to their personnel director:

> (We) visited, I think, 32 (universities) in 1981. In 1982, we're visiting 21.... We conducted an analysis of three parts; firstly which universities have (as a proportion) a higher mix of the type of people we see to employ (we're talking predominantly about engineers and technologists). Secondly, a university would retain its place on the list by virtue of having provided us in the past ... (with)... a high number of suitable applicants. Thirdly, and probably most important, have historically provided a high number of employees of the calibre and discipline we require.

A very small firm of technical employers:

> If the work level takes off again, we'll consider graduates.

A large business machine manufacturer:

> On the good side, if you take programme products division, that now has 140 people. This time last year 90, so a 50% growth in 1981. This time next year 180 people. This department is paying no attention to the recession at all. At the other end, the marketing division this year, recruiting is staying still — they would expect to take 25 trainees which would replace the expected 25 departures.

A spokesman for a large consumer product manufacturer:

> (Q: Could we touch on how far (your) recruitment has been influenced, if at all, by the economic fortunes of the country?) That varies, but it is

certainly true that the research division ... (which)... is funded by the operating groups (detergents or whatever) who will say they have a certain amount of money to spend on research programmes, amongst other things, and so the funding of the research division will tend to go up and down a bit according to the economy – although not enormously.

One general consequence of deteriorating economic performance was that employers seemed increasingly concerned with making their graduate recruitment processes more cost-effective, and in a number of different ways:

1 They may spend less for each graduate recruited, whether the numbers are maintained or decreased as compared with previous years. This may be either through a decrease in the activity of their milk-round or an increasingly rigorous pre-selection.
2 They may not recruit any graduates, or decrease the number.
3 They may delay making decisions about how many graduates to recruit until relatively late in the recruitment year.
4 They may change the distribution of their recruits between jobs.

The effects of the recession were felt differently by different units within each organization. While one might have reduced its recruitment of graduates overall, particular units within the organization might have maintained or even increased their demands for new graduates. It is difficult to infer the recruitment needs of particular groups within an organization from the recruitment demands made by the organization as a whole.

Changes in recruitment policies are not necessarily a function of the general economic recession but of the performance of a particular sector of the economy, or indeed, of an organization within a particular sector of the economy, or of a division within that organization. And many organizations have maintained or increased their recruitment activity during the period of economic recession.

A large diversified manufacturer of paper-based products:

(The)... economic downturn is misleading. It is the total rundown of the paper industry in the UK that is important, and that will happen whether the economies go up or down.... It is extremely important to recognize that we are dealing in part with an industry where we are talking about world market changes that are permanent, ie that you make the stuff in America or Scandinavia and ship it rather than make it out of indigenous material.... We really aren't going to make paper in anything like the bulk grades that we used to. So it is an economic thing, but it is a permanent one, not just the recession.

However, a medium-sized manufacturer of computers:

I think it's a combination of factors... (but) I don't think the economy has played a part because the micro-computer industry we have been in is buoyant, and we've been particularly buoyant, so I don't think that would be a reason.

A very large, diversified industrial organization which is a very large graduate recruiter:

> (Recruitment is) on a plateau now. We anticipate over the next two or three years — as much as you can anticipate in this business — that you will be recruiting around the 230, 250 mark or stable levels typically taking engineers and geophysicists and geologists and we've just got to keep it going.... We have a long-term manpower review which looks five years ahead, and that is the kind of figure we're talking about, asking departments how they see the graduate intake over the next five years.... Certainly the companies who chopped back very hard on their recruitment will find it very difficult to get going again. You know, to get some credibility back in the graduate market. I think (this company) is very conscious of that. Even (the chemicals group)... are still recruiting at about the 40 to 50 level a year, even though they are going through quite an extensive redundancy programme at the moment. They believe that it would be quite wrong to stop and have this gap that everybody talks about. That in five years time you find you've no people coming through at the age of 27 to 28.

A very large consumer product manufacturer:

> We don't want to drop below a certain recruitment level because we've got to run this business in 30 year's time, and we have got to keep the stream of people coming in. What has happened to the economy in one year is almost irrelevant to that issue.

A large holding company representative:

> I don't think it (the recession) has affected numbers greatly. The main board of the company has made a conscious decision to increase our overall numbers in (the) management trainee scheme from 40 this year to 140 next year.

This philosophy towards recruitment is based on company projections and the perceived need to have a constant flow of graduates each year to achieve future requirements. Some organizations had been hurt by radical cut-backs in the past.

A spokesman for a footwear manufacturing and retailing organization which is a large recruiter of graduates:

> Like many companies in the early 70s, we cut back recruitment, particularly for internal consultants. We have been regretting it ever since. It has not formed part of the policy this time round. We are expanding and, OK, closing plants like others, but believe we'll be here in 10 years and do not believe we should destroy the sequence.

Similarly, a representative for a very large manufacturer and distributor of food products:

> ... I think most people are taking a sensible approach; if we stop

altogether, it will cause problems in about five years' time.

Overviews such as these may miss important variation in perceptions and practice in a single type of employing organization or economic sector. Throughout the study, therefore, mini-case studies are presented to illustrate, where possible, this variation or lack of it. Included in the sample of employing organizations were a number of accounting firms, together offering about a quarter of the positions open to new graduates in this sector. Several are among the largest recruiters of accountancy graduates (ie students who have studied accountancy) as well as being the largest recruiters of students who go into accountancy (ie students who enter accountancy independent of course studied). Several are based predominantly in a single region and several are national or international organizations.

Accountancy firms, unlike many others, have not suffered the same effects from the economic recession as have many other firms. Of those included in the sample, only one indicated that numbers 'were down'. This was partly because the recession had made them more efficient in the use of labour. One firm showed a small reduction in the main (London) office. One firm argued 'If anything (there is) slightly more business... no change in the number of students.' One large firm noted that numbers had been growing:

(The growth is due to) forecasts of new business, which is going to require more managers and partners in the future.... We are very dependent on keeping a flow in of students, partly for our future security. It's like keeping a blast furnace burning, partly because there is a job to be done in the auditing world by our students, and I think it would be a waste of high qualified manpower to have people of four or five years post-qualifying doing stock counts which a student is better suited to doing. Against that, auditing is a long-term relationship with clients, and if 60% or 70% of our business is in the auditing areas, that means to some extent we are cushioned from the recession at the student level, and the major effect of recession has tended to be pressure on client fees which might lead to a less thorough job than we would have done if we had been able to command the level of fees we have had in the previous year, which may mean that we've got the same people working less hard, commanding less income and therefore having more time on their hands. Now that's a bit patchy, it varies by regions....

Another large firm reported the past year's recruitment as fairly constant over recent years:

(Recruitment) had been increasing probably by five to ten per cent through the later 70s. If you took 1979, 1980 and 1981 it represents really a fairly level intake in real growth in management consultancy, real growth in tax and cut-back in audit.

What has changed as a result of the recession, a change reflected in many firms, is a re-evaluation of the process of recruitment. Most of the sampled firms had a large recruitment operation in the past year. As one firm reported, however:

> We have cut back because we have had such a large deluge of applications this year, that it really seems silly to go around the country.... (In years gone by) you would be working to attract applications. This year we are struggling trying to get through them all.... For 50 vacancies, this firm has some 2,000 applications.

Another firm reported direct applications coming in:

> ... at the rate of about 300 a month (for 12 vacancies).... More and more are applying in their second year. In terms of cost and use of time, we just sit here this year, and we hopefully get the right calibre of student.

There are several possible explanations for the good fortune found in these firms. To a degree there may be more 'business' in times of economic trouble; some firms may be buffered by their international divisions. Another and likely expalanation is that accountancy firms as a group have well-developed and thoughtful recruitment strategies and realize that an abrupt change in policy will disturb the flow of manpower in their organizations as well as affect their important relationships with higher education institutions.

In most organizations the recession did have an effect, if only on marginal numbers of new recruits. However, the most significant and long-lasting effects are likely to come from the evaluations which many firms made of their recruitment exercises, in particular from their decisions to cut back on the number of institutions they visit and the number of potential recruits they meet.

SUMMARY

Employers expect higher education to provide them with the recruits they judge they need to continue their various corporate activities effectively. Whatever they may say in the abstract about the nature of the higher education experience (see Chapter 6), it is in their recruitment decisions — how many and which individuals to take on — that their expectations are expressed and realized. The evidence in this chapter shows that there is a very great variety among employing organizations, both in terms of their overall size, and in the extent and character of their graduate recruitment exercise. The particular recruitment strategy used by an organization may be seen as a set of responses to the specific demands which it has for graduates, and may take one of a number of forms. It may be a centralized, decentralized or federal strategy. The particular strategy adopted reflects the way the organization feels it is best able to realize its demands. In those organizaions in which authority to recruit graduates is delegated, any one of a number of individual managers of different status, different experience and different expertise (some personnel specialists, some technologists) will be involved in the recruitment process. Crucially, this often carries with it the implication that no single individual can be seen as speaking for the demands and expectations of an employing organization.

As one would expect, recruitment policy will change in a period of economic recession, with changing organizational demands for graduates. It is not just that in bad times fewer people are recruited, but they may be rather different people, recruited in different ways. Organizations may also in such periods choose more cost-effective recruitment methods, involving a smaller range of educational institutions, with a reversion to more conservative, less innovative decisions. Again, however, we saw considerable variation in employer responses to the economic recession in terms of recruitment.

Sponsorship and sandwich courses provide an alternative recruitment strategy. Sponsorship is generally seen as having advantages both in terms of developing the educational qualifications of the organization's own work force and as a way of pre-empting shortages of particular graduates by recruiting them at the end of secondary education. Opinion was more divided on the benefits of sandwich courses. Whilst they were seen as providing valuable work experience for the undergraduates, they may do so over inconveniently short periods, may not attract the higher quality students and tend not to be provided at the high status institutions.

3 The Value of a Degree 1: 'A Degree and What Else?'

CRITERIA FOR EVALUATION OF A DEGREE

'A degree and what else?'[1] What are employing organizations looking for in graduates from the higher education system? What does the graduate have that the non-graduate does not have? Are the qualities identified as desirable by employers likely to develop further or even emerge for the first time in the three or four years spent in higher learning? Do employers value the degree for its academic worth, as a graduate school might, or is it 'value added' to other non-academic qualities? These are some of the questions which are explored in this chapter. A substantial research literature exists on the value of the degree to the individual graduate in terms of such factors as life-time earnings and achieved social status. Much less is known about how employers perceive the degree and put a value on it. A former senior recruiter in industry outlined the problem:

> The question really boils down to what the recruiter or employer sees as the advantage to the person of 21 who's done three years at the university and got a degree.... There is not just the knowledge but the ability to cope and handle the subject itself. Secondly, the general intellectual critical faculty, the ability to judge and assemble information presented in various ways. And thirdly, the sort of personal maturity that he has gained from an opportunity to be, for example, cricket captain and decide on whether they are going to buy new sight screens, or go on a tour to Jersey.

There are several analytic questions involved. How important is the degree as a credential? How important is the specific knowledge (including knowledge of the profession) which is acquired? How much importance in recruitment is given to extra-curricular and social activities which under-graduate students alone have access to? Are employers clear about which qualities graduates are likely to have? More importantly, would the employer have received equal 'value for money' by taking on a reasonably bright 18-year-old school-leaver, rather than a 21-year-old graduate, and training him or her with the firm?

Whereas some of the other material gathered in the survey was straightforward and relatively 'reducible', responses to the questions asked on these issues were neither. Employers know what they are looking for in a graduate recruit (although they are by no means all looking for the same thing) but the expression of this is difficult. For many it comes down to saying: 'I know it when I see it.'

A spokesman for a large public sector organization:

> Even if you can draw up your list of desirable qualities (in a graduate) you can't actually identify them.... You're going to have to recruit them... and rely upon picking out, in the course of time, the type of chap who will be working on special management jobs.

Similarly, a firm manufacturing toiletries:

> What we are looking for is potential and that is obviously the most difficult thing to evaluate.

A senior recruiter for a large nationalized industry:

> You know when you see it... (the right mix of qualities).... At interview it's different because until you actually meet him and discuss with him, you can't say 'There's a high flier'. But when he's there he'll sell himself to you.

The personnel director of a manufacturing and retailing firm:

> A girl I interviewed... was a marine biologist and somehow got through our paper pre-selection, and I interviewed her and she talked for an hour and a half on the sex life of the octopus. But I did not throw her out after five minutes because she had a lot to offer,... because there was something there which rang a bell, to say that there is something here which is good for a lot of initiative, which has to be one of the things we're looking for, she was certainly reacting to what I was saying − not in a complimentary way but in being able to understand and make sense of what I was saying about industry and about our company.... We are really looking for people who will make good as entrepreneurs or will make good as very good managers of people.

For some employers the knowledge gained in the degree course − technical proficiency and substantive knowledge − is essential. For others the choice between a non-graduate and a graduate is less clear-cut. In some organizations a degree is not highly valued and, indeed, may be irrelevant or even disvalued.

A personnel officer for a firm of poultry processors:

> Most of our people come up from the shop floor or have already had supervisory experience in another factory or another type of industry... a lot of people here in management have come from engineering and shipbuilding.... (Q: So in terms of recruitment, the possession of a degree is pretty irrelevant?) Oh yes, it's totally irrelevant. Absolutely, I mean, it wouldn't even tip the scales.

A small food processing firm's managing director reported that they, too, felt graduate status was an irrelevant qualification for the job:

> Ours is a one-off business and very practical process rather than requiring special academic skills, needs common sense and relatively broad education, a business sense when you move into management strata but a lot of practical training, then years and years of built-up experience. Anybody who comes here with a degree will be starting at exactly the same level as one with five O levels. I doubt whether this is a business where you can compare it with other industries as a whole. Compared with the petro (chemical) industries where you need degrees, it's unnecessary here and graduates possibly are wasting their time spending three years at university. The graduate would have gained as much by practical experience during that time. We don't employ any graduates.

The representative of a firm supplying precision engineering equipment felt that perhaps graduate status − at least at early career stages − was over-valued. Indeed, the inflated expectations and lack of work experience of graduates made them less valuable to the organization than non-graduate entrants:

> I'm wary of the education system. If we had a young man capable from the normal apprenticeship to achieve HND, he'll be better for you than a university degree. I don't see a great deal of difference in academic requirements between a BSc and HND. A good OND should go straight to university if his interest lies there. Why do HNC for two years and then another two years to do a degree − doesn't make sense to me.... I have two things against graduates in our experience. One restriction is pre-set ideas and we engage them and tend to find they are not satisfied, despite their lack of knowledge − they are rising too high too quickly. That's the major feature. A young man of 22 without the experience ... is at a complete loss compared with an apprentice who's spent six years acquiring experience in industry with part-time education. He's streets ahead.

A local authority employer noted of social workers:

> If they've got their diploma, we don't mind whether they're male or female, whether they're graduates or non-graduates, whether they're young or old. We want the diploma, the CQSW, and then we look for the appropriate personal qualities. We are finding that a number of them are young graduates again, and we're appointing those with previous social work experience and tending to reject those who have no substantive social work experience.

Many employers feel that they have been forced to recruit graduates because the pool of good A level candidates has 'deteriorated' or 'dryed-up'. That is, few students who get good A levels choose to leave formal education at that point. The representative of a large bank noted this and noted the bank's change in recruitment pattern. While they retained both graduate and A level entry schemes, they did expect graduates to move higher into the organization because of the maturity and wider experience they typically displayed.

We moved over this year to recruiting more graduates into our A level stream in which the top position we expect them to get is middle management — management of a branch with, say, 25 staff, because we were finding some brighter A level people were going to university, and we weren't picking up quality A levels. We've extended our net at the university entrance this year to recruit two tiers: one (of) which is our normal top level entry of some 50, and another 100 who are graduates, but coming into the management stream with A level people.... In a normal year we would require, I suppose, something like a fifth of our entry to be top level people and mainly graduates. The other four-fifths to be made up of graduates and A level people. If they come in after university they have acquired something at university over three years — maturity which the A level people take a longer time to get, and they have an advantage over the first five years or so.

A spokesman for a manufacturing and retail organization explained that they had only recently begun taking graduates and that this had been not only because of their firm's expansion but also because of the deteriorating pool of A level applicants. He also described a major problem in the establishment of a graduate 'fast track' — namely the resentment felt by the non-graduate, non-fast track managers, a theme which recurs in many interviews.

Around five years ago, the growth of the company changed gear almost so that we're now talking in terms of opening 15 to 18 stores a year. Now every time you open a supermarket you're looking for a management team of 12, something like that, 10 to 12.... I think one of the reasons we started taking graduates was because the pool of A level applicants was deteriorating. It's rather a negative reason but it was partly true, I think... traditionally, we've gone for the well-educated youth who before the war was the 15-year-old. After the war there were still... people coming back from the forces who'd been with us before the war, but then we went into the A level scheme in some numbers because that was a group of people who had all these qualities (we required). Yes, the graduates are the next stage beyond that.... But certainly it's true to say that we do feel there is something in the discipline of further education that gives a broader outlook, a more innovative outlook to the graduate managers we have. I was speaking to... the senior manager for the systems department, and he said even three years after taking on a group of graduates and A level trainees he can still tell the difference between the graduates and the A level trainees.

Some organizations which recruit graduates do so rather reluctantly. Graduates have 'pretensions' that non-graduates do not have; they face a difficult period of adjustment when working in an organization alongside experienced non-graduates.

A large public sector representative discussed some of the problems associated with '18-year-olds' and degree level recruitment:

In many ways, a bright man or woman coming in at 18 getting down to things and living locally, is probably more willing to accept the challenge than a graduate who has perhaps not done so well as he or she hoped to do at university and has gone into a convenient post nearby home and is perhaps somewhat reluctant to accept the challenge of moving around.... Our problems are much more of a management kind. (Graduates) have got far greater pretensions than their colleagues and we are therefore posed with quite a difficult problem — which we haven't solved — of how we handle their career within a group which is dominated, in trade union terms, by a very egalitarian leadership.... I think that from (our) point of view, we would much prefer to get people a little earlier — perhaps straight from school — and offer them some training of their own; together with, on their part, a greater willingness to accept the challenge and get down to it.

The personnel director of a wholesale firm sees first-degree courses as taking the place of the old A level entry schemes, but outlined some of the disadvantages of this change:

In some ways we have devalued the graduate. So the graduate, instead of being looked at as someone special, he's just a normal intake, equivalent to the old matriculation lad who didn't get a degree... if you take an 18-year-old A level student, there's a great deal in doing that — giving them a year in industry. We would see that as THE preferred route so I think we're saying there's an immediate shortfall with the graduate coming straight out of school and into university. Very often there's an unlearning process which we have to go through which we don't if we take 18-year-old A level people and expose them to industry for 12 months. They will say, yes I can stay with this and then go to university rather than discover at the age of 24... (that they don't like it).... The 18-year-old can join us, stay with us, takes day release work, moves up the promotional ladder much more quickly. The graduate comes in, has a much more difficult adjustment period but he sticks with us and likely to reach a higher level in the managerial hierarchy. (Q: Why?) I would hope that we got someone with a better capacity to use what he's learned that he might have a better IQ anyway. They are not exclusive. We have graduates who don't make it and 18-year-olds who do.

The majority of employing organizations do positively value the degree. For most it is 'value added' to A levels. It is difficult, however, to separate this perception of value added from the fact that higher learning institutions are communities which happen to have within them a ready source of talent; they are a 'cost-effective' way of finding 'good people'. The director of a large manufacturing and marketing firm noted that, while uncertain about the value of going to university, he did feel that the pool of graduates was more likely to include people with the potential to progress in the firm than the non-graduate pool, although the academic attainment of the graduate was relatively unimportant to the firm.

We obviously look for potential, that's why we look for graduates. We're not looking for a graduate to be a sales rep for the rest of his life. We're looking for someone with certain intellectual capability and record of academic attainment. Someone who will hopefully be in senior management in maybe a shorter period. We take on a sales rep at the age of 20 — he might make a decent sales rep and general manager in a very long period of time but that's remote. If we take a graduate with a good degree and level of maturity, he's going to be able to learn and contribute — the probability is higher that he's going to make it.... I don't personally regard the level of academic attainment as being important. There are so many people these days with degrees that if you can't spend three years at college and pass a degree of some sort there's something very wrong somewhere....

If they are a graduate, one thing is that they are not the only people who were bright enough to get to university but they are bright enough to have got to university and bright enough to have stayed there. But some selection has gone on, to say at least these people have met certain criteria. What they would have been like had they not been to university that's the big issue. You get the feeling when you go back to what happened to yourself that people are able to stand back a bit more, that they have been exposed to the need to think things through and then defend their case or whatever. I find it terribly difficult for two reasons really. One, the problem of distinguishing between the quality of the person initially at the time of going to university and what's been added by the university itself. The second problem to that analysis is that it is not valid to say what is the difference between somebody 'zero university' and somebody 'plus university'. That isn't the honest question. The honest question in our terms would be what is the difference of A + no university + 13 years in (the company) say, compared with A + university + ten years in (the company).... I don't think we can measure it. I think you are back to acts of faith. So if you say am I reasonably happy that we should continue in the long run going to universities to look for people, then I think we should, (a) because the good people — very many of them go there and it is a cost-effective way of getting at good people, or at people who were very good before university got at them if you like, and (b) because I think the university would do good rather than harm.

A personnel director of a manufacturing firm:

Well, there's a big difference between university and school, in that in school you're spoon fed and in university it's very largely teach yourself, isn't it? You've got to study and you're under a lot of pressure as well. I mean the body of knowledge is increasing and so when you get a university graduate you get somebody who's been self-motivated, whereas you get a school-leaver and they've not been.... Another thing is that if somebody has had the bottle, the nerve or the stamina, to go through the A level course and then through a university course then the academic environment has weeded out all the lazy ones and drop-outs. So you're using the university course as a weeding out process. So for these reasons I would in the future prefer graduates.

Relatively few employers evaluate the degree in strictly academic terms. Those who do are often closely associated with academic life, and themselves have degrees. Even these employers also look for non-academic qualities of personality and initiative.

> (A degree is) essential for the higher grades... the higher scientific posts. It does, after all, indicate you've reached a certain educational standard. Now, its very rarely that we take on people without postgraduate qualification.

A spokesman for a national theatre company:

> (Q: Does higher education make more thoughtful actors?) I think so, because my background is academic; since I went through the university circuit, I suppose I do have a university prejudice. I think a lot of actors go to Oxford and Cambridge because they want to be actors,... a lot of intelligent teenagers regard Oxford and Cambridge as a very possible springboard into the profession. I think, on the whole, that passion for language, the easiest way for it to be learned is to read English at university. It would be easier to learn and develop that passion in that context than at a drama school.
>
> (Q: Is it the English Department or the theatre experience you're talking about?) I think it's both. Especially for a young actor, it's quite good to get somebody who knows what iambic pentameter is, does understand something about Shakespearian verse, does recognize it as important. That is frequently the case with young actors who have had some academic training and sometimes not the case with actors who come straight in.

A spokesman for a national museum:

> There are certain departments that are recognized as supplying... the things the Museum wants. More, say, concerned with material culture rather than social background. Say in anthropology and archaeology courses, for example, something that is very socially biased wouldn't have so much relevance.... The Oxford Egyptology course specialization is much favoured.... In our Department, they tend not to like first degrees in the history of art. They like something like a history or classics degree – plus postgraduate qualification in the history of art. For oriental antiquities, they might want someone with a degree in Japanese, and evidence of interest in the material culture.

This statement is typical of the minority of employers recruiting graduates for employment closely and finely greared to specific skills and knowledge acquired in higher education, often with a requirement of postgraduate study. It is closely tied in with the academic organization of universities, but the employer still requires something more than academic ability.

> Often it's enthusiasm for the subject which wins over the technical ability to do research. That's what I'm looking for... the person who's absolutely keen to get that job and do it properly.... If you've been trained as an

archaeologist, then you have a very good start... for a job here as an archaeologist, but... (it) doesn't give you a God-given right to be an archaeologist after you've finished your training, even if you've got a good degree. I've known people with very good degrees I wouldn't give the time of day to, let alone a job in archaeology. They can go into merchant banking or whatever.... What I am looking for, and what I think any sensible person who is employing graduates is looking for, is a person who is potentially dedicated to the job they think they're going to get.... You're making a very expensive investment in a graduate and therefore you've got to be pretty clear that you've got the right piece of machinery to put into the system.

THE QUALITIES REQUIRED: SPECIALIST OR GENERALIST?

Large employers, indeed most employers of graduates recruit from a number of disciplines into a number of different types of job. Many recruit graduates for both technical and non-technical work; with different expectations of long-term tenure and with different expectations of speed of movement through the organization. All of these factors affect the employer's perceptions of the value of the graduate to the organization. This is illustrated by three examples.

The personnel manager for a medium-sized private company which recruits between twenty and thirty graduates each year argued that he looked for certain characteristics in degree holders:

The subjects (of the degree) are essential to the job in research and development. And when we come into management services we do insist we only look at computer sciences/maths degrees which show very marked ability to deal with logic. Outside of these specialist areas we look at any degree. For example, in marketing we seek two young graduates. There are degrees in marketing and if we found a graduate with the right kind of personality to make an impression on hard-headed directors then the student with a degree in marketing would be at a distinct disadvantage, but we will give the person the individual training, since what we're looking for is proof that we're dealing with an individual who's proved that he has the intellect and mental ability to cope with the problems and make contributions. I'm willing to take arts graduates who will follow a career in production but we don't get too many of that type and if I'm concerned about anything it's the number of graduates I meet in the course of travelling the milk-round who are most insistent that they wish to be involved in work that is related to their degree.

The chief recruiter for a large industrial company had expectations of recruiting three different types of graduates, each with their own particular value for the organization:

If one looks at the overall graduate recruitment, one can broadly split three types of individual that one is looking for. We're looking for firstly specailists who may be, for example, metallurgy graduates to go and work in (the company's) central research, or electronics engineers to work on the control system and they will as likely not continue in that specialist vein. Secondly, one is looking for a comparatively small number of high flyers. These are people who may not be recruited so much for their academic ability as their personal characteristics. And, thirdly, one is looking for graduates to enter the lower middle management activities.... We (have in) the group a centrally organized management development philosophy that includes annual manpower audits where graduates are dealt with as a separate category and where each graduate is viewed in terms of what is the best move and when he or she will be ready for that move. Then, either within a division in some areas of the company, or centrally within the remainder of the company, having assessed that person with potential, the avenues for that individual's growth and contribution are then assessed and moves made accordingly ... the ones who enter the management development ladder, as it were, are any graduates who enter the group. Some of those graduates may be in specialist roles but even they could be viewed in terms of their future potential. In other words the job that they first enter is a specialist role but at some point they may leave that specialist field to a more general one.... At the time which we recruit we may have ideas as to those who are worth looking at, either because of the way they impress in terms of personal characteristics or indeed on the basis of their academic performance. This is not to say that any one of the graduates who enter the group is not considered for any future development.

A spokesman for a large chain of retailers made a distinction between those recruited for general management (the majority of their graduate entries) and those for specialist functions.

What we're really looking for (in our management trainees) is a strong personality with management potential, somebody who's fairly intellec- tual but on the other hand, who's probably made good use of their university opportunities over and beyond their academic studies ... we've got a highly established data processing department, attracting sufficient numbers where we can pick and choose, and we're typically taking those with practical computer science degrees ... although we find that an awful lot of computer science degrees are no more value to us than taking somebody with classics or history. They've got to be the right kind of computer science degree with a practical commercial bias, not highly theoretical....

Such employing organizations are not looking for one 'sort' of graduate; the value they attach to the degree differs according to the job for which they are recruiting. For example, a firm may look for one sort of graduate for recruitment into a specific technical function while valuing very different characteristics among their fast track 'general' graduate entry. As the spokesman for a very large chemical manufacturing firm noted when asked what qualities they look for in a graduate:

You will find different answers to that question in different parts of the organization.... In research (we are) looking for high calibre research people ... (on the) ... marketing side, degree subjects are irrelevant ... personal qualities are absolutely paramount. We're looking for confident, creative mature people who have been educated for capability.

In order to simplify the picture, we limit the variation in perceptions by grouping employers who, broadly speaking, recruit 'generalist' graduates and contrast them with employers who recruit 'specialists'. The following examples are taken from several technical recruiters:

> It's inevitable (because of the nature of the firm to) regard the learning in the main subject ... (however) we don't disregard the importance of general intellectual and some personal development provided by university education.

> In an industry like this, the technological component predominates.

> Obviously, 98% of our management recruiting is heavily discipline dictated.

However, this can be contrasted with some quotes from representatives of large non-technical organizations:

> Specialisms... what they learn at university is useful. (The area of) broadening the intellect, yes, that really is important, to bring into the company someone who's mind is developed and can look at issues in greater depth and with greater vision.

> Given that they have the intellectual ability − a 2i − to cope with problems, we're looking for people who will make good professionals. They've got the experience and ability to put across their point.

> The (particular) 'ology' doesn't count. Analytic development which can be transferred to whatever field he or she is dealing with is very important.

> We are looking for people who have demonstrated their capacity to cope with volumes of information, and learning under some stress, and I think *any* university subject provides that.

There is a clear distinction here between the value of the content of the degree for technical recruiters and the value for non-technical recruiters; the former require first and foremost able specialists while the latter look to much broader evaluations of a degree. Nearly half of the jobs advertised for graduates do not require any particular degree.

Employers recruiting generalists typically note a number of qualities they are looking for. Some are seemingly independent of higher learning, eg 'brightness' or 'flair'; some are developed in the years spent in higher education, eg 'interests', 'initiative', 'flexibility' or 'social skills'; and some are the particular skills and knowledge acquired on the degree course; while added to these are the experience of living away from home, work experience, achievement. The relative weight employers give to such qualities varies, as the following examples show.

A large manufacturing and marketing firm's spokesman explained that they would look for people who would 'fit' into the business:

> We look for potential: in my view every graduate we see is going to have a

common background in terms of education, level of intellect, probably social background, so we're looking for potentials that fit into our way of doing business. That is largely going to be a factor of the individual's personality and a factor of probably their involvement in consumer selling, maybe vacations, entrepreneurial flair that they showed at college, maybe contacts with parents, friends, relatives; they tend to be the better person we're looking for.

A large chain of food retailers had found that they looked for a solid, although not necessarily outstanding, academic training, but more importantly, the right sort of personality:

We're really looking for a strong personality with management potential, somebody who's fairly intellectual, but on the other hand who's probably made good use of their university opportunities over and beyond their academic studies. So, roughly, on the application form we're looking for a fairly stable academic history, because we're looking for people who're going to be stable in their work careers, who're going to be supportive of other people, so we don't want people who're not stable themselves. We're looking for people who, on the other hand, are perhaps not over high flyers because we want them to have done other things, ideally to have had some relevant work experience, though that might not necessarily have been retail but it will have some sort of manual work experience.

For a representative of a manufacturing firm:

The degree to me is simply saying they have a certain level of intelligence which ensures generally that they will deal with concepts, systems and procedures.

The personnel director for a large diversified manufacturing firm looked for both academic achievement and more general qualities, but recognized some of the difficulties associated with finding the latter:

We're looking for personal quality which we see as particularly evidenced in extra-mural things rather than academic achievement, per se. I think the handling and processing of knowledge, coupled with what I call pragmatic intelligence, which is a frightfully difficult thing to measure, rather than a chap with a double first or a very great knowledge of the subject.

A director of a large consumer product manufacturer stressed the importance of identifying the attributes of present senior management and trying to decide whether new graduates possessed or could develop the same:

What we try to do is to apply criteria that seem to characterize fairly successful people at the level we think of them getting to and trying to infer whether that is there in people of the age of 21. You will make an inadequate judgement but you have to struggle and try. As to what those criteria are, it would be reasoning ability, an ability to influence a group. Stamina maybe – not just physical stamina but the sort of remorseless pig-headedness to keep on beating your head against the same wall which is necessary for anybody in any big business. Ability to get engaged with what they are working on – whatever the argument is about. The ability described as the helicopter quality. The ability to concentrate on something but to get enough away from it to put it in some sort of logical position. So you are not so close that you are forever involved in the detail and you are able somehow to stand back and say the really important one is that one.

Ability not to give in, not to be overruled on the one hand because at some time in any big organization you have got to stand up and say, 'No, I don't believe that is what should happen even if 329,000 think one thing, but sod it, I've got to say what I believe.' You need that. But at the same time you don't want someone who is sniping for ever more and wingeing about the way it has been done.... So you have got to get the ability to make the point and they say, OK from now on this is what we are going to do and let's do it but at the same time, somebody who is going to fight for what they believe sensible.

(Q: The characteristics you have identified are very interesting ones in that they have nothing to do with the courses that have been taught at the universities or directly applicable to the jobs they are going to be taken on.) I find one of the most interesting things is that if you are saying 'what are the characteristics you need to be a very junior accountant' and 'what are the characteristics you need to be a very junior industrial relations manager', let us say, they are very different animals. But if you say, what are the characteristics to be of the general manager (personnel), general manager (commercial), general manager (marketing or whatever), those are much closer together. If you are trying to make judgements about people at this level, which is what we are doing to people at 21, then it is not so surprising that the criteria we are using are really general managers' criteria rather than criteria for a specific function....

We would use the interview as a way of checking biography because one of our criteria of selecting people would be Michael Edwardes' 'will he deliver?' And however glossy the package looks, you still have to feel at the end that if I gave this man or this woman something to do, whatever it was, how confident am I that in three weeks time it would be actually done rather than elegant excuses which they have been trained to do for the last few years. One way of taking a judgement on how will they deliver has to be how have they delivered so far on what they have set themselves to do, and so I think it is perfectly logical to go through an interview and ask what has happened to you but not just to build up a picture which says that if he has done so many of these things that is so many value points and so many of those, then that's negative points. Not that. It's saying he set out to be captain of house. Did he get there? If he did, what did he do? But the sort of question I always ask at an interview in that sort of situation is, What did you change while you were there? What mark did you leave on the hamster club? It almost doesn't matter what it is but what they change. In a big business you are looking for someone who can actually turn the Queen Mary just that little bit.

One spokesman for a large public sector organization:

> Any second class Honours degree is our minimum requirement....
> Personality is just as important, or more important than academic
> qualifications.... I can't recall many cases where we found someone who
> was intellectually up to the job and had done the various (entrance) tests
> well but whom we rejected because we didn't think he had got the
> personality.
>   What we do say is that a degree is prima facie evidence of intellectual
> ability and intellectual discipline and that's our starting point. We don't
> really care what the degree is in.

While another in the same organization said:

> What I don't think I would want would be a lot of chaps who are jolly
> good all round generalists but (are) not of the highest quality in their
> discipline. It does seem to me that this is the first requirement and on the
> whole our universities really do quite well. But... employing some of them
> for the latter part of their career is a very real problem and I think it's
> going to get worse in the future... because we find it difficult in fact to
> employ a chap usefully for life.

Such expressions of employer expectations revolve around a set of broadly
non-academic criteria, including participation in extra-mural activities,
general intellectual aptitude, the ability to sustain social relations with
different sorts of people, having gained pre-graduation, 'relevant' experience and having lived away from home. They are typically expressed in a
multi-dimensional way.

As we have seen, employers who recruit into specific technical functions
within their organization primarily expect to see particular technical abilities
in the graduate. However, within this second major grouping of views about
the value of a degree, particular technical competence is seen as but one of
the elements in evaluating the potential recruit. As with the group who look
primarily at non-academic qualities, the opinions of employers are complicated and reveal varying configurations of expectations, distinguished by the
importance attached to particular 'technical' abilities but still balanced with
the more general qualities.

According to a light engineering firm's spokesman, the firm looked
primarily for technical competence but also for the 'right' personality:

> Normally, if we're looking for someone at what we would call 'technical
> officer', which is the minimum point for someone who could work with a
> limited degree of supervision, (we would be looking for) a 2ii degree....
> Having looked at the degree, we will look at experience and try to match
> that with the requirements of the job. Some areas where we employ
> people, we look for specific knowledge and for strong analytical bias in
> their chemical course, or someone who's done a BSc in analytical
> chemistry.... We would take it from there to see if, personality-wise,
> they're going to fit into the environment. We work in a closed
> environment so we tend to look at people who are going to be an...

outward/strong person. If you are looking for someone who's going to work in a more fundamental field, then we might find an introspective person, but(if) generally talking to them, we consider yes they have the ability to do the job (they may be shy but their personality will develop later on), we would consider these people....

The personnel director for a detergent manufacturer, in contrast, explained that they looked for the 'best' people including technical competence as a more limited consideration:

> We're interested in hiring the best people and we don't much mind where we get them. Certainly with some, there are technical requirements. Obviously in research and development you need good chemists, etc., that doesn't mean we hire people purely because he/she is a good chemist — we take other things into consideration. There are two layers, (we) take good people wherever we can find them and on top of that our technical recruiters will probably put a higher value on people from a particular engineering department which is known to be good than they would on another.... On a broader basis we need people who know how to think, and had their minds stretched a bit and yes, we are very very interested in people developing their own personalities over the university years and very interested in the success with which people pursue their own activities. I would add a fourth factor that (in my experience), a three-year university course is an experiment to try a few things; to be wild if you like and test yourself. An opportunity which you are allowed to have at university because students are expected to be like that, and much more difficult for someone to have if they joined the company at 18 (with) their training being much more directional.

The first of these two quotations shows technical competence to be the most valued element in the graduate's training and consequently to be used as a first 'screen'. Criteria of 'personality' come into play later as a secondary screen to distinguish among those who have passed the tests of technical competence. The second quotation suggests a different approach, in which the more general considerations of personality are used as the first screen and technical competence the second.

There are few simple dimensions which can be identified from these examples. From the employer's perspective, the mix of qualities is more like a web into which a particular graduate will hopefully fall. It is noteworthy in how many cases the organization places clear reliance on the intuition of the individual recruiters in identifying a good graduate. It is also noteworthy that so few of the qualities are those mapped out by the academics who taught and trained the graduate.

THE CASES OF ENGINEERING AND ACCOUNTANCY
In the next section, the views of two types of employers are presented and compared: those recruiting in engineering and accountancy. By narrowing the focus once more the variation in perceptions and expectations is reduced. To a degree this also controls for some of the economic factors which may affect employer perceptions. Both areas of recruitment are still

graduates, although both recruit an increasing proportion of graduates to starting positions. Both, too, are growth areas. As we would expect, the views of engineers about the value of a degree are more similar to each other than to the views of accountants; however, in both groups of interviews considerable variation in perceptions and differences in emphasis remain. Engineering firms vary in the extent to which they value practical experience, first-class academic credentials, personal factors — indeed, they differ among each other over the value they put on having a degree at all. Work experience plays a greater part in the recruitment into engineering than it does in that into accountancy; extra-curricular activities appear to be somewhat less important; engineers are expected quickly to fit into and work in a group and to show a practical bent. Specific aspects of the engineering course were only rarely mentioned by employers.

A spokesman for a medium-sized consultancy firm felt that a graduate engineer should be both academically well trained and also practically experienced. Personal qualities were also important:

> What we're looking for is basically a good civil engineer, not necessarily consistent with getting a first class honours degree, though most of our intake tend to have 2is or firsts (occasionally 2iis...). The good engineer is a man who has the technology at his fingertips and also has the sense of vision and the sense of commonsense.... And of course, in (our work)... the personal factors are important as well. But we're looking as much at that stage for team work abilities as for leadership abilities. We're not trying to select the managing directors of the future or project managers of the future. We know that they'll be there, but most important we're looking at whether he's the kind of person who's going to have the knack of getting on with the client.

Similarly, a representative of a firm of manufacturing industrial products thought that

> Provided the university has done its homework and selected people on more than just A level results and provided the specific degree course has done the right thing, you *should* have, at the end, a person who has not only got the technology but has got the brain tuned in to using the technology and thirdly the university by its extra-mural activities should have given the person the opportunity to develop into an adult.

A senior recruiter for a firm of engineering contractors felt that there was a degree of uncertainty about the balance between a theoretical training and practical experience, and, indeed, the value of degree-level training in either.

> I think that there is a problem here, the practical route that used to produce chartered engineers produced engineers who were very good at problem-solving but who lacked a good theoretical background. To some extent we're now going the other way, we're getting engineers who've got a very good theoretical background and are very good academic engineers but are lacking a lot of the practicalities and this, of course,

tends to prejudice the older engineers against them; an older engineer still sees a degree as being quite important and quite a rare qualification.... I think there must be a balance somewhere and we're not getting it, we're see-sawing about, we've gone from practical engineers lacking some of the theory right across to theoretical engineers lacking a lot of the practical knowledge until they've been in industry for six to ten years.... I don't think you can say 'Yes a graduate is definitely better than an HNC, HND qualified man with a lot of practical training.' The real test will come when you reach the engineering manager level and to be perfectly honest the graduates who came through from the initial expansion of the engineering departments in the early sixties are still just reaching that level. I think an awful lot depends on the individual, it's difficult to generalize.

A personnel officer for a firm of manufacturing engineering goods stressed work experience:

As far as I'm concerned, people who've been in industry have an advantage. They've gone through the work situation and are definite about the choice of job as they've dabbled in it for a bit and there's evidence of how they relate in a work situation.... The course content is important, the more knowledge they have the less time we have to spend on the basics.... Something like President of the Union, Saturday jobs, some kids are completely subsidized by parents, not even working on summer jobs. So they haven't a clue what a work situation is like – all theory. They don't realize the world is imperfect. We find people who have been in industry are more socialized towards practice.

A large engineering process firm noted that at the initial interview they were looking for:

... technical and personal qualities, and also to a large extent what interests they've been involved in re leadership, and what they've got out of their institution. You are bringing someone into a team who will fit in and hopefully lead later, they should adapt to this role while they have been at college. So the person who's going to get a poor degree might have done a lot of work in sports (and has the intellectual level) is going to be of interest.... (We are) looking for a much more rounded person who holds with interests and responsibilities who can talk logically about things.

The director of a heavy marine engineering firm:

One prefers anything over a 2ii upwards. We are not looking for research people but practical people to manage the flow of men, materials and goods through a factory.... I think attitudes (are more important) than skills. Industry is not glowing excitement.... But I do expect the fundamental basics of engineering, production and management.

In these interviews, the importance of technical training is apparent, although not all employers see it as necessary to first degree level. In addition, employers expect that degree status should bring with it associated non-academic traits such as leadership potential and a 'suitable' personality. Engineering employers also look for evidence of practical aptitude from degree holders, and to some extent related to this, for the graduate to have had some 'relevant' work experience. They hope to see a balance between the theoretical engineering knowledge which higher education provides and the practical engineering competence which is normally gained through work experience. However, finding the right balance of these attributes in graduate recruits may involve considerable compromise. As we say in Chapter 5, perceived shortages of 'appropriate' or 'good' graduates often are the result of the inability to find the balanced graduate. In part, this derives from requirements which are difficult to balance: practical experience and theoretical training.

Those responsible for recruiting accountants express views on the value of a degree which are more similar to each other than to those of engineers. However, parents, graduates and educators will see enough variation in accountants' views to prevent creating a simple picture even here.

This is illustrated by statements from two of the largest recruiters of graduates into accountancy. Both firms are particularly prestigious employers, both are 'training' firms, both recruit primarily from universities and have a disproportionately large Oxbridge intake. In the first extract, the recruiter emphasizes the importance of extra-curricular activities and personality. In the second, the singular importance of academic achievement is made plain.

Major recruiter; graduates only; recruits primarily from 'major' universities:

> We are certainly looking for young people who have demonstrated their capacity to cope with the volumes of information and learning under some stress, and I think any university subject provides that up to a point. I think there is a case for arguing that we would be on safer ground looking for people with some numerate or quantitative aspect to the subject or some heavy volume of sifting complicated material.... The personal qualities: I think we are certainly looking for these more than the students often realize. We are looking for somebody who can very quickly be Mr. (company name) to the client. If we have bright people who can't say boo to a goose or who are terribly prickly as personalities, our clients are just going to say − 'I can't work with these people'.... That's where the tour of Jersey or whatever (comes in).... The demonstrated achievement at university outside their subject, can be a measure. It's not infallible. There will be people who haven't achieved very much who seem to have the right building blocks of personality, they just haven't really come out yet, despite three years at university....
>
> In an interview, I'm looking for a general level of presentation of which appearance and dress is a part, not more.... The way they come across, by the attitudes they strike and by their capacity to handle dialogue − that's at one level and you'll never know that until you meet the person. On paper the sorts of evidence I would seek fall into probably three areas: one is the personal statement about level of achievement at university.... It may be sport, it may be JCR or college or hall orientation; it may be the

Students' Union; publications; charitable organization. I'm looking for some sign of taking the university by the scruff of the neck and saying, 'I'm going to do something' and not merely say, 'I was a member of this or that'.... Vacation work — I simply don't accept even in today's world, with the range of evidence in front of me, that students can't get vacation work and I look more critically at someone who's done no vacation work than at someone who has gone out and got work....

The second firm is a major recruiter which also takes graduates only, from 'major' universities:

(Our firm looks purely at the) level of achievement at the 21-year-old stage: indicating what they've done at school — predominantly academically; and what they're doing at university in terms of academic achievement. The *sine qua non* is 'nous', and application thereof, coupled with motivation to actually do the job; personality factors are very very subsidiary in our experience: they can be extroverts, introverts, but they've got to have the track record of achievement. Academic achievement is the overriding achievement.... I suppose I'm terribly prejudiced by an élitist mainstream education which concentrated heavily upon exams and Oxbridge scholarships at 17 and so on and it's what most of my close friends and colleagues went through and I do believe in pushing teenagers and early twenties people very hard to high level achievement.... There are, of course, more liberal ideas of absorption and continuous assessment and a little bit of this, that and everything. I don't think on the whole... this is necessarily a good thing: I'm not an educationalist. Certainly for our purposes we want products'of a straight educational system for taking exams.

Few employers, recruiting for any positions, discussed specific course content or differences among courses. Accountants were not exceptions. However, accountancy presents a particularly interesting case in which there is a dramatic difference between the number of graduates trained and the positions available in the field. Approximately 1,000 students graduate in accountancy each year for about 4,000 vacancies. The profession, however, appears undecided about the value of the specialism of the degree. One senior recruiter noted his firm's ambivalence:

As it happens, if you look at the intake, very roughly 20 to 25% of our intake is going to be of accountancy students.... And at the other end, 5 to 10% will be scientists and engineers, if you exclude mathematicians in that. Chemists and engineers (about whom, in the mid 70s, industry was saying 'they're all becoming chartered accountants').... I don't think it ever was the case and it's not the case now. The very obvious pattern is that the preponderance of people are economists or with an economics aspect; the social sciences — not sociology, psychology, virtually none of those. Quite a lot of lawyers.
    Historically, the early intakes of people who did accountancy were not academically very distinguished. That's not necessarily the case now.... (Some accountancy departments rank among) the toughest departments

to get into, so in that sense the academic base line has probably been increasing and that ought to mean that accountancy students will qualify at least as well as non-accountancy students.

In another large firm, the recruiter notes that 30 to 40% of management consultants are engineers, and computer scientists. That number is expected to increase although he notes that 'we still take pure arts people also'. For tax some are trained as accountants, a good proportion are lawyers. He notes, 'this is more of a lawyer's than an accountant's job'.

> I would say that with competition as it is, we're aiming at 30% of our intake to be graduates in accounting. Not that we are necessarily achieving this. I'd like it if we were moving towards 40% through the 80s. (Graduates from) the numerate sciences are increasing... as the professional exams include more of it and are much more heavily technical than they used to be.

As a senior partner in this firm notes: 'we are quite happy to take someone who has done a completely non-relevant degree. We have found that they perform equally well, if not better, than the relevant graduate.... People at university say: 'Should I have done an accountancy degree?' And I say: 'Not at all, if you enjoy doing astronomy, so be it.' I believe at university you should be broadening your whole outlook; we don't look for accountancy graduates specifically.

One large, well known firm put no special value at all on the accountancy degree:

> They compete equally with anyone else.... One wouldn't want to put too much importance on it, but one finds that scientists − chemists, physicists, engineers − tend to do rather well. I wouldn't say that (this) is *because* of their training − it may be that they are correspondingly better individuals (than the corresponding arts graduates) in any case − their basic talents are possibly a bit higher.... Also, their training in investigation is rather similar... to that needed in accountancy.... But the door is certainly *not* closed to arts degrees, and there have been a lot of successes with such graduates.

The large accountancy firms plan to take on the professional training themselves. Several investigated here are 'training firms', that is, they will take on large numbers of graduates with the knowledge that they will lose them in a relatively short period of time. A small accountancy firm will not have the resources and opportunities for a similar scope and intensity of training. Thus, existing training opportunities within the organization will affect a firm's evaluation of the courses and the degrees which potential recruits will have read.

Although some members of the profession perceive a need for a common standard of training there is apparently little consensus about what that training should be and how well contemporary accountancy and business studies meet any standard. Over time, the accountancy degree may well be the significant degree as it changes to meet the needs of the profession. The employers represented here are uncertain as to the value of it or business degree, and several remain unwavering in their belief that a degree-level education to a high standard in any subject is as good an initial training as any other.

Turning back to the question we began the chapter with, 'What is seen as the advantage to the employer of the three years spent on a graduate degree?', we would have to say that any gains to the employer are clearer among those recruiting engineers than accountants. For many of the latter the value added by the degree is not sharply distinguished from good A levels, an outgoing personality, skills in communication, and evidence of some intellectual development in the post-A level period.

SUMMARY

It is clear then that for many employers the value of a degree is not something which can be assessed solely in terms of the degree itself, but derives from a comparison with other available forms of experience and training. The results of this comparison range from firms in which the graduate is thought to bring no added value to the organization, to the other extreme where only graduates are able to satisfy requirements. The most straightforward form of evaluation lies in assessing the specific attributes which are gained during degree work, which non-graduates lack. Examples given are the ability to learn, relative maturity, the level of training. However, there is no consensus among employers about this; some argue that such qualities might as easily be developed by non-graduates and indeed some argue it is preferable for people to undertake forms of training other than degree work, even though they still recruit graduates.

Some include in their assessment a time dimension, making comparisons at different times between graduates and non-graduates. One employer will compare the 'value added' of a graduate entering the organization (at 21 or 22) with an 18-year-old entrant. The graduate is seen as having 'potential' and is consequently afforded more opportunities for rapid promotion. A second employer will compare a graduate at the time of entry with a non-graduate at the same age who has 'worked his way up'. Some organizations see the non-graduate as being superior, some argue the reverse – that graduates have an all-important something extra. Another type of comparison is made between graduates and non-graduates at some time in the future (as one respondent succinctly put it: 'A + no university + 13 years experience, compared with B + university + 10 years experience'). Again employers differ: some arguing that one can always tell the graduates from non-graduates, some suggesting that after some years there is really no difference.

Many of the employers express difficulty in establishing solid grounds for these sorts of comparisons. One felt that it was largely an 'act of faith' as to whether in the long run a degree added anything to the value of the employee. The conclusions reached often depend upon subjective views of the value of the higher education experience to the individual graduate rather than the usefulness to the organization.

On the evidence, three factors contribute to the value added by a degree. The majority perceive it as adding some value beyond A levels, though some do not think it is very great. Mostly, this value derives from a mix of academic and non-academic qualities which graduates are believed to acquire. Secondly, a minority put a very high value on the substantive content of the degree. A third perception cross-cuts these. Whereas the first two see values as attributes of the individual graduate, the third sees a value in the degree as a useful (if not wholly accurate) screening device. The 'screen' of higher education selects a group of people who, upon graduating, will provide a richer source of potential recruits for the employing organizations than the cohort from which it was selected. For this reason it is more cost-effective for employers to tap the 'richer' graduate source than the whole age group.

This view relies upon the assumption that graduates as a group are likely to have desirable qualities which their contemporaries do not have. Some of the employers who expressed the view recognized that using higher education as a recruitment screen is a blunt instrument, for many people who could have achieved graduate status chose not to do so.

This view of the cost-effectiveness of the value added by a degree lies in an appreciation of the changing (and deteriorating) value of other qualifications, especially the impoverished pool of 18-year-old applicants. Employers argue that the increased proportion of the age cohort of 18-year-olds going into higher education has had the effect of generally lowering the quality of pre-higher education applicants. Hence the value added by a degree lies not so much in the qualities developed by reading for a degree but in the effects which increased access to higher education has on the quality of the pool of manpower which enters the labour market at eighteen. (Perhaps this should be regarded as 'value substracted' in recruiting 18-year-olds, rather than a real 'value added' by a degree.) Amongst employers expressing this view, we again find differences in response: some arguing that the increase in the pool of graduates allows for more potentially 'good' applicants to join their organization, some bemoaning the demise of the 18-year-old market for qualified manpower which had in the past been valuable to their organization.

A cost-effective recruitment exercise is geared to finding the largest number of appropriate graduates in as few institutions as possible. Employers attempt to control for as many as possible of the academic and non-academic qualities they seek in graduates by the choice of institutions and departments from which they recruit. This singularly important aspect of the evaluation of degrees is discussed in the next chapter.

4 The Value of a Degree 2: The Eclipse of the Public Sector

Some 150 higher education institutions in the UK grant first degrees. Every year some 80,000 graduates are potentially available for work. Given the later average age of marriage in the past two decades, and correlative changes in the status of women, increasing numbers of women graduates seek work experience or full careers. Thus record numbers of graduates are seeking jobs at a time when employers are looking for more efficient and cost-effective strategies for recruitment. 'Cost-effective' recruitment often means reducing the number of institutions visited on the milk-round or, in some cases, not increasing the numbers on an already attenuated list. Employers concentrate on institutions which have given 'best value' in past years, depending on perceptions (and prejudices) from past recruitment. The effect of this is to create vastly different opportunity structures for graduates from different institutions. The type of institution attended — university, polytechnic or college — emerges as perhaps the single most important determinant of the value of the degree in the market place.

Early interviews with employers showed a marked and consistent preference for university graduates. Indeed, 'university' was often used as a generic term describing all graduates. The preference takes a number of forms, as can be seen from the examples below. Employers' views on the differential value placed on degrees from different institutions is shown in their discussion both of recruitment strategies and of the qualities of particular institutions and their graduates.

A very large nationalized industry which is also a very large recruiter of graduates:

> Universities are the main hunting ground, and I think that's becoming increasingly so. People who are what you might call genuine degree material, and therefore getting the sort of A level grades, etc. to enable them to go to university, will go to university.

One large public corporation:

> In the past (we) preferred to recruit from universities, although polytechnic graduates are looked at on the same basis. Recent entrants

have come from London, Cambridge, Glasgow, Manchester. We do look at poly people. To be frank, we found that we don't normally select them. I think it's a part of the system, isn't it?... Somebody goes to university if they can, and therefore, whether you like it or not (the polytechnic students) are not of quite the same high standard.

Similarly, a personnel manager for a large computer systems consultancy:

(We have) a heavy preference for universities.

A small manufacturing firm:

We would want someone who'd done a really good engineering degree, someone from Imperial College or Cambridge, or somewhere like that, with a really good engineering degree and who has experience. But usually, if you're hiring graduates from university you're not hiring them for particular projects like that, you're hiring them to beef up the staff.... There is a hierarchy because they're the ones who get all the best kids.... I don't draw a line after those two (Imperial and Cambridge) actually, I'm sure there is a pecking order, but not one that I know about. All I know is that when you're at achool, if you're really good at science subjects then you apply to... one of those two: Cambridge or Imperial.

The senior recruiter for a very large diversified industrial firm:

We are talking about 250 recruited; divide that by 45 universities and you would expect to get four or five people from each university, on average. The top ones being Imperial College and Oxbridge... the other big three are Bristol, Durham and Manchester.

A personnel manager for a firm of food manufacturers:

My personal prejudice, in terms of my own experience was for universities.... They (polytechnics) still are, in many people's minds, including my own, a superior technical college.... I still believe the Oxbridge qualification carries clout and I would like my son to be exposed to what are, after all, top academics.... But I must confess to an appalling lack of knowledge of the other universities and the polytechnics.

A large manufacturer of engineering products which is a medium sized recruiter of graduates:

We were particularly concerned about the engineering guys, so we really got our list (of institutions) together on the basis of our personal experience in previous years, on the basis of our contacts and our gut feeling about those universities.... Last year we went to in the order of 20 universities. This year we've actually included one or two polys... (and now go to) 23 or 24 institutions... (and this) is to some extent fairly revolutionary.

A senior recruiter in the motor manufacturing industry:

> We tend to look at the more traditional universities for the more creative
> type of individual experiences. They don't necessarily come good
> immediately, but seven years on, provided they stay with us, we look on
> them as people who are more senior.

A spokesman for an electronic engineering firm said:

> I suppose looking at the available talent, Oxbridge and Imperial, but... we
> would look favourably on what we quote as a 'local university'. Given that
> much manufacturing was in the west, we would always feel obliged to try
> and develop a close relationship with Liverpool (university and poly),
> Salford, Manchester and with people in the area.

In the same vein, the personnel director of a very large firm in the fibre and
textile industry, which is a medium-sized recruiter of graduates, said:

> You would probably go to Cambridge if you were a technically based
> company because, at Cambridge, you have the pick of the best brains....
> There are bound to be good fishes in the sea. You can't get all the good
> fish out; but what you have to do is get a selection of the big ones; and we
> know that some pools are better stocked than others and where you drop
> your line.... One infuriatingly rich pool we don't get our share of is
> Imperial College. It has very strong connections with the oil companies
> (and) they constantly take the best fish.

A senior spokesman for a public sector organization with limited responsibility for graduate recruitment noted:

> I would know about the academic grade recruitment, which is Research
> Assistants. In every case it's a university with a specialist course on the
> subject in question.

The emphasis was the same for a small research establishment:

> Principally from the universities (Cambridge, Oxford and Manchester)
> and one rich source of recruitment from universities has been from
> people who have taken a one-year MSc course.

A spokesman for a very large industrial production firm which is a small
recruiter of graduates said:

> We have had people in the past from polytechnics. For example, Trent
> Polytechnic has a very good reputation for engineering. But... competi-
> tively, we would be looking for people from the engineering universities.

These early interviews suggested the need for an extended analysis of
employers' perceptions and expectations of university graduates as com-

pared with those of graduates from public sector institutions. They showed a surprising lack of evidence about public sector institutions. To compensate for what might have been a university bias in sampling and questioning, new employing organizations, known to recruit public sector graduates, were added to the survey; the 'problem set' was also revised to call attention to the public sector. The difficulty remained, however, and it became apparent that one explanation lay in the understandable ignorance (and perhaps indiffer- ence) of those outside the educational world to the distinctions of terminology and function within it. The binary line; universities, polytechnics and colleges; further education; advanced further education; higher education; 'sectors' which may be described as private, autonomous, voluntary, public, maintained; all are distinctions which many employers do not hold in mind. Many who have employed graduates over the years are only vaguely aware of the changes that have occurred in the nature and names of the institutions at which they have studied. As one employer noted: 'When I talk about universities, I mean all higher education institutions.'

The interviews show great variability in employers' knowledge of types of institutions, content and quality of courses, and experience of the institu- tions about which they express opinions. One technical recruiter who had a generally positive view of polytechnic graduates also expressed the view that 'people at polytechnics tend to be of lower ability'. The evidence for this is his view that 'Salford is notorious for its low entry requirements.' Salford is, of course, a university; a similar error is made by the interviewee who described Solihull (a further education college) as a polytechnic. Another admitted: 'I don't know anything about polytechnics... they seem to do more arts and social science subjects than universities.' Some others confuse polytechnics with technical colleges and believe they are concerned primarily with technical subjects. A senior recruiter in a multinational manufacturing firm observed: 'I must confess to an appalling lack of knowledge of the newer universities and polytechnics.' Very few employers, indeed, were aware of the graduates of the recently diversified colleges of higher education, even in some cases when a college was at their doorstep.

With these differences in knowledge and experience in mind, we can nevertheless look at what employers say when they do differentiate between institutions and their students. The distinctions were, after all, intended by the government which established them to have important policy implica- tions. As background to our evidence, we can consider what were the stated policy objectives of those who established the present public sector categories in the late 1960s.

In his speech at Woolwich in 1965, the then Secretary of State for Education, Anthony Crosland,[1] outlined the policy for public sector higher education which was the basis of the next year's White Paper. He argued that the government wished to see a system of higher education composed of an 'autonomous sector' (universities) and a 'public sector'... 'with each sector making its own distinctive contribution to the whole. We infinitely prefer it to the alternative concept of a unitary system, hierarchically arranged on the "ladder" principle, with the universities at the top and other institutions down below.' It was the foundation of what became known as the 'binary' policy and, as a first step, amalgamated some sixty colleges of technology, art and commerce into thirty 'polytechnics'. They were to incorporate degree and non-degree programmes, full- and part-time students; they were intended to cater for students in a wide range of social circumstances and of mixed ability, and to offer both academic and vocational subjects. (The conversion of many former teacher training colleges into colleges and institutes of higher education was to follow later, as the demand for school teachers declined.) In his Lancaster Speech in January 1967, Mr. Crosland defended the new policies:[2]

> I believe there will be great educational advantage from the existence alongside the universities of more broadly based higher education institutions in which full time, sandwich and part time students at all levels of higher education work together. In academic as well as human terms, there is no hard and fast line between the different categories....
>
> Secondly the inclusion of full time degree work carries on the historic and invaluable further education tradition of providing opportunities for educational and social mobility... no wonder some other countries envy what has come to be called the open ended role of the technical colleges — the role of providing the second chance, the alternative route.
>
> Thirdly the inclusion of full time degree work is the best way of avoiding a most undesirable and social division at 18.
>
> These are the reasons why we see the polytechnics as comprehensive in their student intake....
>
> What we see as the role of the polytechnics is something distinctive from the universities and more comprehensive....

Some two-thirds of the higher education institutions whose function it is to provide courses for first degrees are in the public sector. Their main formal distinguishing characteristics are that they are not chartered to award their own degrees, as universities are, and they receive most of their funds from local education authorities. Of all the first degree students in England and Wales, about one-third are enrolled in these public sector institutions. It is a proportion which has built up rapidly over the last decade. In 1970, 6% of the total of first degree graduates (UK) were in the public sector, in 1975 18%, in 1979 23%.[3] This means, among other things, that some employers' actual experience of public sector graduates is necessarily very limited and very recent.

Public sector institutions include thirty polytechnics and some sixty colleges and institutes of higher education. They also include a large number of colleges and schools which are involved in advanced further education but not primarily with degree courses. Among these, for example, are many colleges of further education which offer one or two degree-level courses among many other lower level ones, and some specialized colleges of music, drama, art, argriculture. Such institutions receive little attention in this study as the focus is on graduates and the institutions which educate them.

From the evidence here, what can we see, from the employers' perspective, of the comprehensive reform of higher education which took place a decade and a half ago? There certainly seems to have been success in what was earlier perceived by the reformers to be the comparable policy of establishing comprehensive secondary education. Our interview evidence shows very little concern by recruiters for the type of secondary school attended (comprehensive, independent, direct grant, etc.) and, in particular, no sign at all that the comprehensive school student is disadvantaged on that account in the job market, provided he has the A level results. (It may be, however, that the continued preference for Oxbridge graduates by many employers is in part an indirect preference for independent secondary schooling.)

Public sector higher education, however, does not appear to have achieved the status intended for it. There is nothing approaching parity of esteem; instead a 'hierarchy' of institutions has developed and remains.

There appear to be two explanations. First, most employing organizations continue to attach the highest importance in selecting graduates — or at least, in shortlisting them — to the A level grades they achieved three or four years earlier. Public sector institutions are seen as consistently attracting students with lower A level grades than universities; and employers, concerned to use their total recruitment resources economically, therefore concentrate their activities in universities. Second, the effect of this is not balanced by any general perception on the part of most employers of any special academic, vocational or social value in a public sector degree. Indeed, except in the case of a few courses at particular institutions which may be judged comparable to similar university courses, degrees from public sector institutions (which are, of course, formally CNAA degrees) are generally seen as decidedly inferior. In the words of one large employer:

> The polytechnics and the technical colleges doing CNAA degrees have much lower acceptance requirements at A level. Anybody with an A level of respectability at all seems to be dragged into the degree or degree equivalent course. These people quite rightly say we are graduates. We can fit a number of these people into the organization very comfortably. (However) a number of them cannot compete on terms with the conventional academic graduate.... If they cannot they go into what is really a technician's job they get disgruntled because you are using them as technicians and they see themselves as graduates. (The system) provides more degree people but the quality... is more uneven... people are now labelled as having second class Honours degrees but when we interview they don't sound like second class Honours degree people at all.... In terms in which we have to judge they are not really comparable to the second class Honours degrees that you get from Durham, Imperial, Bristol... (however) it would be unfair to bar everyone who comes out with a BSc from North East London Polytechnic. You have to interview carefully because they are a variable animal whereas the upper second class Honours from Bristol — we know exactly what they are. We have got used to that standard.

Those employers who do see particular value in degrees from both sectors may nevertheless still orient their recruitment towards universities for reasons of cost:

> We reviewed the situation three years ago — on a cost benefit (basis) — mostly that we couldn't afford the time and effort to visit all departments in all universities.... We drew up a short list of departments and

universities which we felt were best able to give us the type of graduate we required. These would vary according to discipline. That decision is made from a combination of factors. Obviously, a relevance of the course to our particular needs — you can teach chemistry from a highly theoretical viewpoint or from a more practical point and the same with molecular biology. So the factors are the course content, the practical element, the general reputation of the department. When it comes to the post-doctoral level, it is the type of research carried out, the quality of research, the quality of supervision of PhD students. All of these factors played a part in the short list drawn up... (a list heavily weighted toward universities).

In the following sections we review the survey evidence which bears on the employing organizations' relationships with and attitudes towards universities and public sector institutions. This analysis uses a rough typology which is not exhaustive but which suggests the variation in relationships and attitudes and which incorporates most of the organizations in our survey.

A TYPOLOGY OF EMPLOYER PREFERENCES

We return to recruitment as a basis for creating a typology of employer preferences. As we have argued above, the process of recruiting new graduates is the clearest indicator of an employing organization's perception of and relationship with higher education institutions. Any other 'links' most employing organizations have with higher education institutions are minimal. Where they exist they tend to be with a single institution: for example, in having a member of staff on an institution's governing body, or, more rarely, in collaborating on a research project. Thus, it is to recruitment that we turn to observe the cumulative experience of organizations with institutions of higher learning. In this chapter the excerpts from interviews cover a number of question areas rather than any specific set of questions. We have looked at the interviews for any point where comparisons were made between types of institutions or where perceptions of the public sector institutions, specifically, were offered.

Discussions of these relationships prove to be sensitive for some employers. As one interviewer noted: 'My own experience as a recruiter was that an employer could gain nothing from being nice but stood to lose heavily from any perceived insult to an individual or group of institutions of learning.' Some employers' representatives are very positive toward the public sector in principle, but appear to recruit very few of its graduates. Few representatives admit, as did one representative of a multinational petrochemical firm: 'we visit polytechnics because it is politically important.' Further, a number of organizations argue that they have no particular preference, although the institutions they visit are primarily universities and their comments indicate a preference:

We don't have an overall preference for universities. The best polytechnics are capable of sending out graduates comparable to virtually anything we see from the conventional universities. We have a number of examples of successful recruitment. Having said that, one has to acknowledge that if you take a mean value — if we would (evaluate) the candidates that we see from both sides, then the poly candidate by and large shows some deficiencies. It tends to be in the breadth of their knowledge. In many ways in their practical ability and experience they are ahead of the universities. We are getting concerned about the practical element in university courses.

As the evidence will show, some employers were extremely forthright. The large majority offered some observations and the typology below is created from these.

Type 1

The largest single category of employing organizations represented in the study is of those who say they recruit very few graduates from the public sector. Many of these are regarded as 'blue chip' firms and many are household names. They are typically large and have corporate images which will attract the 'best' graduates. They have received good value from universities in the past and, by and large, see no reason to change their orientation toward higher education institutions. Many of these employing organizations are not primarily recruiting scientific, engineering and technical graduates although many recruit some. The excerpts from interviews presented below cover a number of question areas. The separation into paragraphs indicates where the argument is not a single sustained one.

A large manufacturer of electrical and domestic appliances:

> (Q: Polytechnic graduates in the last few years?) Not that I know of, they are all from university. You don't get the credit if it goes right and you get heard about if it goes wrong so we stick to the tried and tested (institutions) without innovation.
>
> (Q: What is the difference in training?) Polytechnics are more practical. Probably it is just prejudice if we are honest about it. (We feel positive about a university graduate) and suspicious about a polytechnic graduate. You try and work out your own biases – we all have them in one way or another. Whether we will stop putting them into practice, I don't know.

An international computer and business machine manufacturer:

> We are not really in the business of picking up large numbers of those whom you would expect us to pick up. I am not enthralled by the vast numbers of computer scientists who are on offer here and there. We are after the best people we can find – we find many of those in the old universities... we conduct a milk-round in 26 universities, 3 polytechnics (one polytechnic because it's local, one because we take their people on industrial training, and one other).
>
> (I think there is a difference in graduates from polytechnics and universities). A very high proportion of the people we recruit come from Oxbridge. Of the 67 we recruited this year (half were recruited from Oxbridge), the rest are scattered throughout other universities and polytechnics.... We usually pick up some polytechnic graduates.
>
> I think there is a feeling that a computer science degree is an automatic entry into (company name) – if someone has a computer science degree (it is a negative attribute).... It is still true that (a classics degree) provides some very good people into the computing industry.

A small chemical engineering firm:

> We haven't recruited anyone from polys; that's been a matter of response to ads — they have all been from universities. We're great university people.

A small accountancy firm:

> There is a big Oxbridge bias about who we see and who we take.

Three large accountancy firms:

> I suppose we have a natural preference for Oxbridge which are our biggest source — 15 or 16 of the partners are Oxford; 11 to 12 Cambridge; 11 LSE. Those are our biggest three sources. Oxford remains our biggest and most loyal source of all in the practice and also the biggest source for outside London offices. Cambridge is also a major source but not quite the same — not quite so fertile. Beyond that we are looking at the Bristols, the major universities.

> There is a traditional prejudice (toward) the upper middle class — Oxbridge class such as myself, not that I have the prejudice — we love to have men like myself — historians and whatever — and indeed they make very good chartered accountants. (However, universities other than Oxbridge, which have very high standards for their accountancy courses are looked on with favour) the major universities — and the major universities are Bristol, Manchester, Exeter, East Anglia then followed by Kent and Warwick, Leeds — tend to have higher entry standards for accounting courses than they do for other courses. Bristol demands three A levels at A grades for accountancy. Exeter will demand two Bs and an A currently. So will East Anglia. So you're getting a good calibre of undergraduate for a start.

> We have, like everyone else, certain biases that you pick up. You see students from polys and other universities and probably to a degree, if you're thinking about it rationally, they're probably not fully representative of 2,000 to 3,000 people.
> Nevertheless, we've had two or three (polytechnic graduates) in and they seem to be a waste of time so we don't bother encouraging other applications. They still get the directions — we obviously don't dry them up, so applicants with persistance are still going to get through to you. However, we regard ourselves as a fairly high class firm and think we're able to get a good calibre — therefore we try to get most of our graduates from universities that subjectively are likely to provide good students.

An international computer manufacturer:

> We would always go to the universities as a block. This year, even though we are not recruiting as many, we have gone to all the universities. We have not gone to many polys... the numbers we recruit are small and it costs a lot to recruit from the polytechnics.

We have got our prejudices about universities based on experience... but not enough that we could do a statistical analysis on it.

Course content matters. Some of our technical people are very keen on some universities because of course content. But more generally, we would follow our prejudices about what we would regard as a good university.

The special thing polytechnics do give us is graduates as industrial trainees... helps spread the recruitment load.

A large firm producing photographic and technical equipment:

We see 20 to 25 universities, because they give us a good response, because the careers services are well geared, because the quality of the people they attract are the right sort of people for our needs.... Half a dozen universities won't meet the particular need because of the nebulous reasons for students going to particular institutions... so at any university you can meet the next managing director.

The (sandwich) model of higher education is non-proven because they have not attracted the top quality people. I can't see it being proven.

An insurance company:

Whereas 20 to 30 years ago when I was a young school leaver, if you went to university it wasn't so much what you had done at school but what you were going to do if you went.... You were going to university because you wanted to become a doctor, a dentist, lawyer. You had to go to university before you could continue your profession of choice. Recruitment within our organization was from very good quality A levels. There were still numerous A level holders who didn't want to become doctors, etc. and were quite happy therefore, to look for a career in our organization. These are no longer available because they've been encouraged to go to university to take a variety of degrees and therefore I, over a period of time, have brought this forward and say that I think we should be looking at graduates, not so much because they are graduates, but because they are of a certain academic standard that we should be interested in, albeit that they are three years older than they were 20 to 30 years ago.

(Q: Do you recruit from polys?) We go to polys. I go to Liverpool Poly. Providing there are sufficient applicants for me to interview, we will certainly go to the polys. One's got to always to be a bit cautious. I'm not going to make comparisons between universities and polytechnics – that's not my province. But certainly in the specialist areas there is no doubt that the person who's taken his maths degree at the university, from an actuarial point of view, stands a better chance of getting accepted by us than the one who's taken a maths degree at a poly. On the other hand, if you're talking about business studies, certainly poly business studies graduates would be considered. Don't ask me how many we have had from polys – it would be very very few. No, there's not an exclusion. But universities could provide us with what we want and in practice they do. This is just the way the cookie crumbles.

A merchant bank:

> People may say, why should we stick to the two supposedly best universities? Why can't we go to non-Oxbridge? The answer is that the level of excellence is higher than the level in any other individual universities — the numbers are much greater for a start. As it satisfies our recruiting needs, why should we change?
>
> (Q: Is the level of excellence through the people who go there — they are the brightest people — or is it the teaching?) I don't think it's necessarily the teaching — to have got to Oxbridge you need something extra than to go to other universities. Bristol, for example, is better at teaching some specific subjects than Oxbridge. If someone goes there for that reason, we respect that and if they have all the other qualities we take them.... Nothing against polytechnics — it is simply that we can find the right people we want from the universities we go to. So why make life more difficult...?

An advertising/marketing group:

> I've resisted the idea that Oxbridge produces better candidates... but I have had to admit since being involved in recruitment myself that we have had some extremely good applications.
>
> (Q: Any bad experiences?) Only polytechnics, unfortunately.... We certainly didn't in any sense prevent people from polytechnics applying.
>
> (Q: Did you send application forms and information to polys?) If they asked us for them. That's the difference. We sent them out to all the universities... and I don't know, going back a long time, whether there was ever a mail out to polytechnics, but of course I have been involved for four or five years I suppose.... I must say that we found on the whole that we didn't get as good a standard of applications. I don't know why. Maybe it was because we didn't have close links, maybe we weren't getting the best graduates directed towards us. But, you know, we'd look at an application form, and often you'd try to judge it before you looked at where somebody was from. And we tended to find that, without preconditioning ourselves, we didn't get as many good applications from polytechnics. So given that we had limited resources we just chose not to seek them out.... In fact, I can't think of anyone we have ever recruited from a polytechnic. It sounds terrible to me because, I mean, I sympathize with the polytechnics when they say 'People discriminate against us', unfair and so on.... I do think, personally, that a lot of the courses they do are very good, and very orientated towards the more practical side of business. I mean languages with business studies, and this sort of thing. And potentially it sounds just the sort of thing that we'd normally be looking for but... whether it's partly because we haven't concentrated on them or we tended not to get their best people, I don't know.

An armed service:

> When you come down to selection, immediately you leave (training) we

have to judge that he's going to be capable of doing the right thing at four o'clock in the morning in Belfast and it's that potential we're looking for.

(Q: Outstanding polytechnics/colleges of education – are they accepted?) We don't get a lot from polys. We have pushed ourselves very hard for polys in the past. Again many come from the background where commissioned service isn't really considered when they're at school. The problem is to get them to even consider the services within the polys.... We are sponsoring within the polys. That has a long term effect... but not in great numbers.... The last time I was down at Portsmouth, there was quite a lot of interest, one or two but we don't get a large number from the polys....

An accountancy firm:

I tend to prefer the better established universities: certainly universities are preferred to polytechnics. (For non-graduate recruitment) I look for people who have got sufficient A levels and could have gone to a good university but have decided for some reason not to.

An international office equipment manufacturer:

(Q: If candidates from university and polytechnic applied for the same job, would one have an advantage over the other, all things being equal?) Yes, the candidate from the university would have better A levels almost by definition.... He would at the end of the university course undoubtedly have more maturity.... I am sorry to say this because polytechnics struggle, but nevertheless there is a greater ease and communication of skills at the end of the university course.

(Q: It's been suggested that degrees differ in the labour market. Sometimes because a particular course is thought to be good. Could you comment on this?) I would have said we are commercial gents here and ignorant of the minutiae of that type of thing. We wouldn't say that a first class degree from institution X is really only worth a second class degree from a superior institution. Yes, we recruit from polys – any job – just the same as the universities except that the odds are less. There are fewer 'capital' fish per gallon in a poly compared with universities so therefore if you have half an hour you would prefer to consider five university graduates than five polytechnic graduates on the grounds that the odds were better. If you are limited in time, you pan for gold where there are more bright things.

A multinational petrochemical company:

(Q: The nature of your milk-round suggests that there is a very strong preference for universities. Is that based on experience?) It's a fact of life we do a milk-round: it's very difficult to choose which universities to go to so we go to the lot and when you have all the applications from universities and also applications from people from polys/colleges which we don't visit, as well as people who are out of work, it is just a fact of life that you are likely to say these are the good people. There is just a huge pool − why should we bring someone else in? Those people on application forms have got to look rather good − they have got to have done something and have got to indicate some entrepreneurial skill, perhaps to go into our commercial areas.... We can't be totally fair with the numbers we have got − we have got to get the best we can. There's not a total prejudice, it's just an unfortunate fact that we have this huge application pool.

A large firm of solicitors:

We send out literature to the various universities, particularly those who apply to us. We have close contacts with universities with good law faculties. We don't do a milk-round.... If you look at the applications, a lot of the students have either not talked to their tutors or their tutors have advised them badly. People want an interview here with three Es at A level.

We are satisfied that we get enough good quality applicants to have an arbitrary ruling that it is not worth coming to see us if you are not likely to get a 2i or a First... however good your personality, you might as well not apply.

(Q: Which institutions have you recruited from?) Belfast 1, Birmingham 6, Bristol 20, Brunel 1, Cambridge 56, Durham 7, Exeter 7, Hull 2, Ireland 1, Keele 1, Kent 4, Leeds 3, Leicester 1, Liverpool 2, London 36, Manchester 1, Nottingham 4, Oxford 70, Reading 3, Sheffield 5, Southampton 5, Surrey 7, Sussex 2, Wales 4, Warwick 4, York 1. Polytechnics 2. Not many people come to us having got a degree at a poly but quite a lot come to us having taken the Law Society final course or the CPE.

As some of the above comments show, employers do not operate on the basis of an undifferentiated conception of university graduates. They often concentrate on particular universities, operating from a perception of the characteristics of the institutions, or past successes in recruitment or both.

A senior partner for a large firm of accountants:

By and large, we would tend to avoid sending our literature to those universities which have the reputation of being academically unsuccessful. We can get on quite well at Manchester, and this is the only university to be visited this season.

The personnel director for a large insurance firm:

In the past we visited universities according to whether there have been large numbers of applications or not. (Manchester and Bristol have proved 'happy hunting grounds' in the past.)

A medium-sized computer manufacturer:

Our best six are something like Oxbridge, Manchester, Bristol, Leeds, Salford, Liverpool.

A retailing firm which is a medium-sized recruiter of graduates:

> (Our visits to universities) change a little bit from year to year, for
> example, in 1982 we are going to Manchester and Durham for the first
> time. (Q: First time to Manchester?) That's because of the number of
> applications we had last year. We've knocked out a couple of universities
> we did last year where we didn't have sufficient numbers. It's self-
> perpetuating but.... I suppose we've got about six universities that we
> would reckon to get one or two people from.

Wholesale reshuffling of the list of institutions visited for recruitment does
not typically occur if the graduates coming forward are satisfying the
organizations' recruitment needs. 'Favoured' institutions tend to be the
result of the historical development of a particular organization's recruitment strategies. Changes in preferences for institutions tend to be marginal.
The stability in recruitment strategies, in itself, seems to indicate that these
employers are reasonably satisfied with their recruitment. This is reinforced,
in the current climate, by the need for economy of effort.

Type 2

A number of engineering, scientific and technical firms suggest that the
public sector graduate provides neither the perceived superior academic
training of the university graduate nor the qualities of the HND/HNC
student (higher national diploma/certificate). The significant recruitment
problem for these firms is to find the good technician. The polytechnic
graduate is not seen as a satisfactory compromise between hiring a
technically trained non-degree student and a university graduate. While
some of these firms admit to problems in using university graduates in lower
level technical jobs, they tend not to see the solution to their problems in
recruiting a polytechnic graduate. Generalizing, these firms would prefer to
recruit either technicians of good A level quality who have chosen
non-degree training or university graduates.

A major motoring manufacturer:

> We are employing graduates in occupations that would be more
> effectively done by technicians. (We even face situations in which)
> someone will pick up the 'phone and say, 'Have you a graduate to spare?'
> They don't want a graduate but a technician. It is questionable whether
> we really have the (appropriate) number of graduate jobs (which we call
> graduate jobs). Technicians in those jobs don't get as disgruntled as
> graduates.

A recruiter of engineers:

> Because the pattern of the old style OND etc. has almost disappeared
> from the scene, it is accepted that most (young people) go to university.
> There are now more placed.... We have got to get the better academic
> standard of engineers so we go for university applicants... (those with
> high) academic standards go into universities and not industry.

However, it is argued here as well:

> It doesn't mean we need a degree-standard boy to become a professional engineer. In my judgement HND is adequate as a degree.... If we had a young apprentice... capable of achieving an HND, he is better than a university graduate. I don't see a great deal of difference in academic requirements between a BSc and HND.

A pharmaceutical firm which recruits a large number of technicians (a third of the firm's positions) primarily chooses students with HNC or HND, noting:

> Graduates are probably not going to get the satisfaction, and we don't want problems. We think they would cause difficulties.

When recruiting graduates:

> We go to universities that have some reputation in disciplines which are of direct interest to us. Probably six or seven, full stop.... We get a number (of polytechnic graduates)... not good ones (and) very rarely. In the main, even with chemists... they are not normally the brightest.

Typically these firms are somewhat reluctant to take a graduate, fearing conflict and problems of retention. Fitting the graduate with high expectations into jobs shared by or previously held by technicians creates dissatisfaction. As one of these employers notes:

> Within a five to seven-year span, we are losing 75% of them.... If you suddenly bring in someone expecting a certain level of remuneration and responsibility – who is relatively green compared with the experience of all these other people – it causes problems. We never really cracked it....

Solutions to recruitment problems in these firms include sponsorship or an insistence on some industrial experience before or during degree work. One, however, does not see the solution in polytechnic recruitment.

> We tend to look at the more traditional universities for the creative types of engineers. They don't necessarily come good immediately but seven years on, provided they stay with us, we look on them as people who are more senior.... We insist that all undergraduates spend some time in industry before going to university... we want undergraduates to go to university as an employee of this company (although) he is not contracted to us... a successful degree is 2i or 2ii or even a pass. We are not looking totally for high fliers, (thus we do not put) all our eggs in any one university basket. The undergraduate goes to the university of his choice, ensuring that we have a wide range of different university experiences from university courses coming into the company.

Another large technical recruiter:

> We have (visited polytechnics) in the past but we find that the numbers do

not justify the visit. Principally, we look at high calibre technical people and that means, in most cases, the major universities.... The standard of entry (in polytechnics) is very much lower and generally the standard and expectations of people are lower. If they end up with a degree, they expect to get a graduate job but very often those who have managed to get to a poly are not qualified personally – I'm not expressing this very well – they don't really perform as we expect graduates to perform. They are very much super-technicians.... We expect a graduate to move into a much broader base taking a much more management attitude. That's a generalization.... People only go to polys if they can't get to university. A levels are not a bad judge of a person's academic ability.... If someone is capable of getting three Cs at A level then they are capable of, normally, getting a good quality degree. If you get someone who's only capable of getting two Es, they normally can't get a university place but they can get a place at a poly. Normally, the academic world is not theirs. If they've forced themselves into the academic life, they tend to be very much the technician rather than the general graduate. Their academic ability is limited.... We have links with a number of polys with specific interests....

Possibly I have a personal bias, I would much rather take a first class degree graduate who had done a relatively classical course than a highly applied course. I would rather take a natural scientist or a chemist who had done a straightforward course than I would a modular course.... I am sorry, in a way that we have moved a bit away from the ONC and HNC approach of combining day release studies with practical experience. This still happens, of course, but the better people do go to universities. I've a lot of time for the BEC and TEC courses, but I just don't think that they are attracting the high quality people.

Type 3

A number, a minority, of employing organizations which were interviewed have highly specific and technical manpower requirements. These firms focus their recruitment efforts and their relationships with higher education almost entirely around the courses offered. They take graduates from any *appropriate course* in any institution in which the course is offered, independent of the type of institution or educational sector. Such firms particularly value courses which offer an industrial training component. Firms of this type, while primarily dependent on course-based recruitment, like other employers have an eye out for 'good people'.

A manufacturer and retailer of dairy products:

We go to a selection of universities – no relationship geographically. (As our demand has grown, the number of institutions has grown). University of London, Brunel, Oxford Poly (for the food technology course), Weybridge College of Food Technology and Reading University, Silsoe College, Bath University, Manchester Poly (which has been a very useful supplier of graduates in computer sciences) and Southampton University for engineering.... Apart from the obvious like between those specializing in food and other scientific subjects, they come about more by chance than thought.

A food wholesaler:

> (Q: Do you concentrate on one group of institutions?) It is as wide as the universities are... (actually) they are not mainly universities. We give polytechnics a fair share.
>
> (Q: How do you select?) It has something to do with where good people have come from and (also we concentrate on) institutions which specialize in fields like agriculture.... (There is a problem of company image.) The fact that we recruit from Salford is perhaps indicative of the fact that in the engineering world we are not normally regarded as an engineering company. Good engineers will go to Rolls. They see us and say, 'engineers, how come?'

An electronics manufacturer:

> What I want from an individual in his first six years here is technical excellence and a man tends to get promoted on that basis. His technical contribution controls how fast his career progresses.... I personally have not been very impressed with engineering students from Essex, whereas someone who comes from Aston or Bradford is very good. (We) think more of graduates who have done a sandwich course. There are two factors: (i) (they provide) cheap labour; and (ii) when they come to finish, and if they decide to join us, which 80% do, they start work on day one. And the ideas they have about industry are ones that we have put into their minds. They have no bad preconceptions − ideas, etc.... our best relationships are with Brunel, Bradford, Aston, Loughborough − this is because their courses are relevant.
>
> Other things being equal, the university graduate would have a slightly higher chance (of being recruited). One would look back to O level and A levels and the academic attainment. But I'd look for the growth and rate of learning. Someone might start poorly but do very well later.

A small technical and engineering firm:

> The main way we choose universities is to look at our particular requirements.... The disciplines we are looking for... (in polytechnics and universities) are pretty similar, certainly in the engineering fields and the (accountancy field).... No we don't see any difference in calibre.

A large construction firm:

> We would not like to recruit a lot from the same university. (Although) we have just started a continuous association with one university, we like to... spread recruitment. We usually get enough applications to allow us to do this.... Polytechnic graduates − these would only be associated with sandwiches.... We don't take a deliberate decision that we will have a percentage of those and some of these. Over the years we have built up an association and understanding in places of learning. If you took building, for example, we support the Polytechnic of Central London, the

Polytechnic of the South Bank, Aston, but at diploma level there are also several institutions....

(Q: Would the graduate intake be from polytechnics?) We don't think that way. It is pure chance. I think (the polytechnics) produce a slightly different animal... the product of the polytechnics is rather more practical.... They warm more readily to man management... there is one other thing and that is the entry into these places.... City University, which we use a great deal, is looking for three Cs and perhaps a B. In a poly they are looking for two Ds.

A household products manufacturer:

We are interested in hiring the best people and we don't much mind where we get them from.... There are two layers (of recruitment). We take good people wherever we can find them. On top of that our technical recruiters will probably put higher value on people from a particular department which is known to be good.

A manufacturer of electrical equipment who visits almost every university and two-thirds of the polytechnics:

(Q: Any particular preference?) No, we have no particular preference.... Half a dozen universities provide half our intake... but it is difficult to find one consistent pattern.... It is not usual for us to analyse who is coming from a polytechnic and who is coming from a university. They are all treated equally on milk-round visits. We keep no records — I don't know what the percentage will be when you add those numbers up. But you have got to use discretion on the numbers because the percentage that will come from polytechnics in a five-year period will be understated. In the early years, we did not make *separate* visits to places like Liverpool Polytechnic and Solihull. We could see people from local polytechnics on our visits to the universities and we always log applications according to the place where they are interviewed. So if someone from Sheffield University last year was looking for a job and he lived in Exeter and presented himself at Exeter University on the milk-round — this year he would be counted as a success for Exeter. (Recently we) have found it worthwhile to pay separate visits to Liverpool Polytechnic and University where hitherto we had seen them jointly.... We have never distinguished who is from a polytechnic or university and I have never been conscious that one is the guy who is a little bit inferior.... I would say that increasingly, the polytechnics are being shunned (in sponsorship). Although the number of sponsorships has increased dramatically, very few students will be sponsored to polytechnics.... We are inundated with applications for sponsorships and therefore we tend to go for the guy who got five As at O level.

A spokesman for a very large consumer product manufacturer which is a large recruiter of graduates:

Yes, we tended to go to polytechnics where we have been successful... only four or five... we regularly went to Bristol Poly because we had some success there a little while ago. We regularly went to Sheffield Poly, again, we had some success there.... I think we started when we found that a couple of people applied and were successful.

A similar argument was made by the senior recruiter for a detergent manufacturer, whose firm is a small recruiter of graduates:

We visit polytechnics in particular cases. We don't visit all universities, we decide which universities to visit purely on the basis of past experience. A new university gets on our schedule by having produced direct applicants of interest to us. After a couple of years, we see they're good applicants so we should add to the list. That's been very much the case with polytechnics.... Some polytechnics will produce a number of such people and at that point we say 'let's have a look at them'.... Polytechnic people are invited because they are good enough to be invited.

Type 4
Only a small number of firms could be said to have a positive 'prejudice' in favour of the polytechnics. One firm, which manufactures office equipment, recruites only polytechnic graduates. 'If you are a graduate, you are a graduate.' This recruiter's advice to secondary students was:

... strongly to go to a polytechnic rather than a university because polytechnics are more practical.... (This firm is looking for people who will) fit in... personality is very important.... Outlook on life is important and that they are prepared to work hard.

Reflecting the firm's recruitment policy, he continued:

I think it's very important in these days to choose a course that's got some practical value to an employer. I think that to do, say, take a degree in English or History, unless you are specifically doing it for the pleasure because you like the subject or because you want to be a teacher, I don't think that sort of course offers anything to an employer and I think graduates should realize when they're finished that they've no more to offer than they had when they left school and that if they go into a job they will have to start at the bottom and learn about the company and learn how all the routine functions are carried out, which we do with all our graduates. They go through the whole department and do the most boring jobs, because they have to know how the company works. A lot of graduates, I find, tend to think that the world owes them something, and I don't think that's the case at all. I would say that it's important for people to acquire skills, whether it be typing or doing some sort of electrician course; I think that's very important.

A medium-sized computer manufacturing firm, which recruits primarily from polytechnics, emphasized the positive attitude toward work life held by polytechnic students. Again, however, it is difficult to separate the value of work experience from the 'polytechnic experience' generally:

Particularly with the software support organization where people are dealing with customers, it seems to help the graduate, because they've had some industrial experience. We find... particularly in terms of confidence and being able to deal with people and communicate...that three industrial periods of six months each is a tremendous help in boosting their confidence. And generally being more aware of industry... more aware of the opportunities available. For example, as I explained earlier, there is a lot of difference between software support and software engineering, and I find at universities it's very difficult to get this across to students because... they just have no experience to relate to. I find with the polytechnics, that, generally speaking, the students there pick up the concept much quicker and are able to say, well, software engineering will be more interesting because I've actually worked in that environment or I would find software support more interesting because when I was out working for an organization for six months I actually dealt with customers and I loved it; or conversely, I hated it and I therefore think I would prefer to go into a backroom job. I think they're much more aware of the opportunities and the sort of job they'd like to do.

(Q: Do you think of the university graduates as less practical, more theoretical?) A lot of university graduates I interview have a very practical streak in their nature and they're very keen to go into industry and they understand about industry in general, but specific opportunities − and I'm generalizing terribly − they really don't have any idea. And that's totally understandable because they have nothing to relate to.

The managing director of a large building and civil engineering contractor noted:

We sometimes find the poly applicant is more mature that the university person. The university person traditionally goes straight from school; the poly applicant does occasionally move on to poly after being at work... we get some very mature and competent people from polys, which is less likely to happen at university.

However, when institutions are dropped from an organization's milk-round they are more likely to be public sector institutions, as this interview with the personnel director of a large diversified manufacturing firm illustrated:

(Q: What about polytechnic (recruitment)?) We receive applications and they are considered in the normal way.

(Q: I see you've got Newcastle Polytechnic down on your list. Is that the only polytechnic you go to?) It's the only poly we go to this year. That list is subject to change year by year, we've always had a very good response from Newcastle Poly.... We've been to many others, we've been to Portsmouth, Trent, Hatfield. Last year you'd have found a number of other polys on (the list), but in contracting down, I think I made the decision... that we need only go to Newcastle Poly.

Type 5
A number of employing organizations which actively seek university graduates still have a decidedly open mind towards public sector graduates.

Some of these are firms with a strong emphasis on personal qualities in their graduate recruits and they are prepared to take a good look at candidates from all sectors. Of these organizations, however, some are still 'finding their feet' in recruiting graduates, and appear not to have the organizational tradition which is such an important influence on patterns of graduate recruitment.

A new but large charitable organization reported that they began their first year recruitment programme within the university sector, with a milk-round of twenty universities. In respect of public sector institutions:

> If they show an interest, we will come.... I have no preferences as regard which university produces the right products.... We are looking for the person, not the university.... Having said that, we have planned our recruitment programme for next year and there is a greater tendency to move towards universities that offer PGCE courses and BEd.... Working for a charity requires commitment to a cause. A lot of people going through a university become much more aware of social issues and are keen to work in a worthwhile, altruistic environment.... So as part of a university education, they have a greater social awareness which makes them keen not to work in multinationals.... Secondly, they are keen after their university degree to prove themselves.... We offer them just that. (Thirdly) we offer them creativity.... We are saying within certain guidelines you can do what you like.

A large retail clothing firm reported: 'no favourite recruiting places.' However, 'of the people we interview, polytechnic people are weaker' and 'Oxbridge people tend not to think of retailing as a career.' Though in terms of coping with the firm's training, polytechnic graduates are as likely as university graduates to 'cope' well.

A large and important retailer:

> We select universities and polytechnics on the basis of either past track record of similarities to other (institutions). If I was only allowed to go to one group of institutions, I would go to universities and not polytechnics, and redbricks rather than either Oxbridge or the modern universities.... The status of universities is higher; therefore the majority of parents who wish their children to go into higher education... are opting for universities. The ones who don't make it are the ones who end up in the polys. The reason I go into universities is the calibre of entry not the value of the education they receive there. I go to a fair number. The polys tend to be established: Sheffield, Newcastle, Manchester and Liverpool spring to mind quickly....

However, this firm is open to graduates from all sectors:

> I don't know what a good graduate is. We are looking for skills with people, not academic prowess.... (We ask) 'Has this person got the personal qualities to enable them to manage in a pressurized environment with lots of interruptions and build a team that will work for him/her?' I don't believe the higher education system has a great deal to do with these qualities.

Type 6

A few firms, often smaller firms or divisions of larger firms, form relationships with particular higher education institutions on a regional basis, recruiting from local universities and polytechnics.

A building and design company:

> We recruit mainly from Midland universities and polytechnics.... (We have contacts at) relevant construction departments... our needs are so small that local departments – especially through sandwich placements – give us what we want.

A supermarket group:

> We go for universities where the company image is strong.... We are much more successful in the Northern and Scottish universities. We include polys, for example, Birmingham. At Durham and Newcastle we pick up Sunderland polytechnic.

A marine engineering firm:

> We just use our connections with the local polytechnics and universities – Newcastle and Durham Universities, Newcastle Poly, Sunderland Poly and Teesside Poly.
>
> (Q: Do you generally recruit from one type of institution?) No. The polytechnic lad needs less of a training course and he has usually come from a working background whereas the universities concentrate on the lads from school and their experience is totally different.... Therefore from university, it is longer to train but at the end of the day they are no different.... We are certainly not looking at their degrees.... We use the local institutions because they understand our industry.

A large multinational, also a large recruiter:

> We have a philosophical approach to this. The universities are likely to attract the academic person who from our experience makes the better (company name) manager. The skill of the polytechnic is in producing the technician and doing retraining. Our divisions have close links with some polytechnics for just that purpose – training.

A medium-sized firm of chartered accountants:

> We specifically do not present (ourselves) at polytechnics, but where they have a local university they are generally invited to attend... probably every year there are two or three polytechnic (graduates) joining us.

A local authority:

> We have considerable links as a local authority with the local (institutions). We tend to take from them unless they come from Oxbridge.... Obviously, we are in the market for Oxford and Cambridge.... I am a little biased there because my son is at Oxford.

We are more than satisfied with the major red bricks.... Polys do a good job but are the next layer down... this is a generalization... it might be unfair....

The way things are, perhaps the brightest people are not attracted to us anyway. The public sector being under constant attack, nobody's friend... possibly we have a very short life (it is questionable if) we are going to survive for much longer. In that sense we are probably not getting the brightest people.

The Atypical

An over-rationalized portrait of perceptions of differences between and among higher education institutions can easily be painted. However, there are many mavericks among employers and employing organizations and a number have a noteworthy lack of consistency in their perceptions. For example, the chairman of a large holding company argued:

The reason I have never had a graduate entry scheme... is that I regard it as inequitable that graduates should have a special right to anything − it is a question of philosophy. I regard it as entirely equitable that anyone who requires further education should be in a position to get it. We sandwich quite a number of people through polytechnics and universities.... If I were running one of my groups, I would regard the situation as perfectly OK. If I wanted something, I would get it − there is no lack of resource. The industrialists cannot complain, and if it's not working for them, they are lazy − they are lazy in not approaching the university saying 'Listen, I want a dozen guys trained in the next three months' or 'I want six of your best students within the next two years, and they have got to be able to do this, that and the other.'

(Q Perhaps industry is not encouraged enough to do this?) I'm not a personnel manager so I'm not interested in principles. I'm paid to run a group and make money. All my interests stem from self-interest, which is cruel and hard but that's what it's all about. If I want people, my view is that there's no lack of resource. I am surprised by the educational system − if I want specialists in exchange for money, I can get them trained. If the UK can't provide them I can get them from the USA − which is also what I have done. They just happen to be specialists in a certain area in which UK don't train staff. If I have money, I can get a resource: it's not difficult. I won't have my people complain to me about a lack of anything. If I can pay for it, I'll get it.

One of the group managers within the same company, however, said he liked mostly graduates from universities, although:

... we have people from Cambridge down to a little college of technology.... My knowledge is that people from the older universities − Edinburgh and the good English ones − tend to be the best employees because, although not the high fliers of Oxbridge, they have more determination.... The universities give (graduates) a wider background than polytechnics. At the end of the day, the polytechnic people fit into jobs just as well but they may take longer to adjust to the outside things we do.... The universities seem to have a wider social backgroung if nothing else and it makes it easier for them to adjust to people from overseas and that sort of thing.

Another example of this difference of view within an organization can be seen in a nationalized industry where a top manager involved with graduates at the final selection stage could not identify any difference between university and polytechnic graduates, but in practice, recruited mostly from universities. However, a senior recruiter in the same organization pointed out that 'Oxbridge has its own special magic' and that 'the universities, at least the better ones, provide a better education for life.... Overall, polytechnics tend to attract the slightly less able student.' Another senior recruiter in the same organization was even more specific about the differences:

> Well, obviously there are differences in the abilities of students, otherwise they wouldn't have fallen into the polytechnic trap. The reason that we, and I personally support very much polytechnics is for the industrial experience they have to offer. There are people who have failed to get into university, and those are ones which generally speaking are down the queue, but there are also those who have gone to polytechnics for very deliberate and positive reasons where they have identified a course that no university offers. There are polytechnics offering some very very good sandwich placement courses and so forth and with the right motivation and the right commitment the slightly older, slightly more mature polytechnic student can be very good material indeed.

A number of organizations could not easily fit into any of our 'types' of relationships with any higher education institutions within or outside the public sector. These firms take few or no graduates; often their senior managers or personnel directors are not themselves graduates. They, in short, have had little experience of the higher education system. Some scorn it altogether. One medium-sized firm recruits no graduates straight from higher education:

> We don't see recruitment in ready made graduates... if we recruit a ready made BSc from university, more often than not they have frittered away four years... there is a missing link with graduates who go straight from A level − with a three year course − and all they have to offer is a good academic brain with no industrial experience.

One clothing manufacturer noted:

> A degree might be valuable on the manufacturing side but not on the retail side.... Three years spent in a retail shop would be much more beneficial than three years spent in university... on the entrepreneurial side you don't necessarily need a degree.

The firm occasionally visits one university and sometimes takes students on work placements but the recruiter seemed uncertain what a graduate was.

THE SPECIAL ROLE OF THE PUBLIC SECTOR

Few employers recognize a special contribution made by the polytechnics or the colleges of higher education in offering a second chance to mature students or in giving the particular value of part-time courses. These are, of course, extremely difficult questions to put directly. We expect that few employers would, if asked, say they did not favour these aspects of public sector education. However, given many opportunities to propose changes in educational policy or to comment on the adequacy of current provision, these social and educational aspects of public sector higher education were rarely mentioned.

There were some exceptions. One employer, asked his opinions about polytechnics, observed:

> Brutally, some of these produce rubbish and there are one or two polys that I wouldn't touch with a barge pole. As against that, the thing that polys do well — and no one else does — is to reclaim the guy who has only had one or had bad A levels, whose achievement at A level stage was below his normal level of achievement. Polys do a rescue job on people who should have gone to university but whose A levels let them down. I had a case the other day of a man who had a good school record, bad A levels and a good record from the polytechnic. When you inquired he was firm that his A levels were poor because he had suffered under a couple of nationalist eccentrics in Wales who spent all their time ranting and burning places down and not teaching him. I would have said there that the poly had rescued a man who'd been hard done by at A level.

A senior recruiter from a nationalized industry noted the vocational orientation of the polytechnics:

> The point initially was that the polytechnic student in the past has been a failed university entrant. I see that's changed slightly. Some polytechnic students have opted now to go for a 'career' and I see that there's also been a change in youngsters in the sense that they worry about their futures. You get 18-year-olds who are really worried about where their future lies and their job prospects. This is reflected in some students, in the fact that they go to polytechnics and are taking career-oriented courses. I see a slight change there.

Against these views, however, are a number of statements like the following, which argue that the public sector has not been responsive enough. An accountancy recruiter said:

> There are a narrow range of polys who provide a very good course... and there are a much larger range — based on the applicants we have seen from time to time — who are in a totally different class, just not up to the mark of the handful. (These better courses have a good reputation, and so get more applications and can set a higher standard. They have the reputation that they) run courses which more nearly meet the needs of the accounting profession. (The polys generally have) very jealously

guarded their independence in putting the elements... of a foundation course together, and the Institute (of CAs) has come up against a blank wall (when trying to suggest what should go into the courses. Some of the best courses are City of London, Kingston, Hatfield). Once a reputation gets going it feeds on itself. (But in some polys it seems as if the course) had been cobbled together from available elements and students may emerge with almost no relevant technical knowledge, for example, on book keeping.

A few employing organizations stand out from all others in their attention to and knowledge of differences between types of higher education institutions. For example, a retail food chain noted some interesting characteristics which the firm perceives in graduates of colleges of higher education:

(Q: You suggest that you have a picture of colleges of higher education that makes them suitable as recruiting grounds.) Yes, I do.... I've spoken to other people who have recruited in colleges and I've spoken to some of the principals of the colleges, too. There was a study done about two years ago about the class split of people in colleges of higher education as opposed to university and typically, and I know this is very crude, they will tend very often to be people who will have come from either lower middle class or working class families, they will come from parents who are used to working life, to physical work, to shift work. They have to be prepared to work odd hours, be used to fairly long hours of work and they probably have brothers and sisters who haven't gone into higher education at all. So they have probably got a better expectation of what it is to be in what is a fairly physical management job − certainly this is true of the early stages of retail management. They have better expectations and will adapt more easily. Retail management is, I think, an area where a lot of satisfaction comes from working in a fairly close knit group, which the branches are. Working in a team.... It is very supportive, almost cocooned in a way. (It is said that many) people actually positively want to go to colleges rather than university or polytechnic, even if they have got the grades, because they prefer the more family-like atmosphere, the smaller groups of colleges.... And so there is a correlation between the reason they want to go to colleges, the (work) environment that we can offer them, and their own expectations. Crudely, also, I think (college graduates) appreciate that in many people's mind they are the third tier of further education and therefore they differ from those coming out of university in their expectations from that fact alone.

It is important, however, to note that responses such as these were relatively rare. The colleges of higher education played little part in this survey. Apart from the interviews quoted above, few employing organizations appeared aware of the colleges and their recently diversified courses. Asked whether college graduates had been recruited in the recent past, the majority of employers simply said 'no'. Other responses included:

Not in practice.

No.... I wouldn't, speaking from my own personal experience, expect to find many people from that source.

We do, but very rarely.... We find that the numbers we are seeking are adequately met from the higher education institutions higher up the league table. We rarely find the necessary degree standard coming through.

Seldom.

We have, but I don't know now.

I can't honestly say we do contact them.

We don't use colleges because it's just not what we're looking for. We're looking for the graduate trainee who will go up to management fairly soon.

No. If we had an appointment out of the blue, yes. But we don't positively extend our list to them.

Very rarely.

In practice, no.

We do not generally recruit HNCs, our graduate programme is exclusively for graduates.

(There)... is some chance that someone from colleges will come knocking on the door, join the staff and work his way up.

I can't recall doing so.

The Law Society effectively precludes them.

THE BINARY SYSTEM

Becher and Kogan[4] have described the creation of the binary system 'as a dramatic intervention in both the norms and operations of higher education, and as an affirmation that public purposes should be determined outside higher education proper. It can also be seen as a governmental assertion of the antimony between academic independence and conformity to social demands.' They go on to say that 'the case of the polytechnics demonstrates, however, that the basic characteristics of higher education cannot easily be overridden', that 'the polytechnics steadily moved towards the modes and aspirations of the universities' in a process of 'academic drift', and that 'the universities in their turn moved towards adaptations of their course offerings designed to meet identifiable market needs. The distinction between the two types of institutions had... become embarrassingly blur-red....'

Certainly this is a view widely held within the education system itself but one which is also hotly disputed. Harold Silver[5] has reviewed the various competing claims about differences and similarities of the curriculum, teaching methods and student characteristics and concludes that 'statements of clear role difference ... and the various ways in which it is attempted to define and categorize these roles, are in fact surrounded by uncertainty and ambiguity.' But he goes on to say 'there is a widely perceived university-polytechnic hierarchy, whatever the distinguishing characteristics to which appeal is made.'

What light does our evidence throw on this? First it suggests that *most* employers are not at all concerned about, and are probably not even aware of, the functional distinctions observed by those within the educational system. They see little overlap or 'blurring', little 'academic drift'. A few firms which hire highly technically trained men and women are those most likely to ignore institutional differences. However, what most employers do think they see, and what they are, for the most part, overwhelmingly concerned about, is a very clear, and often oversimplified hierarchy. They argue that because the intake of students to universities (measured usually in A level grades) is superior, their output must also be superior. Add to this A level factor the conviction that the 'university' experience produced better personality characteristics and there seems abundant support, from a rich variety of interviews, for the conclusion in an earlier smaller study quoted by Silver that 'polytechnics are viewed as producing second rate graduates both intellectually and socially.' And this is what appears to matter to many employers, regardless of the educationalists' small print.

What explanations of such perceptions (or expectations) might there be? First, they may lie partly in the background, attitudes and perhaps lack of knowledge − in a strictly neutral sense, the 'prejudices' − of the employers themselves. Few have had public sector degree level education. We do not have complete information on the academic background of every employer interviewed, because some interviewees were reluctant to give it. Some interviews were conducted with two interviewees present and it was difficult to handle personal background questions. To complement the information gathered in the interview, however, a short questionnaire was sent to the employers we had interviewed, and nearly three quarters of them provide information in one form or other. Of those who responded, slightly more than 70% were graduates. This proportion is greater than that which would be found in a larger random sample because the non-participation rate of firms was considerably greater among those which recruit few or no graduates, and these are the most likely to have non-graduates in senior positions. Of the employers who are graduates, slightly more than a third were educated at Oxford or Cambridge, while only four were graduates of polytechnics.

This pattern, of course, is strongly related to the ages of senior managers and recruiters and the structure of higher education during their youth. As late as 1970 only 6% of graduates − today's 33-year-olds − were from the public sector − yet of those employers we interviewed, the largest proportion (slightly over 35%) were between 36 and 45 years of age, and the second largest group (22%) were those between 46 and 55. Twenty years ago one-fifth of all degree-level student were at Oxford and Cambridge and another fifth at London; fifteen years before that (today's 56-year-olds, and still influential in management) 40% of all graduates were from Oxford and Cambridge. The educational background of the employers interviewed was therefore much what would be expected in their age group, and did not include personal experience of higher education in what are now public sector institutions.

Given the fact that most employers in our study appear to prefer university graduates the nevertheless relatively high level of employment of polytechnic graduates needs some explanation. Nearly 65% of both university and polytechnic graduates find employment in the first year after graduation, although the unemployment rate is considerably higher for polytechnic students.[6] (A greater proportion of university graduates do not directly enter the labour market.) In 1982 13% of polytechnic graduates were unemployed a year after graduation and 5% of university graduates. Comparing the short-term unemployment rate of university and polytechnic graduates we find a similar pattern of employment as between subjects for the two sectors; but higher rates of unemployment for polytechnic graduates in most subjects. Thus, in both sectors students in engineering, computing, management and accountancy fared relatively well in the market, but even in these areas unemployment among polytechnic graduates is slightly higher than for university graduates. Polytechnic graduates coming out of the social sciences, law and humanities had extremely high unemployment rates. Subject to subject the employment statistics suggest that employers do prefer university graduates.[7] However, given the evidence presented above this effect is not as strong as might be predicted. There are a number of possible factors at work:

First, the graduate labour market is highly differentiated and stratified. Any single employer sees only a relatively small number of graduates. A close analysis of the graduate labour market would require accounting for differences in courses of study across sectors and the consequent differences in first destinations for men and separately for women. The following data are suggestive of these differences, although by no means comprehensive. For example, fewer than 3% of all university graduates and male polytechnic graduates studied education; of the polytechnic women, however, nearly a quarter studied education. If we combine all science and engineering (but not medicine) we find that 45% of men in universities studied these, but only 22% of women. Of polytechnic men 41% studied science and engineering compared to only 12% of polytechnic women. In terms of broad disciplines, therefore, the composition of the male graduating population at universities and polytechnics is similar, but for women it is markedly different in both sectors.[8] There are other differences between the two sectors. Medicine is only taught in universities (although pharmacy is taught in polytechnics.) Art and design courses are more common in polytechnics and have a preponderance of women students. There are also very great differences in absolute numbers of students on courses. In 1979-80 there were ten times as many first degree graduates in medicine, dentistry and other health fields coming from universities as there were from polytechnics; fifteen times as many science graduates and two and a half times as many engineers and technicans. Employers will see many more university then polytechnic graduates.

Further, university and polytechnic students may be moving out of dissimilar courses to dissimilar jobs. There is some evidence for this in the first destination statistics. Nearly 30% of university graduates will enter public service (other than education, but including the National Health Service), contrasted with about 18% of polytechnic graduates. While between 15% and 20% of polytechnic graduates will enter education, this is the case for just over 5% of university graduates. Roughly equal proportions will enter industry and commerce; however they may not be competing for the same jobs.

When analysing the movement of graduates into the world of work account must be taken of the course of study, the institution attended and its links with local employing organizations, the sector of the economy, and personal characteristics, eg gender, class of degree. Employers do not typically evaluate the graduate labour market using these categories, but they are what refine the picture dominated by institutional preference.

Second, while the overall employment rate of public sector graduates is relatively high, there may be more underemployment of these graduates and fewer in their first choice of job. Further, first destination statistics are not complete; there may be a higher rate of public sector unemployment than these statistics show.

Third, given the decentralized nature of recruitment in some firms, organizations may be taking on public sector students at the 'periphery', whether the head office is aware of it or not. There may be, as suggested by some of the evidence, considerable within-firm job stratification. Top jobs for graduates may be filled in a different recruitment exercise. Interviews like those presented here may see a focus on jobs the firm is most anxious to fill.

Fourth, given that the rate of employment is high for polytechnic students in certain subjects, the proportion of employers which recruit on the basis of course (for example, our Types 3 and 4, pages 80-83) may well be greater than our sample suggests.

Fifth, many jobs, at any one time, will need to be filled very quickly, for example for work on a project basis. A highly rationalized picture of recruitment may well not operate when an employer is in a hurry to recruit. Whoever is available may get the job. Further, at any one time, many jobs will depend on special factors which will override a more general judgement, an example being knowledge of the geographical area in which the job is based.

All or some of the factors listed above may explain the relatively high level of employment of public sector students. Nonetheless, employer preferences come through strongly and clearly in this study and in others. A questionnaire survey of employers carried out by Alan Gordon in 1982 showed employer institutional preferences to be consistent with those found here. Using a quantitative ranking system, Gordon found Oxbridge to be most preferred, followed closely by the old civics. Polytechnics and colleges were least preferred. Two other surveys in the Expectations of Higher Education project support these data on institutional preferences: that of careers advisors[10] reports that twenty-four out of thirty-two (75%) of universities were visited in 1980/81 by over 100 employing organizations. A third of the universities were visited by over 200 organizations. Only four of twenty-seven polytechnics and no colleges reported this level of visitation. (Although half of all institutions reported a decrease in number of employing organizations visiting their institution, the universities are starting from a much larger base). Undergraduates, too, perceive employer preferences for university graduates.[11] Nearly 80% of students agree that employers have a preference for university students. Asked about their satisfaction with the numbers of employers visiting their institution, 73% of university undergraduates *disagreed* that 'Not enough employers visit'. This contrasts with 32% of polytechnic undergraduates and 20% of college undergraduates. Looking only at Oxbridge, all but 3% of the undergraduates agreed strongly (75%) or agreed with reservations (21%) that 'The careers service does a good job encouraging employers to visit the institution'. Only 20% of polytechnic undergraduates strongly agreed with this proposition and only 8% of college undergraduates. In the race for employment, 77% of polytechnic students and 78% of college students rated Oxbridge students as having the 'best' prospects; 67% and 71% of those respective students ranked other universities as second best. Again, this holds for course: asked to rate the employment prospects of graduates on courses similar to your own, nearly 80% of all undergraduates ranked Oxbridge 'best'. There was, however, an important minority of polytechnic students who ranked their own course highly. For jobs in which field of study is not specified, 83% of university undergraduates and 71% of polytechnic and 59% of college undergraduates indicated that university graduates have an advantage. Asked whether recruitment procedures of employers were unfair, only 7% of university undergraduates strongly agreed but a quarter of all other undergraduates.

The perceived advantages accruing to university students are no doubt reflected in the fact that while three-quarters of university undergraduates were in the institution they most wanted to attend, this was the case for fewer than half of the public sector undergraduates. The majority of public sector students would have preferred a university course. Even among polytechnic students who were inclined to or had decided upon an occupation, a majority were not in their preferred institution.

A persistent theme throughout this study has been the importance of A levels to employers. They argue that the students with the best A levels go to universities and not to public sector institutions, and that *therefore* university graduates will be likely to be superior. There is no objective way of checking the second perception – that better A levels at 18 mean better recruits at 21, regardless of what intervenes. The first proposition can, however, be illustrated from external data. The table shows the data on entrance characteristics for the 1975 cohort, men and women who graduated in 1978 and 1979. It shows that the A level 'scores' of university entrants are indeed significantly higher than those of entrants to public sector degrees. 58% of all university A level entrants had scores of 9 and above, compared with 12% of CNAA entrants; 84% had three A levels compared with 50%; only 5% were in the lowest entry group (two A levels and a score of 4 or less) compared with 30% of CNAA entrants. These figures apply across all subjects. It is the case that a much higher proportion of public sector entrants came in by a non-A level route (23% compared with 12% in universities) but it does seem that, strictly in their own terms, employers see this situation correctly: for the 1978/9 graduates, it was indeed the case across all subjects that those from universities would have tended to have significantly better A levels than those from the public sector. If, then, it is A levels that are important to employers, the universities are the places to recruit. (This begs the question of how sensible a test this is for recruitment years later). As against lower A levels, however, the student survey shows that a larger proportion of polytechnic students have had work experience, or have spent a period of time outside higher education; and a larger proportion are attending their local institution. These are all qualities many employers also say they favour.

1975 Entry to Degree Level Courses: A Level Scores of 2 Plus (percentage)

	3 A Levels			Total 3 A Levels	2 A Levels			Total 2 A Levels	
	15-13	12-9	8-3		10-8	7-5	4-2		
UNIVERSITIES									
All	22.2	36.3	25.6	84.1	3.2	7.9	4.8	15.9	100
Engineering	19.1	30.0	33.4	82.5	1.1	5.9	9.5	16.5	100
Social Studies	16.1	39.8	26.5	82.4	4.3	10.4	2.8	17.5	100
CNAA DEGREES									
All (excluding BEd and Art)	1.4	10.7	38.1	50.1	2.3	17.2	30.4	49.9	100
Engineering	1.7	11.7	40.9	54.3	1.4	11.7	32.6	45.7	100
Social Studies	1.2	10.8	38.3	50.3	2.7	18.7	28.2	49.6	100

Source: Statistics of Education Vol. 3 Further Education Table 58 (HMSO, 1975);
Statistical Supplement 1974-75 Table G1 (UCCA, 1975)

SUMMARY

The statistical evidence, so far as it goes, seems therefore to support the dominant voice coming over from the employers in our study. Employers do for the most part, and with the exception of some particular courses and jobs, operate a rough stratification system, which considers most university graduates before most public sector graduates (and for that matter, most Oxbridge graduates before most others). And one of the consequences of the economic downturn has been to exacerbate this situation, the 'milk-rounds' are decreasing in size and importance, while the 'paper sort' – with its crude emphasis on 'objective' histories and qualifications – is becoming more important.

Reliance by employers on A level grades provides a screening mechanism which from their point of view leads to efficient selection of the fewest institutions and departments to be visited to provide the numbers of graduates needed. However, the system is highly stratified and inequitable from the point of view of many individual graduates who, whatever their achievements and qualities, may be excluded from consideration because they have not attended the favoured institutions. Less able graduates from higher-status institutions ('status' in this context determined largely, though not entirely, by A level grades) are relatively advantaged in the recruitment exercise when compared with more able graduates from lower status institutions.

There is little, perhaps all too little, 'blurring' in the way employers and students perceive the sectors – students with good A levels choose universities because they know that employers will turn there first, while employers rank institutions by A levels of entering students. If the UK system were more like that in some other countries (West Germany, Sweden or Australia, for example), where students normally attend their neighbouring institutions, or the 'planned economies', where employers are less free to exercise their recruitment preferences, there would be more constraints on the operation of this market system, and perhaps more leverage for government policy. In the UK, the creation of the binary system may indeed have been an affirmation that 'public purposes should be determined outside higher education proper . . . in conformity with social demands.' But what has happened so far in practice seems equally to demonstrate the impotence of government policy makers. They cannot themselves, by adjusting structures and incentives, influence the nature of those social demands. It is perhaps, beyond the capacity of a government to 'manage' a change in the status structure so long as students remain free to study where they wish, institutions remain free to admit the students they wish, and employers remain free to recruit the students they wish.

5 Shortages

DEFINITIONS OF 'SHORTAGES'

In this chapter we take up the question of shortages of highly qualified manpower – perhaps the most difficult of our topics. We come closest here to having to confront the traditional problems of long-term manpower planning, in a climate in which most approaches to it have been discredited. As Williams[1] points out, however, the felt need for planning remains: 'We can expect another Crowther-Hunt in every decade.'

Manpower plans recur as governments respond to myriad reports of shortages with ever renewed efforts to find efficient, cost-effective strategies for educating to meet demand. The following offer only a few contemporary examples. A recent report in *The Times* asserts:

> Computer and electronics staff have been in short supply ever since the computing industry was born. Even the recession has not obliterated the demand for more computer staff; last year British companies were short of 16,000 programmers and 6,000 computer engineers, according to a recent survey.

The Finniston Report argues:[3]

> Manufacturing is a complex, multidisciplinary activity which depends for success upon the balancing of specialist contributions and their co-ordination to satisfy constantly changing market demands. The response of many British companies to these demands is handicapped by lack of an adequate engineering input to marketing and business planning activities and by lack of sufficient market input to engineering activities.

The report *Manpower Implications of Micro-Electronic Technology* (1980) argues:

> A shortage of electronics engineers was widely reported... in the course of its research.... It is important to recognize that, in purely manpower terms, the problems of initial innovation are rather less than the continuing ones which the company will face when it has successfully innovated. In short, initial innovation creates manpower problems largely

at the level of the professional engineer. Subsequently, once the innovation is operational in a plan or incorporated in a product, it will give rise to new manpower requirements throughout the work force as well as leading to further requirements for professional engineering skills... so far as the supply of electronics engineers as such is concerned, almost all firms have mentioned difficulties.

Against this we have to set the evidence gathered for this study, which shows very little indication that employers perceive serious shortages of highly qualified manpower in the graduate market.

These differences in perception and estimation may lie in the different definitions of 'shortage' used by employers, economists and governments. They range from the commonsense meaning reflected in high vacancy rates:[4]

A recent study by the Californian Society of Professional Engineers showed, for example, that Hewlett Packard had 2,500 unfilled technical jobs and Hughes Aircraft 2,000.

to the more complex definition that economists use:[6]

Without considering all the niceties, it would be fair to say that there is a consensus among economists that if the salaries of one group have been rising/falling relative to other groups for some time, this can be taken as evidence that a shortage/surplus exists, or has recently existed.

Our purpose here is to review the ways in which employers experience a 'shortage', use the concept, and implicate higher education. What emerges is a conceptual framework for analysing perceived shortages rather than a new definition.

Drawing on the work of western European economists, Fulton et al.[7] distinguish among 'needs', 'requirements' and 'demands' for qualified manpower; all of which are parameters in discussions of shortages:

... many writers in Western Europe have drawn a distinction between *needs, requirements* and *demands* for qualified manpower.

(1) The *need* refers to the number of workers considered desirable to achieve a general policy objective such as economic growth or particular kinds of cultural development.

(2) A *requirement* refers to the number of workers technically necessary to achieve a specific objective, for example, a given level of output in the motor car industry or a target teacher-pupil ratio. It is assumed that once economic and social targets have been set, the *requirement* for particular categories of manpower is determined through the available techniques of production or through demographic development or something similar.

(3) The *demand* refers to the relationship between the wage rate and the number of jobs for which employers are willing to hire people at that rate.

According to the critics who argue along these lines, manpower planners make a logical mistake in assuming that the *requirements* for qualified manpower are necessarily the same as the *effective economic demand*.

This statement outlines some of the perspectives from which shortages can be viewed. At the national (or some other aggregate) level there may be a felt 'need' for more engineers, for example; at the level of the firm a 'requirement' may be put forward, usually in the short term, for more engineers. Aggregating these 'requirements' would, if possible, yield short-run targets for particular types of manpower. 'Demand', defined in this way, is the (theoretically) measurable number of specific jobs for which employers will hire at a particular wage rate. The most difficult of the parameters to define is 'need', based as it is upon aggregate estimates projected into the future. However, the difficulty in defining it does not apparently affect assertions that it is important to do so. The brief for the present project argued:

> It has often been said that the higher education system should seek to meet 'the country's needs'. If, as seems likely, this will be heard with increasing frequency, it is important to take steps now to give the formula some definition and focus....

The brief for the Finniston Committee included:[8]

> ... the following terms of reference: To review for manufacturing industry and in light of national economic needs – the requirements of British industry for professional and technician engineers, the extent to which these needs are being met, and the use made of engineers in industry.

Attempts to define 'needs', however, are often less than clear, as this excerpt from Finniston shows:

> Before addressing these questions we must distinguish statements about *needs* from those about *demand*. Employers' demands for engineers refer to their stated requirements to fill identified jobs, either existing or to be created. They are thus more specific – though not always more reliable – than statements about industry's needs, which usually refer to judgements about the numbers of engineers required to achieve corporate national goals. It is thus not incongruous to suggest that, '... in the light of national economic needs', some organizations might need more engineers than they currently demand, while questioning whether other employers are not demanding more engineers than a wider view would suggest they need.

Estimating 'needs' will depend, in part, on the adequacy of each firm's own estimate of 'requirements'. However, as the evidence of this survey suggests, firms have considerable difficulty in assessing requirements, even in the short run. They are victims of shifts in business cycles; they use multiple strategies for substitution of manpower and for meeting manpower requirements. Moreover, manpower shortages in a firm are often described as deficiencies in 'qualities' and 'characteristics' rather than in graduates trained in particular areas. They are often expressed as there being something missing in the firm rather than as there being a requirement for 'x' engineers within five years. Further, because firms vary in their ability to project requirements into the future, there is, at the aggregate level, hidden variability in the precision of statements. And as the interviews here show, firms differ in what they mean by apparently simple job categories such as 'engineer' or 'chemist'.

'Need' can also be taken to mean, as the National Economic Development Council (NEDC) has said:[9] 'a gap between the future/present supply and the future/present demand for qualified engineers.' This is the definition employed by the Jackson and Zuckerman Manpower Planning committee in the 1960s. The methodology is to project future supply by extrapolating existing enrolments, and to estimate future 'demand' by asking employers about their employment plans. Another, frequently used method defines need at the national level in terms of manpower profiles, relating them to profiles of countries similarly situated with levels of economic activity which a nation has or hopes to achieve. Using this meaning, the 'need' for engineers in the UK might, for example, be defined in terms of the necessity of having a proportion of an age cohort with engineering qualifications equivalent to that of the UK's major competitor. This assumes that either country can realistically estimate 'needs'.

The use of employer experience and opinion in estimating needs and identifying shortages is not without its critics. Mace argues, for example:[10]

> There is also a problem about using employers' opinions of the current manpower structure of firms to determine educational spending. If they are optimal, the market left to itself is providing the right answers. If they are not optimal, the market is an inadequate instrument for determining the optimal use of manpower. This means that the present non-optimal structures cannot be used to determine future 'needs' and employers, who in large part have determined the present structure, are the last people who should be asked about future 'needs'.

Further, as Mace and others contend:[11]

> In order to give a satisfactory answer to such questions, firms would need to have manpower plans for the ensuing few years to which they rigidly adhered; to have a precise definition of what an 'engineer' is; to form a view about their future share of the market (which implies a view about the future state of the economy); to form a view about future levels of prices and wages; to forecast future technological innovations and to form a view about their effects on the input mix, implying knowledge of the present and future elasticity of substitution between labour and capital, and between different labour inputs.

Summed up by Sir Solly Zuckerman, the argument is: 'One of the least reliable ways of finding out what industry wants is to go and ask industry.'

Yet in the last analysis, and whatever the paucity of previous research on employers' opinions, it will have to be employers who outline and act upon their own requirements and perceived needs for qualified manpower. This does not mean that they can do so in a clear and unambiguous manner or that their assessment of what will promote their own prospects or national economic growth is necessarily correct. It may be the case, and contemporary evidence supports the proposition, that current fluctuations in the world economy make difficult effective intra-firm manpower planning, even in the short term. If this is the case, then policy planning in education and industry must take place in a climate of great uncertainty. And then uncertainty becomes an important factor to take account of in any policy analysis and in future planning; and is not an element to be 'overcome'.

THE EMPLOYERS' VIEW

The purpose of this study was to explore the meanings which employers themselves attach to such concepts as 'shortages' and 'needs'. The method we used allowed for a number of ways of expressing shortages: 'Have you experienced shortages of qualified manpower?' 'What is your major recruiting problem?' as well as more indirect questions such as 'Are your recent recruits sufficiently numerate?'

We argue that inter-firm and intra-firm variability in perceptions of shortages, conceptual differences in meaning, or use of different imagery to express a perceived need do not mean, as some writers suggest, that employers simply do not 'pay attention' to significant economic categories. The variability is an important economic fact of life, and as such is an essential element in describing manpower requirements. The questions which were put to employers were therefore intended to allow the maximum opportunity to express the shortages they felt their organization had experienced, in their own terms. Their responses would, it was hoped, assist in unpacking the rhetoric of the debates surrounding 'shortages'.

Most interviews began this area of investigation with a general question:

There has been a lot of talk and writing in recent years about shortages of qualified manpower. Could you say something about whether this has been a problem in your organization and how it has?

Among the follow up 'probes' were: 'Do you get enough top quality graduates?' 'Are graduates specialized enough/too specialized?' Another problem area was expressed as: 'Are there some examples of skills that your organization would have liked graduates generally to have that you felt they lacked?' with probes to look at the specific nature of the skills they were lacking and whether this related to specific sorts of graduates. We dealt particularly with one much-discussed skill shortage ('numeracy') by asking whether employers felt that graduates lacked confidence in their ability to use figures or reason quantitatively, and whether employers attempted to assess numeracy or use it as an indicator of other personality characteristics. We also asked: 'What was the most serious recruiting problem for the organization?' with probes to investigate if this had changed over recent years, and the extent to which these changes were, in the opinion of employers, the fault of higher education.

Evidence such as this does not often reach the level of provision that a planner would wish for. Few employing organizations could express themselves as specifically as this one:

There is a shortage of graduates in civil engineering with sandwich experience and local ties, who are prepared to move around the country and work at a starting salary one half that in the United States. Only men will be considered and a second language is a must. Must be highly personable. Polytechnic graduates are not favoured.

Rather, firms' assessments amount to a 'Dance to the Music of Time'; aware of the sharp variations in internal requirements, of present and past competition for graduates, and of the vagaries of the economy, employers look back at the past and forward to the future. Describing Poussin's painting, Anthony Powell[12] evokes images of Time, 'of human beings facing outward like the Seasons, moving hand in hand in intricate measure: stepping slowly, methodically, sometimes a trifle awkwardly, in evolutions that take recognisable shape... unable to control the melody, unable, perhaps, to control the steps of the dance.' It is the human, tentative, sometimes flawed assessment of shortages that is portrayed here.

ARE SHORTAGES A PROBLEM?

The majority of employing organizations drop out of any analysis of 'shortages'. Either because circumstances are favourable or because they are unfavourable and out of their control, they are not in need of additional manpower. The majority of firms in the survey were able to recruit the manpower needed for their identifiable future. The following extracts are from a building materials manufacturer, an industrial products manufacturer, a clearing bank, a firm of traders, a charity, a manufacturing firm and an engineering firm respectively. They demonstrate both the variety of employers reporting 'no shortages' and the different jobs for which there are said to be 'no shortages'.

We don't find any scarcity.

None really for successful applicants.

(Q: Is there a general shortage of skills in graduates who come to you?) No. From my experience — we don't have periodic assessment. Each line manager looks after his own graduates. The comments I get from graduates and managers about the graduates, I can't fault them in any way... for the most part, graduates have been a highly successful introduction into the company.

(Q: What is your most serious recruiting problem?) We haven't one. Probably to maintain the interest and continue to increase the interest of the more ambitious graduate to come to us.

The biggest recruitment headache is the actual administration of all the applications that we get in. I am a one man band.... I do the whole personnel function from company cars to payrolls and to get time to handle 250 applications and make sure we acknowledge them... it takes about an hour to write a standard form. If you have done that you have the right to have it scrutinized pretty thoroughly.

I can only look at the score card. We think we get too many applying. We invited for interview 251 people (for about 50 places), we received applications from a further 186.... We would rather not have the numbers. We would (like to) retain the quality and reduce the numbers.

(Q: The product you're getting: are there particular areas where you find graduates lack when they join?) I can't think of an example where a graduate has turned out to be what the company didn't think him to be. Certainly in latter years most graduate recruits have been first class people and are instrumental now in companies' growth and prestige contributing to imaginative, original design work which is taking place in a company of this sort.

Thus we find employing organizations representing widely different economic sectors with a range in size of graduate intake and in types of recruitment that are satisfied with the number of graduates available and with their training.

For a substantial number of firms, 'shortages' are not seen as a problem, because of the sharp fall in recruitment in current economic conditions. A number of the firms which declined to participate in the survey reported only limited recruitment; others were going out of business. Several firms which did participate felt they could not take on fully qualified manpower because of the economic recession.

A nationalized industry:

... it is a climate within a department. If you have got people being seen to be redundant, there is a climate in which you are cutting back, there are tight budget constraints, the easy thing to chop is the recruitment of a trainee for each future vacancy. If you like, you are eating last year's corn, and it is a very natural and easy thing to do.

An entertainment firm:

Because of cutbacks, the first thing to go have been trainees.

A small publishing firm:

If the work level takes off again, we will consider graduates.

A large civil engineering contractor:

We like to base our training scheme on actual work going through the company... and clearly when our work load is low, the actual opportunities to do that are low... (recruitment) is less than half what it was.

A large paper products manufacturer:

I would like to be clear. Economic downturn is misleading, it is the total rundown of the paper industry in the UK that is important and that will happen whether the economies go up or down.... We are talking about world market structure changes that are permanent.... Unless something goes quite crazy with (exchange rates) which it often does, we really aren't going to make paper in this country in anything like the bulk grades that we used to.

On the other hand, a few employing organizations have weathered the recession well, and find graduates more available because of it. They also do not feel shortages acutely, although they may face shortages in the future, or anticipate them.

A nationalized industry:

This year we will meet all our targets without too much difficulty. We normally have a problem in the electrical, electronic field, it has improved by virtue of the job market and no other reason. When the economy picks up we shall still have a problem.

A large civil engineering contractor:

If there is a great deal of work about, the Oxbridges of this world would not come to us or to industry in general because they don't associate it with (a proper) career. Because of the recession a great many people have looked to us. The recession has done both of us good. In the past, one has wished for better quality people to apply to us.

An organization's perception of manpower shortages will thus depend critically on past experience, future expectations and the current state of the economy or the economic sector of which it is a part. The following interview suggests that all of these time-related factors play a part in an assessment of manpower requirements.

A medium-sized pharmaceutical group, recruiting many graduates:

We're always under criticism as an industry for complaining the universities aren't turning out enough of the people we want: for example, chemical engineers. I know there are something like 700 chemical engineers who graduated last year. We say, why can't the colleges get the forecasting right? They say – tell us what you want so we can take it into account when forecasting. We sit here and say – not very easy to do. It's a simple example, but we're going out to universities in January – vacancy list already sent out. Those numbers will change and quite radically because our review procedure of work in progress doesn't take place until after Christmas. So we know we want certain disciplines, but how many? We can't assess a year in advance, so trying to plan long range is taken up at meetings – can we not as an industry get together and tell the universities what we require? We try but we're not always aware of the exact commercial pressures. We don't know if business in three to four years will boom or be bad. A company like ours – multi-national, British-based, British-owned – helps but many companies are American/European based. We don't know if we're opening new factories or may be closing factories. Business is booming but if the products of the factory are mainly for the international market and the exchange rates go against us, it may be uneconomic to continue operating the factory. We don't know.

For some organizations, forward planning is nearly impossible. Either they have not felt sufficiently stable to plan for the future or they are not sufficiently large to take on new employees and cushion against possible future shortages.

A large textile manufacturer:

> I don't really think you know you can make any deductions about what has been an extremely unstable state — starting really from the fact that in the late 60s the group built up... with the oil crisis in '74, the over capacity of the textile industry, the recession and then decentralization... there have been several factors affecting everything over the last 13 or 14 years — no two years have really been the same.

Instability affects even the very large employers. In the public service, for example:

> Our recruitment is very volatile. It has to respond to changes in demand from government departments for different types of specialists. Where the administrators are concerned, the problem is with numbers — the numbers go down but you still require the same animal in different quantities. Where we are concerned (is at that point) that you get a need for a different breed. It means there has been a change of emphasis which reflects the government's priorities.... This may be a reflection of government policy... where there is a change of emphasis from doing work in-house to doing work with outside consultants.... For example, in one year we wanted 200 graduates for valuation, but the following year we didn't want any at all. That imposes difficulties (all around). There are not vast numbers (of qualified graduates) and to chop off 200 vacancies is quite significant.

Organizations which continue to recruit are involved in assessment of employment prospects in their industries or economic sectors, as well as in assessment of their competitive position in the market place. A grasp of the employers' perspective of shortages depends on identifying factors in the past or anticipating those in the future which determine a present perception of a shortage.

A partner for a very large firm of chartered accountants:

> I think and hope we are moving towards a situation where the (recruits into) chartered accountancy will level out.... If you look at the top 10 (accountancy) firms... there is a slight levelling out and even a slight reduction, which is being topped up by smaller firms coming into graduate recruitment for the first time.

The spokesman for a multinational company:

> We've done a bit of analysis going back over the years trying to see the

percentage of high-flyers we have taken on in each year, and the percentage does fluctuate (but) it doesn't fluctuate very much. In other words, we don't seem to be recruiting more than a very small percentage of the real high-flyers.

Many large firms and firms with past experience in graduate recruitment try to avoid shortages by maintaining a relatively high level of recruitment. 'Planting the seed corn' is a recurring image.

A footwear manufacturing company said:

> Like many companies in the early 70s we cut back recruitment... we have been regretting it ever since. It has not formed part of the policy this time round. We are expanding and OK (we have) closed plants like others, but we believe we will be here in 10 years and do not believe we should destroy our seed corn.

A very large diversified industrial organization said:

> We see graduates as a long-term investment. You can't suddenly stop recruiting now because in five years' time the economy may have picked up and you need people with a certain amount of experience... (another company) has cut back on their recruitment; they will find it very difficult to get going again. They will have to find credibility in the market. (One of our subsidiaries) is recruiting at a (fairly high level) even though they are going through an extensive redundancy programme. They believe it would be wrong to stop and have a gap in five years' time when there are no people coming through.

Large firms like this are able to create a cushion against future shortages by forward planning. Similarly, an accountancy firm reported:

> No we are keeping (recruitment) up on the principle that if you tried to stop planting your seed corn now in order to reap it in three or four years' it won't be there. We have ploughed on.

Another large and diversified multinational:

> (We) will go up and down a bit according to the economy although not enormously. One of the advantages... we have is that we have so many industries that they are not all down together and so if one industry decides to pull its horns in, the chances are that another one comes back up the cycle. There will still be some variation and that particularly affects the recruitment at the lower end when you really are recruiting for the job. We don't want to drop below a certain recruitment level because we have got to run this business in 30 years' time and what has happened to the economy in one year is almost irrelevant to that issue.

We can conclude that at any point in time the majority of employing organizations will perceive no shortages of qualified manpower because they are able easily to meet current requirements, they have stopped or reduced recruitment, or upheavals in the organization or the economy preclude future planning. In the following section we turn to the minority of employers who do identify shortages.

WHAT KIND OF SHORTAGES?

There are a number of explanations given by employing organizations for shortages of qualified manpower. Conceptually these allow the analyst to disaggregate shortages into a number of different dimensions. In some cases, cited below, the problem is a failure to attract any candidate for a job, but more often the perception of shortages relates to the quality of the graduates a firm sees and the belief that there are not enough good ones. Employers' perceptions of their attractiveness to graduate recruits will, as we have shown earlier, influence their definitions of the shortages their organizations face. Organizations with 'good' reputations are seen as attracting the 'quality' graduates. 'Shortages' are seen as the shortage of 'good' graduates which they are unable to attract in the face of competition in an often segmental labour market. The two examples below illustrate this. The problem the first company faces is coping with 900 applications for 25 positions. The second company has suffered from shortages of good graduates in the past and is trying to change its image in the graduate labour market.

A medium-sized engineering consultancy:

> The majority of our graduate recruits are civil engineers and there is over-production of civil engineers by the universities in relation to demand and has been over the last five or six years, say since 1977/78....We're fairly well known, certainly in the trade; any graduate who is thinking of going into consultancy, and quite a lot of them do, is bound to include ourselves on the short list. So that for our 25 places this year we have had something like 900 applications. Now that doesn't mean to say that the quality is there, but in fact we refine those 900 down to about 60 for interview and there are very few of those 60 who we wouldn't be glad to employ. Perfectly true, we do not always get all our first offers accepted... some of them go to Shell, for example, people look at us, they look at the oil companies and they say 'I'll take the oil company's salary', but the short answer is 'there is no real difficulty'.

A medium-sized manufacturing firm:

> The good graduates are in strong demand by the companies who are prepared to pay for them and who are also attractive enough to them to get them into the company. On the whole, we have not been, up to the last two years, an attractive company to the outside world, which is why I stressed earlier that (we are) now split off from the original parent company. We now have a much tougher, stronger, more enlightened managerial style, and we're trying to change our image in the UK. The fact that our share price has doubled over the last two years is probably a significant factor in this, it demonstrates that we are showing that we are now a growing company rather than the old 'auntie' image. This does

mean that we are more able in the market place to start to attract the better graduates. Now, when I say better graduates, I don't necessarily mean first class Honours degree graduates but what we're really after is the graduate who has got the personality to become an effective manager at an early stage from largely an engineering discipline.... When we do identify them we do everything we possibly can to see that the offer we make to them is going to be sufficiently attractive in terms of not only just the financial aspect but also the opportunities we offer the potential graduate.

Company image in relation to the graduate labour market is clearly a 'soft' problem in determining shortages, one that is difficult for firms to assess because it is often measured conceptually by the (sometimes hypothetical) manpower an organization does not see. The belief exists that there are more and better qualified men and women than the employer has seen; it is therefore a matter of complaint that they are 'short' of such people.

A very large consumer product manufacturer:

I don't think we have got a largely serious problem but I suppose the most serious would be engineers... (it is a problem of) not being equally attractive in all functions.... The other big issue is that it is just not an easily understood organization. How do you get it across in a real way (that we are) (subsidiary name) frozen foods; (subsidiary name) ice cream; we are meat, cardboard boxes, animal feed and chemicals? It is difficult to present that picture and yet you have to get people's attention.

A large textile group:

Textiles are a declining industry... this group is thought of as a textile group. We have suffered about it in terms of the numbers of people that come forward for interview.... We can do our damnedest with those who come forward... what we can't do anything about is those that don't come forward.

A large employer in the photographic industry:

We have a problem with engineering recruitment, because we are seen as a chemical company... (however) we recruit a lot of engineers as well as chemists.

A nationalized industry spokesman said:

We have not presented ourselves well to the higher education system as a potential employer. A lot of the fault is of our own making.... The image of the (service name) industry is an old fashioned one of the fitter who doesn't turn up by appointment. We have not done enough to present ourselves in terms of the modern technology of an industry like this. (As a result, we miss out on really top graduates.)

Another manufacturer complained:

> The work we appear to offer is not really attractive... other companies appear to have much more attractive work than being involved in the design and manufacture of cables.

A multinational organization which is a large recruiter of graduates:

> We have some difficulty in recruiting the top drawer of engineers because the first thing they think of is (other companies). And they may be right to think that. I don't know. Similarly, we haven't found it very easy (and that's common to almost the whole of manufacturing industry) to attract the very best budding accountants. We have attracted some extremely good ones but not enough, the big accountancy firms have a bigger pull on them. Certainly we would love to get some of the people who are at the very top end of (other company).

As we shall see in several sections of this report, the shortfall of qualified manpower, where it exists, is often in attracting those who are perceived to be 'the best', 'the very good', 'those from Oxbridge'. It is not necessarily the number of applicants with minimal qualifications which precipitates a perception of shortages but the quality of the applicants as judged by the employers.

A very large manufacturing firm:

> The key thing is the quality. In our experience there doesn't seem to be a real shortage of qualified manpower. The shortage is in the suitable personality characteristics of that qualified manpower. If we were going out on the market and were prepared to take in people who just had the qualifications, we wouldn't have any problem.

An international marketing organization:

> We have difficulty getting the 20 people we need of the standard we want. Again, it's not the case that we want people with a degree, we're looking for a whole range of personal characteristics.

A representative for a large holding company explained:

> We have always come very close to fulfilling in terms of numbers the match between the jobs that we have and the graduates we're able to get. Whether these graduates and jobs are matched together to the extent that we have the most desirable... disciplines is another matter. For instance, we have a fair proportion of jobs that we would ideally like to see (filled by) a graduate in production engineering, but because of the shortfall of good − and I say good advisedly − graduates in production engineering, one might find a mechanical engineer or electrical engineer in those types of activities.

A large firm of chartered accountants:

(There is) a shortage of élite of all disciplines who are going into the business community of one sort of another.

A large diversified industrial manufacturer:

We would like to have a bigger pool of applicants to choose from; hopefully then you get more good ones. It comes back to the point that recently the engineering faculties at universities have tended to take people who maybe don't have the academic achievement and broad-based education as other, more competitive areas. Unfortunately, this is reflected in the standard of products that come out of university. Although we're supposed to be in a situation of unemployment, the offers to acceptance ratio for the engineers is 66%. This would indicate that the good engineers are still being chased by all the majors and there is quite a small pool there.

For a number of firms shortages are structural. The flow of manpower over time within an organization has inevitable discontinuities related to the age structure of the firm, changing technology or reorganization of plant. For a very large chemical manufacturer, which is also a very large recruiter of graduates:

In our experience, there doesn't seem to be a real shortage of actual qualified manpower. The shortage is in... people with the qualities to get to the top.

An engineering firm:

It's found that we're going to have a lot of problems in that a lot of senior managers are coming up to retirement.

A personnel director for a medium-sized engineering manufacturing firm:

We have stumbled across a problem because over the last couple of years we have been bringing people in to fill gaps, but we realized philosophically that we haven't got continual people moving up the ladder but tend to bring them in as, say, a level of person who is perhaps a graduate and who has something like five to eight years' experience. Then they can develop into the company but we haven't had that lower level of person coming up. It's found that we're now going to have a lot of problems in that a lot of senior managers are coming up to retirement and we're finding difficulty in providing people to replace them. We either look for senior people to put in at the top (ideally you would like to move up the middleman to the top but you've no one to put in the middle) so if we can have an on-going situation, realistically, 75% of the people are leaving within the first five years.

A number of other dimensions of 'shortage' can be identified. One is geographical location:

... our biggest problem is location. (Town name) is a very expensive housing area and not very attractive in terms of environment.

Retention is another problem for companies with graduates who are in high demand.

A very large textile group:

> Our problem is clearly not a recruitment one, but one of retaining the people who are coming through strongly, the people who are coming up to 30 or something like that who decide to make a career change. That is particularly true of engineers. We recruit enough engineers. What is difficult is to retain them because engineers are becoming extremely mobile and high paid.

Some firms do not identify their serious shortages as concerning graduates at all. A small chemical engineering firm is typical:

> (Q: Turning to more general problems, do you have particular shortages in your organization that you think higher education should have redressed but hasn't?) Straight answer is that I regret the passing of evening classes. The ability (for a man) to go to evening classes and work his way from ONC/HNC. I think that also affects quite dramatically the tradition of supervisors. I think it's the very devil to get a good working supervisor/foreman − such an animal no longer exists. It's a vital tradition because that's the guy at the coalface between shop floor and management.

In summary, a number of factors determine an employing organization's perception of a general manpower shortage. One is the image the organization has of itself as a recruiter of qualified manpower; another and related factor is the effect of company image on attracting the 'best' manpower. Other factors are related to other characteristics of the organization − location and retention. In the next two sections we look at more traditional conceptions of shortages − shortages of specific qualifications and shortages of specific skills.

SHORTAGES OF SPECIFIC QUALIFICATIONS

A minority of employers do experience 'absolute' shortages of people with particular qualifications. These are usually seen in engineering, scientific and other technological areas. Again, however, the quality dimension remains an important one. The point where 'not enough good ones' becomes 'not enough' is hard to define, and depends as much on the definition of 'good' as on the number of qualified candidates.

A medium-sized heavy manufacturing firm's strategy:

> We try to get a good balanced intake towards the disciplines that we really need. Basically there is bias towards mechanical engineers followed by electronic engineers then naval architects. I'm not certain about a shortage, or whether mechanical engineers aren't attracted to ship building; or whether we've directed our recruitment to the right colleges.

The spokesman for a large nationalized industry:

> Within engineering, no shortage of civil engineers at the moment. Chemical engineers, unlike 1970s tend to be plentiful but good mechanical engineers and electronic engineers are terribly hard to find — these are the two most difficult areas — and they happen to be precisely what we're looking for and particularly those 44 vacancies of our quota of 70.... Can usually fill all vacancies — if you want to — with graduates of the right discipline, but of only mediocre quality. It will become a straight question of whether you fill all 70 engineering vacancies — just for the sake of filling them, by dropping your recruitment standards or whether you don't recruit for all 70 and hope for better luck next year in terms of quality.

A spokesman for a firm of traders which is a medium-sized recruiter of graduates:

> The effect of the UGC cuts has reduced the number of people joining electronic engineering courses. Other people must have said this, so that the number graduating in electronic engineering in 1984 will be 10% less than graduated this year. I have letters now from a number of universities saying will you come to visit us in the summer, careers fairs, second bite at the milk-round cherry, please will you make sure that you have sufficient staff to cover the number of interviews and there's a little rider which says basically that if you're looking for electronic engineers don't bother to come, there won't be any.
>
> (Q: So you in fact have a shortfall?) Yes, this year's a reasonable year when you add it all up. I could have taken probably 200, 220. I will be very lucky if I see 70.

A representative of a manufacturer of electrical equipment:

> ... Until the last two years, we've had difficulty in having enough engineers and technologists to choose from. We, like anyone on the scene three years ago, had the same worry as to how we could get engineers to apply to us: to get the ones that apply if they are good enough, or reject them or whatever. The concern is that one year we find for some reason that the universities and polytechnics will not supply us with enough candidates.

A nationalized industry:

> We have experienced a major shortage in electronics. In our signal department we find it difficult to recruit. There's never a straightforward answer to these things because we like to mix people — we grow quite a number of people in signals by sandwich courses and they tend to stay with us. We like to leaven that by bringing in good graduates because signalling covers not just things visible on the track but automatic driving, computers. We have difficulty with them. We also try to make up by sponsoring. Mechanical engineering — up till this last year or so we've had difficulty and even last year the quality was difficult to obtain.

The personnel director for a precision engineering firm:

> There was the 'screaming shortage' — graduates for software where we were bending over backwards. Again, we ran at least once if not twice, a specialist software course where you took an engineering man and turned him into software. It was very successful. So successful that he's now leaving us for an enormously increased salary: always a danger to do that. He's in a shortage area. The area where we were noticeably short we got involved with message switching. We had the utmost difficulty. Message switching is where it's automatically routed to where it's supposed to go untouched by human hand, sort it out in priority and all the rest of it. They had great difficulty in finding people who could do software on that. Again we would much rather have an engineer who has got computer options within the engineering degree than a computer scientist.

A medium-sized manufacturing firm:

> Engineers are difficult to recruit. Similarly material scientists. That was up to 1979 but 1980 we recruited 26 graduates and it was the first year we had more applications than we knew what to do with. Other years we had to take that person because there's no one else. In 1980 they're all very good, what can we do with them? Chemists and physicists have always been OK. Certainly in the last few years we haven't had any problems.

A major broadcasting organization:

> Perhaps the only area where we have any problem in finding suitable applicants is in languages, in particular with the Eastern European languages, where we want perfect language and expert knowledge of the country but we obviously cannot recruit in those countries. Otherwise we are inundated with applications — about 5,000 for 65 training places. Most are not up to the mark and of those selected not all decide to join us.

A small research establishment experienced difficulty in:

> ... essentially metal casting — and a substantial part of one's R and D has to be devoted to process engineering — it is in that field which we find the greatest difficulty in discovering amongst graduate applicants people who are suitable. (They have to have a practical ability, not only theory.)

A medium-sized manufacturer:

> We are interested in very high calibre graduates and it's tough to get these people as there's a lot of competition for them. Typically, someone we offer a job to may have five to six other jobs offered, so those who we consider suitable people are tough to get. On top of that we have specific difficulties. We find that high quality chemical and mechanical engineers are in very short supply at the moment. We also find that the quality of people who read chemical and mechanical engineering is not always as

high as we would want it to be. Another area where we have difficulty is in recruiting excellent people for sales management and that's because in this country, as opposed to other places around the world, sales management isn't considered an attractive occupation – not glamorous. It's a pity because sales offers equally good opportunities. Possibly at this point in time, it's a faster route to reach the top because the competition is less.

The representative of an electrical manufacturing firm:

> When I qualified I was told chemists are in short supply and there was some increase in the number of chemists at university, five years later you read: chemists must not expect to get employment in the field of their study. They get jobs as sales managers. They see the deficiencies, fill them, then reach an over-spill phase, then a drop, a backlash and deficiencies again. We're short of good engineers – they are difficult to find.

Although it is clear from the above statements that there are indeed shortages of qualified manpower, they reflect as often as not a perceived problem of quality. It is most often measured by the 'best' person recruited in a particular cohort. And the question is, apparently: 'Why cannot they all be like him or her?' As we have seen in previous chapters, the qualitative dimension is not necessarily related to what the candidate or the employee knows, but to such factors as motivation, personality, ability to work in a group, personal attractiveness. Some shortages reflect a highly specific market – graduates in 'Eastern European languages', or 'message switching', and some reflect a lag between the rapid change of technology and the time it takes to educate several cohorts of graduates who are familiar with the new technology. The shortfall of electronic engineers is an example. As we shall see in a later section, 'blue chip' electronics and computing firms are not the ones to feel the shortfall, which affects mainly smaller firms and those not well known for recruiting particular types of graduates.

Shortages elicit from firms a number of coping strategies, some of which are illustrated here. Employers facing a market which does not produce enough 'suitable' or appropriately qualified graduates may decide:

i   Not to recruit as many graduates as had been planned.
ii To recruit graduates who have related qualifications in the hope that the 'suitable' graduate will have suitable skills.
iii To impose lower standards and recruit graduates who do have the appropriate qualifications but are in other ways less 'suitable'.

As the following example shows,[10] any concept of shortage will be linked to the relative degree of substitution within a job function.

> In the UK a study of 68 electrical engineering establishments by Layard et al. (1971) showed that employers' use of people of different educational backgrounds varied widely even within the same industry. More recently, a study of engineers in 12 British firms revealed that over a third of the

people in engineering jobs requiring degree-level engineering skills had qualifications below degree level. The same study showed that over 25% of graduate engineers had moved into non-engineering jobs.

First destination statistics support this. As one recent report argues: 'Perhaps the most general message from the data is that graduates in most subjects entered a wide variety of jobs.' For example, 'In the sciences the proportion of graduates entering scientific or engineering work... ranges from 70% to 75% in physics and geology to 45% to 50% in biology and chemistry... a fair minority of science graduates found work outside sciences and engineering fields such as general management and financial work which are typically open to graduates of any discipline.'

The element of timing is also a central one in assessing 'real' shortages. Much scientific and technical work is organized by 'projects' and much engineering work by contracts. The need in a particular year for civil engineers, for example, may be very great in a single firm but be satisfied with a large intake in that year. The firm down the road may need a larger than normal number of textile technologists in the same year. Most employing organizations cannot give long-term projections of these needs. Indeed, the current economic recession shows this clearly, with a large proportion of firms unexpectedly cutting back on graduate intake. Given the very long lead time required to put up new courses and put through a cohort of graduates, the higher education system can only be wary of becoming over-responsive.

SHORTAGES OF SKILLS

Another dimension of 'shortage' is reflected in deficiencies in specific skills, aptitudes or experience. Rather than employers seeing the problem as a shortfall of electrical engineers, for example, the shortage is defined in terms of particular aspects of their training. The following quotations illustrate this.

A large nationalized corporation:

> Universities have still not grasped that people... are going to come out (into employment) to make things, that it must meet a price and make the delivery date, and you have to direct people to do it.

The managing director of a small electronics firm:

> While universities do provide a really sound training in electronics, they don't (or can't) provide the commercial awareness that we expect in recruits.

A manufacturing firm:

> I think the main area where we see the shortfalls of skills is the ability to relate and work within a group.

A very large nationalized industry:

We find the main skills they (the graduates) are lacking in quite often are personal skills, motivation and self-analysis.

A firm of computer analysts:

We teach them how to give presentations; some jobs quickly involve them in doing that and it is something they don't normally acquire at university.

A personnel director for a firm of electrical manufacturers:

(We find shortages in) man management and customer liaison. We don't expect them to come in with these skills. They don't need them for three or four years (and) then we train them.

A very large manufacturing and retailing organization thought they had none of these problems:

None really for successful applicants.

A director of a holding company:

I think the main area where we see the shortfall is in the ability to relate and work within a group.... I think it comes down to selection by bringing in the right people into the activities for which you want them.

A director for a large manufacturer in the motor industry (whom we have already quoted in another context) thought:

There is the fundamental problem of spelling. I don't think they're dyslexic but it worries me because if they can't spell properly they can't do anything properly. I believe it reflects their general approach to life and their work and there's a self-discipline one looks for. I spend time talking in schools to ensure children can spell, do tables, but it's a little bit like the old argument about Latin – training the mind, get a sense of satisfaction that they have got something right.

A charitable organization:

At the moment, we're getting all the skills we need.

A large design and construction firm:

The lack of numeracy in arts graduates is less striking, lack of literacy is common in scientists. It's vitally important for potential managers that they must be able to communicate, argue a case, express themselves.

A medium-sized engineering consultancy:

As soon as a graduate joins us he goes straight on to our report writing

course and then over the next three years will be involved in a programme
of writing a continual series of essays, under supervision.

A multinational corporation:

Certainly on the technical side there may be a lack of communications
skills and perhaps commercial awareness, sometimes, especially in the
research people. The will research a project until the end of life but you
have got to call a halt if it's not going anywhere, you have to be
academically inspired to keep going. I think what you say is right
communication/commercial awareness. On the arts side I would have
thought they had better skills at writing things. On the commercial side –
but they may still lack the communications skills – the ability in a real
situation to argue your corner and be successful in influencing people.
That's one skill in which the company spends a lot of time now trying to
teach. We have a lot of workshops in influencing skills, expression and
this whole area which is vital to us in a negotiation situation.

A large industrial product manufacturer noted:

I would have thought that if the universities are now doing the right kind
of tutorial work then they should be showing students how to write
effective reports. And again talking from the engineering and computing
fields, my concern is that universities are not yet necessarily understanding that reports should be written in a way that can be understood by a
person in industry rather than a professor.

A very large chemical manufacturer summed it up:

The key thing is the quality. In our experience there does not seem to be a
real shortage of actual qualified manpower. The shortage is in the suitable
characteristics of that qualified manpower. If we were going out on the
market and were prepared to take on people who just had the
qualifications, we would not have any problem. The element in our
management and professional levels – people with the qualities to go to
the top – that is where the shortage lies and where we are competing with
other organizations.

One of the most commonly perceived shortages is of people with the right
kind of previous work experience. One obvious solution is to recruit people
who have already spent time in regular employment. There is a trade-off
between the benefits gained through employing graduates (or others) with
work experience and accepting a deficiency in skills which new graduates
might display. The way in which employers perceive and negotiate this
varies.
  A consumer goods manufacturer:

When a vacancy arises, a decision is made whether to bring in someone
completely new to industry, or someone with a certain degree of
experience, or to move an individual from another function of the
business.

A manufacturer of petroleum products:

> If we need a job doing and we don't have an experienced guy to do that job we will go out and get that man.

While for a diversified industrial manufacturer:

> We fish with many nets. We would go on the milk-round and most of the students would not have any significant work experience. But we would be always looking to take on people with experience....It would be where specific vacancies occur.

The need for new or relatively new graduates with work experience is often related to the problem of retention already referred to above.
    A firm of computer analysts:

> The retention rate... used to be 50% at four years, now it's 50% at three years.

A heavy engineering firm:

> People often recruit *from* us because we are so big in the UK. But we very rarely bring anyone in from outside, promotion is internal....

A firm of computer analysts:

> Because of the company's poor position in the industry, we see ourselves very much as a training ground. Many of the graduates do move on after a period. We do not encourage that, but are not that 'anti'. We would welcome them back.

Even here there is variation in employers perceptions. Some do not need or value work experience. For example one employer in the arts said firmly:

> One great maxim I firmly believe in (is) that experience is something and not a duration. We can have people in the profession for 60 years and be totally inexperienced; you can have someone in for six weeks and be very experienced.

The views expressed illustrate some diversity of feeling about the specific shortages of skills which employers miss in graduate recruits. A number of themes emerge. Employees lack industrial experience; or personal skills; some show an inability to work in a group; or to write reports; some have insufficient numerate ability; or have deficiencies in the ability to communicate effectively. Employers varied in their perceptions — none argued that all such skills were lacking in their graduate employees, and many said that they perceived none of these 'shortages'. The lack of skills, aptitudes and experience mentioned here does not typically result in a 'shortage' of graduates within a firm. Rather, employers perceive graduates to be deficient in particular qualities. Many such qualities are aspects of the graduates' higher education experience which educators can address. They stand in contrast to shortages related to characteristics of the firm – image, retention, ability to attract partners material.

STUDIES OF FIVE COMPUTING FIRMS

It is hard to capture from short extracts of this kind the full flavour of the employing organizations' perceptions of shortages, and how, if they are perceived, they relate to the organizations' general recruitment policies and whatever they expect from higher education. We will therefore quote some extended passages from five interviews with different firms. They are all in the computing industry, but they differ in size, structure and opinions.

Firm A

A manufacturer of business machines: international: recruits engineers, systems analysts, marketing (from any discipline): medium to large graduate recruitment.

The interviewer approached shortages through recruitment. There was no evidence in the interview of problems in recruiting graduates other than those outlined here.

(Q: For what kind of jobs does your firm recruit graduates?) They recruit them for varying types of jobs: in the one area we have manufacturing and engineering divisions and they recruit electronic/mechanical/industrial/test-equipment quality engineers. The same division, manufacturing and research, also recruits systems analysts and software programmers to carry out systems software rather than applications software – that's our division. The Marketing Division has an annual requirement for marketing trainees and this coming year, 1982, we expect to recruit 25 marketing trainees. Then there are systems analysts for applications software which is done in this division – the Programme Products Division and this year we have 18 vacancies for new graduates and a couple of vacancies for technical writers. In addition we have what you might call miscellaneous: one or two – this year four – financial trainees in head office, whom we would expect to be working for qualification in ICMA or something like that and we also have customer service engineers who used to be called Field Engineers and this year we have a requirement for five.

(Q: Arts or social science disciplines?) Yes. In the area of marketing trainees: financial trainees, perhaps less so; we would be more inclined to get someone with a degree in one or something like that. So far as systems analysis goes we have a preponderance of people who have been reading computing studies. The jobs demand things like team work and leadership.

(Q: Have there been significant changes in recruitment practices with the economic downturn?) Yes, I should say so, but this has varied from one division to another. On the good side if you took the Programme Products Division that now has 140 people in it, this time last year it had 90. So we had 50% growth in the Programme Products Division in 1981 which was a year when very few people grew at all. This time next year we will be 180 people, so slightly smaller a percentage rate of growth and probably about the same absolute intake. So at one end of the scale you have Programme Products Division which is probably the fastest growing division of the company paying absolutely no attention to the recession at all. At the other end you have someone like Marketing Division who is this year recruiting to stay still. They would expect to recruit 25 marketing trainees and you would get 25 marketing people in the company one way or another, anyway.

(Q: Which degree disciplines do you usually recruit from?) Depends who is recruiting and for what jobs. In Programme Products Division generally, maths and computing science but by no means totally. For factories wanting electronics engineers – a degree in electronics. We are then recruiting for characters with brain/personality.

(Q: Are you able to recruit enough graduates in the disciplines you would like?) We would fill our recruitment needs with the people we get hold of.

(Q: What is the most serious recruiting problem the firm has?) You ask me to speak for my firm, and our recruitment is decentralized so this is difficult to do. In my own case, the most serious problem is we find good people who are quite desparately short sometimes of communication and team work skills. You get a good bloke – with a good brain and never happier than curled up in front of his TV set playing chess against his home computer and never talks to more than one person at a time in his life.

(Q: What should higher education do to take account of the UK's needs for trained manpower?) Don't think they are doing a bad job at the moment. It's been covered in this conversation: matters of teamwork, numeracy and ability to communicate your thoughts is what is on occasion so distressingly lacking. You say why to someone and after they've been talking for five minutes they are no wiser. You ask a question and he talks for five minutes and he hasn't answered it.

Firm B
One of the world's largest computer firms: multinational, large graduate recruiter, with large proportion of graduates in its work force. Recruits for all facets of computing: hardware, software, systems analysis and development.

We are not really in the business of picking up large numbers of those whom you would expect us to pick up. I'm not over-enthralled by the vast number of computer scientists who are on offer here and there. We're after the best people that we can find. We find many of those in the old universities, of course we do, and some may have read languages, history, classics and I should show you numbers of people who've read arts degrees whom we've recruited in recent years. So those able people are attractive too.

(Q: How many did you take on in 1981?) These were new graduates – 112. These are the people I have responsibility for recruiting. 1981 we recruited 112 of graduates seeking first employment after university whether Bachelor or postgraduate level.

(Q: How did that compare with the previous five years?) One hundred and twelve in 1981, 62 in 1980, 84 in 1979, 159 in 1978 and 160 in 1977. This year we're not recruiting many but the reason for that is the tremendous reorganization at the beginning of the year in our marketing division. We took the opportunity to merge the previously separate support functions of finance, administration, personnel and information systems, and there are separate such groups for each of the marketing divisions before we merged them together. When you merge things together you get head-count savings and surpluses and so we have had to absorb people rather than to recruit.

(Q: In a typical year, out of 100 people is there a percentage which you could say were technical and the rest any discipline?) I would say in a typical year 20% of the people we recruit need to have specific backgrounds. This year is a strange year — marketing, developing and manufacturing and because of that the proportion is higher. The development laboratories are developing both hard and software. If they develop software, the degree subject is less important. Within manufacturing a surprising number of those whom we recruit are going into the area we call production control where you have people with business studies backgrounds or indeed anyone could do the job quite well. There are numbers of people who are production engineers and a new need that I can see coming on the market for ceramicists to work in manufacturing and in the development laboratories — electronics engineers.

(Q: Do you get graduates applying for non-graduate jobs?) Yes, we get a lot who are willing to do any job at all in order to get a job within the company. Only to go into that kind of job where it doesn't matter too much I can't conceive for example, a branch office — let me think — a non-graduate type job? The kind of areas: certainly finance because when we recruit graduates into finance we're bringing them into non-graduate jobs initially.

(Q: What would you say — persistent problem with recruitment over the past few years?) That's the biggest problem: I mean, my problem's not connected with recruitment or finding candidates, my problem is concerned with those relationships with universities that, at this time, we are not visiting.

(Q: The higher education system as a whole: is there anything you think ought to be done to it — examinations rather than developing personal curiosity, and so on?) I tend to be a nuts and bolts practical sort of bloke and I'm not too enamoured nowadays of people reading single honours subjects at university, whether technical, mathematics or arts oriented. It is my personal view that we would do far better to have a much broader system of higher education at universities and polytechnics.

Firm C

A large computer firm, developing both hardware and software. The company had just undergone a major internal reorganization. It had recruited no graduates in the previous year and dropped out of the milk-round altogether. It was aiming, however, to resume its graduate recruitment in the following year. It is important to bear in mind that the person we spoke to in this organization was reluctant to discuss many elements in their recruitment or the shortages of manpower they were presently facing.

(Q: Most serious recruiting problem?) The recent history of (company name). Its reputation has suffered a severe blow.

(Q: Sponsorship?) Yes, at the moment only electronics engineers to be development engineers − 25 of them.

(Q: Why sponsor?) We were forced to sponsor in the old days because it's a competitive market place and this was the way to beat competition. We are involved very much in their training for four years. At the end of the day we end up as far as we are concerned with someone who is better trained, better orientated. His attitudes are (company name) attitudes.

This firm is a place-holder for others like it, in respect of shortages. An important employing organization, it, like others, is in serious crisis because of the economy and the competitive nature of the industry. It cannot estimate shortages because it is not hiring. Shortages in the past were coped with by sponsorship. At the aggregate level shortages of qualified manpower must be linked to these fluctuations of manpower needs, and cross-sectional estimates must reflect firms like this who experience no shortages simply because they are not hiring.

Firm D
A small firm, recruiting few graduates direct from higher education. Produces printed circuits for computing, electronics and communications industry.

I would argue that the graduates we take on are really basically very good. Our firm does take on graduates with some experience of employment, however, because we feel that they have gained what you might call a 'commercial awareness', like consideration for clients, meeting deadlines and so on. While universities do provide really sound training in electronics, they don't (or can't) provide the commercial awareness we expect of recruits. I'm really not sure whether universities should try to provide this sort of commercial awareness as it may detract from the electronics training they get. On balance, we're happy − but then we're not so involved in taking people direct from universities and so perhaps we get the best of both worlds.

(Q: Do you recruit non-graduates for any of the major job categories for which you generally recruit graduates?) It's really difficult for me to answer that question. We have a number of jobs which require specific skills but for which higher education doesn't provide courses. Take the example of silk screen printing for circuit boards, that's one of the things we really need in this firm, but we have to do the training ourselves. There is a group of firms operating in the north of England who have come together to provide a diploma course for trainees in this very field.

(Q: Shouldn't higher education do this for the firms?) I don't think so, you know.

Firm E
A small software house, based in London and employing about 300 people: offices in North America and South East Asia: recruits between twenty and thirty graduates each year.

We have done probably not very accurate manpower planning in the past and we are just going through a numbers exercise at the moment based on good market forecast, to see just how many graduates we need worldwide. We start in about January getting response to our very few advertisements which are in the various graduate publications like GO, and so on. We do write to many universities careers officers with brochures on our scheme, we find we get a very adequate response in the UK anyway: plus a few writers from abroad. Normally we get about 600 unsolicited applicants for our graduate trainee programme in London. We then do a sift about March, deciding on who we would like to call in for an interview. We base our selection process on the knowledge that eight or nine people out of 10 failed our 3R aptitude test, which is a pure programming aptitude test. Typically in a year, we bring in 15 or 35 graduates (depending partly on manpower plans.)

We have a major problem in that to get 10 graduates in, we have to interview hundreds of them. We avoid computer scientists as far as possible because you find that in general their degrees are not useful to us directly. They have been taught scientific languages like 'Fortran' and stuff like that, which has no commercial application in our environment. They tend to have − although being highly intelligent normally − a non-commercial sort of view of computing. And our problem here is that people have to produce results fast exactly according to typed programme specifications and so on. The computer scientists we have got are all very good in fact, because we have been able to cross-train them but we find it more useful probably to take in an arts graduate that has passed the test, who will certainly be able to programme, who the test has shown has the logical ability to look at fairly complex accounting systems... and come up with functional specs and eventually programme those specs. Ideal in fact, is an arts graduate preferably in modern languages as we expand in Europe. But we do not often hit that ideal. Most of our graduate trainees have historically had degrees in sciences or maths.... There is a trade off between scanning the whole universe for graduates who are in fact available to us and getting the right sort of people in. We have only recruited 15 trainees in the latter half of this year. I have been following their progress. They have all done extremely well, there is not one guy who is anywhere near a failure. First class people, and that's basically from the applications that we got in. The only place we advertised was in GO, and through a careful sifting of application forms.... So we see no need, in fact, to have any sort of rational process of going to any respected universities.

I am asked by people outside and inside the company why do we recruit only graduates? Firstly because it is a handy screening process given that universities are churning out enormous numbers of graduates, it gives us a vast pool to choose from. There is no point in looking beyond that pool, it is a handy filter, it does show that a person has worked under fairly high pressures and has actually achieved certain mile-stones and targets by certain dates to certain standard, which is what our job is all about in fact, managing computer projects. It shows that they have mixed with a fairly wide spectrum of people, that they may well have lived away from home.

These excerpts from responses to a variety of questions over the whole area of recruitment certainly do not suggest that shortages are a major preoccupation of the companies, all of whom operate in an industry which, more than most, is said to suffer from them. These recruiters had plenty of opportunity to discuss shortages, but spoke instead of how to choose the best. All were experienced graduate recruiters. Shortages which are felt in some other organizations in the study (for example, electronics engineers) were not felt by these firms. This, no doubt, reflects their image and status in the graduate labour market; and underlines the importance of a close analysis of the position in the market of firms which make up any serious study of shortages in qualified manpower. It is important to note, as well, that among these firms one large firm had been through a period of trouble and reorganization. In a single sector, a change in recruitment patterns in one or two firms which recruit large numbers of graduates may have serious effects on the perceptions of shortages in that sector and outside it.

SUMMARY

In this chapter we have examined employers' and not economists' percep-tions of 'shortages'. We have implicitly looked at the *substitutability* of different kinds of manpower throughout the chapter. We have not, as yet, looked at the consequences of this, which we will take up in the final chapter.

Although we have seen some of the uses employers make of substitution and other strategies for overcoming manpower shortages, not all shortfalls will be amenable to this. In a market economy there may be a mismatch between candidates and jobs at any moment in time, in the short run, or over a considerable period of time. Employer and student choice are fundamental characteristics of a market economy and its higher education system. Few manpower requirements can be determined by the combination of demog-raphic trend and policy that can affect medical and teaching requirements. (Given the size of the age cohort and certain assumptions about public expenditure, an educational policy can be drawn up for an estimated number of teachers or doctors.) There is no demographic basis for the number of civil engineers which will be wanted over a five-year period – especially if exogenous 'demands' for technically skilled manpower vary along with endogenous 'demands'.

6 The Higher Education System

The interviews with employers' representatives conducted for this study included several evaluative questions which were designed to move from the specific, questions about the higher education experience of individual organizations, to the more general, questions about the adequacy of the UK higher education system in producing educated manpower both for the country as a whole and for the firms and their associated professions.

This is an inherently risky area of questioning as it requires employing organizations to evaluate the higher education *system* rather than the particular institutions, departments and educational bodies of which they have had experience. Indeed, early interviews showed a marked reluctance on the part of many interviewees to respond to general and evaluative questions. Some employers felt it was 'not their job' to give general commentary on educational issues. Some felt they did not have proper evidence. Some argued – and indeed some demonstrated – that they did not know anything about the 'system' as a whole.

Most common among the evaluative questions asked were:

i   What should higher education be doing better to take account of the UK's need, and your own organization's need, for trained manpower?
ii Let us say you were asked by the Secretaries of State for Education and Science and for Employment to give your views on how higher education could better meet the country's economic needs – what would your views be?
iii In your view, what are the major economic problems which face Britain today and how can and should the work of institutions of higher education contribute to solving these problems?

Questions of this breadth allowed employers to present manpower and other problems relating to the higher education system which were compelling to the organization, whether or not these had previously arisen in the interview. We considered it unlikely that critical commentary on educational issues would go unmentioned here.

Respondents discussed the issues in different ways. Some expressed their views of the higher education system only in terms of courses or institutions with which they were familiar; some outlined a single issue which had been argued throughout the interview — for example the inadequacy of careers advising; some used examples of higher education policy issues in the press in the weeks preceding the interview; a few delivered fully prepared statements. Interviewers were instructed to probe, where necessary, to develop the issues either generally or specifically as reflected in the firm. What emerges is inevitably somewhat disjointed. A fair number of responses begin or end with statements such as:

> This is a very general question, almost too general to answer.

> I would need notice to answer this question.

> It is not my place to say.

> This is a highly personal view.

> It is so complicated a question I don't have examples to answer it.

> (It would be fairly presumptuous for) someone fairly new in the recruitment field to tell the higher education system what to do.

> I just haven't considered... the wider context.

> (Advising individuals is one thing) advising the educational establishment is another. It is a different thing. All we could say is these are our views and ICI can say these our ours and Trans can say these are ours. Any one company's view is biased because you are looking for people to meet your narrow needs because of technological requirements....

Most employers, however, offered some statement about higher education whether or not they distanced themselves from the statements they made. Even when reluctant to discuss such issues, they were co-operative. As one senior recruiter noted:

> ... when I say I don't think it is our place to say what the system should be like, I think this is a bit of a cop out. You can't moan about what people do (and say they don't listen) and then not answer when they ask.

Most such general responses are long and multi-dimensional. Abstracting and indexing them according to relevant policy areas (eg content of courses) tends to distort the clarity and importance to the interviewee of a particular comment. The following evidence from two interviews illustrate the problem.

The first is an articulate senior recruiter from a large multinational manufacturing firm. He mentions the advantages of the German system; the need for the system to change subject balance; the cuts; the importance of more science and maths at A level; the need for arts graduates to have some business orientation. It must be read, if it is to be useful, in its entirety. The question 'What is the simple message?' can only be answered by, 'This is it, complex though it may be.'

I must say that I get the feeling that Germany which seems to me anyway to have more of its education biased towards economics and an economics in business sort of approach, and more towards technology and less towards pure science, does seem to struggle along a little better than we do. If there are cuts to be made, I must say that I would protect technology and business studies and applied economics and take the pain on social sciences, maybe....

I know that the view of the research people, if you take the scientific disciplines in universities and how that would be attractive to (large multinational) scientifically, that would be just to do the basics well and not to get into fashionable mixtures of nonsense which is the danger. Biochemical aspects of sociology or some sort of thing. You can get bizarre combinations — anything to get a few kids in the door — we need that like we need a hole in the head, not just (company name) but industry generally. Outside of that I don't think it is for (company name) to say really. My feeling is that we do need more technological education even if the jobs are not there at this moment. I can only believe that is a good thing. We should get people a bit more versed in business studies, not necessarily as an undergraduate course. But I don't think — not just me — anybody in (company name) could give much sensible advice on it. Yes, probably a bit more bias to practical vocational subjects but I don't think that is as important as just maintaining standards in the particular subjects they are studying and finding ways to encourage people to find out about work before they go into it. What I would not do is shut Salford and Bradford and these places. That seems to me to be as near lunacy as I could imagine.

My instinct is that if you were able to throw a switch somehow it means changing all sorts of attitudes and having many more people in this country do A level mathematics — like every graduate; and, for example, weighting the non-scientific technological courses at the university overwhelmingly towards applied social sciences. If you can make that sort of change, do I think the country would be more successfully economically? Then the answer is, 'yes, I do'. I don't know how you make that sort of change. You would need to move away from purity, and it doesn't just apply to chemistry.

I have interviewed at universities and gone round to chemistry departments and said, can you tell me what you think of so and so.... They say, well, in semi-micro analysis he is very smart. However, I am interviewing him to be an accountant. They just have no perception whatever. It is not just chemists. You go through language schools — so they tell me, I'm no expert at it. If you go through French departments or German departments and say, how well does the programme train people to really orally communicate with a Frenchman — not all that well, It's done on a very, very theoretical adademic basis and that seems cuckoo to me. As it happens, the only schools they are closing in that line are the ones at Bradford which have got a world reputation for turning out translators.

The second piece of evidence is given by the head of a chemical engineering firm. He is critical of 'subsidized' education for some overseas students —

students from countries which are economic competitors; he emphasizes the problems associated with risk-taking in business and the need for government to further help the small businessman; he, too, argues for the need to change the subject balance in the national interest; he thinks tertiary education should be paid for by its beneficiaries.

If it's an inventive guy who starts the company the likelihood is that he will become bogged down with his inventiveness or will get pushed into doing things he's not well equipped to do. It was that last thing that happened here: the more successful he was, the more he got pushed into administering the company with a management team. That he was not well equipped to do. I came on the scene. My skills lie in organization and motivation. I'm a generalist. I like to think I'm numerate and literate. My predecessor was 61, widowed, thoroughly demotivated. Every two to three years we have tried to recruit a mechanical engineer to replace him. We draft attractive advertisements, gulp when we see the salary to attract the right calibre, what anomaly that might create within the existing management, then get two inadequate replies. The nearest we've ever got is head of mechanical engineering at the local technical college. He was getting 20% more than we were offering and working 60% below the hours per annum we were requiring. How do we alter that? Needs an act of faith....

There is only one aspect of this that we haven't touched on. You can't push a piece of string, nor direct labour other than in a national emergency and that puts it down to government to set the scene. Government has got a great thing on small companies these days and in my view most of the people who have set up businesses of their own have done it because they've been made redundant from where they were. We're not here to set up business on our own account but it's more attractive than doing something else. I believe we're in a situation where government has to make positive changes, especially in the sphere of taxation. We must make the successful businessman enviable. There's no shortage of kids wanting to be professional football players because they make money. It's a pity we don't have a lot of small businessmen in the same enviable position.

Further, what happens if one takes the idea that students should take courses that they are best at, mediated by employment expectations? What happens if consistently they don't go into engineering/science/ technology, with the consequences it has for British industry? If you make tertiary education freely available then you may end up with people pursuing their interests at the expense of the rest of society. I don't go along with that.

I got a bunch of very hard working employees and I like to think it's because management set the standard. The fact remains that the amount we pay as employers into the education kitty is frightening and it is to benefit others and few will come back into this company. It's socially unfair to make tertiary education freely available, quite morally wrong when people are pursuing their own interest for their own pleasure. As a nation we make primary and secondary education freely available but tertiary education should be on a loan basis then you get a balance between supply and demand. At the moment you can have the female geologist with five years to MSc and unemployable. If she and her Dad had to finance that themselves they would think a bit harder. We should thrust responsibility back at people and make them much more accountable, then it would be much more self-acting. At the moment you ask how do you forecast demand for engineers five to ten years hence, you can't.

In the following sections we disaggregate such lengthy statements into a few of their component themes — taking statements somewhat out of context and drawing upon answers to more than one question. The reader will discover that whether employers are critical or satisfied with the higher education system, whether statements are long or short, there are no clear explanatory variables which rationalize the diversity of responses. Employers, large or small, technical or non-technical, in public or private sector, do not have common views on either the adequacy of the higher education system or how it could make a more significant contribution to economic life.

SATISFACTION

Satisfaction with the higher education system is, of course, rather easier to analyse than dissatisfaction. As Tolstoy wrote: 'All happy families resemble one another, but each unhappy family is unhappy in its own way.' A large number of employing organizations were satisfied with the numbers and types of graduates that they saw, the division of labour within the system, and the general size of the system. The following comments are representative.

A manufacturer of photographic equipment:

Our system is a good and efficient system of three or four year courses and produces someone who can really go out and do a job. In America they spend a long time doing their courses and then to a lower level. I think the problem we're stuck with is the problem of suitability of people to higher education. The principle that education should be available to all those capable of benefiting from it is an excellent one. What has happened is that institutions have been set up to cope with the need and in order to survive they have had to lower their standards and to take people who really are not going to benefit from that education. That goes back a bit to the schools such that schools have probably got to do a better job preparing people to a level from which they can take advantage of higher education, but opportunities ought to be there.

An advertising agency:

(We are) generally satisfied — would like to see as high standards as possible.

A market research organization:

Our biggest problem is in filtering out good people from an enormous number of applicants.

A local authority:

> Higher education is doing a good job. We are getting plenty of able applicants. The problem for local government is having to justify its needs.

A large diversified manufacturer:

> We have no objections to the present system. We are quite happy with it.

A manufacturer of wood products:

> The system overall can't be beaten as such. Perhaps more on the 'man-management' side. I don't think that is taken up.

A museum:

> I would say (the system) is meeting our needs, but by accident rather than design.

A national theatre:

> I don't think the theatre has a feeling that the universities should be teaching anything different from what they are.

A large shipbuilding firm:

> I've heard in seminars about different courses carried out at universities. Criticism is being made about our standards compared with continental standards. I don't believe there's sufficient evidence to show that the British system is worse than other countries. By and large the system works well. Very large/diverse system of education which gives very good results and compares with other systems in the world. The university degree is very attractive.

An important minority of employers did not, however, see higher education as relevant to whatever problem the firm might be facing. A building and design company spokesman noted:

> Every university and polytechnic runs a civil engineering course − if a few courses are eventually cut out it won't affect us in the least, because our needs are small. But we do feel the general effects of cuts − for example the big cuts at Salford seem crazy, and indicative of a climate of opinion and/or decision-making process which still doesn't recognize the realities and importance of manufacturing and construction life. Cuts like these are a blow to the morale of industry.
>   But most generally, higher education isn't going to affect us − trading conditions are what affect us − the solution to our problems of the moment rest with us. We have to create new markets and opportunities for development.

Another employer, a larger manufacturer which does not typically recruit graduates identified his major training problem as antiquated machinery coupled with the lack of up-to-date skills held by the teaching staff in the local technical college:

> We have the largest single covered (machinery) in Europe in (city name) and we are under an obligation to send our apprentices to the local technical college. The machinery where these lads are being trained... is machinery we presented to the college 15 years ago. The college isn't keeping up with technology. Equally, tutors came out of industry 15 years ago. Their knowledge of present industry bears little relation to what actually happens.

Another employer reflects a satisfaction with the graduates they see because, in any case, they will need further training and enough are found who are not only academically able but are suitable for that training.

> Me? I don't care a damn what they do, what I want is a good mind. I'll do the training, because there is nothing you can do in a university which will provide you with more than the first step. The rest of the steps have to be done by gradually working within the institution.... (We are involved in) all sorts of academic fields.... I don't think we ever worry about higher education, frankly. The point is that we've never had any difficulty recruiting good people. And our needs as far as the universities are concerned are normally those that would be in a university anyway – academic ability, with a slightly broader base than you would if you were appointing a lecturer of the equivalent grade.... I don't think there's anything the universities could do for us, frankly that we would want, as long as they don't cut down their standards too much.

While the remaining sections of this chapter illustrate lines of criticism, this is not the dominant voice of employers. Most were relatively satisfied with the graduates they saw, with the number recruited, and with the general efficiency of the system.

DISSATISFACTION; THE GAP BETWEEN EDUCATION AND EMPLOYMENT

A number of employers made general comments of dissatisfaction, noting particularly a lack of integration, co-operation and mutual understanding between industry and higher education. Some are critical of what they see as 'ivory-tower' isolation, fewer see the problem as belonging as much to industry as to higher education.

A manufacturer of domestic appliances:

> It's very much up to the educational institutions to get the 'flavour' (of our needs), by talking to people and finding out the types of graduates employers take in and the types of disciplines in which they're interested and, indeed, as you have already asked, the types of areas where education is falling short.

A manufacturer and distributor of food products:

> The universities still think they are the seats of learning and not the seats of training. I think there should be bits of both.... But we're still heavily biased on seats of learning.

A widely diversified manufacturer and retailer:

> Higher education has been out of touch for so long it's not true. It's not all their fault, because the basic system has not geared itself to the necessary changes if we are to survive as an industrial economy. (It is a political requirement) to survive in an ever-expanding industrial economy and no efforts have been made to react to this.... It's about time they (higher education)... had the skids put under them because they have been out of touch for so long... it's not all their fault because I think the whole higher education system has not geared itself to the changes that are so necessary if we are to survive as an industrial economy....
>
> I tried unsuccessfully on several occasions to offer the opportunity for lecturers/teachers to spend time in industry. Every time it has been mooted it has been pounded on a rock by the education establishment. They are not prepared to release their personnel. The latest is the South Bank Poly.
>
> I think the academic people should learn what hard work is because they don't know that. They have such long holidays and short hours and high pay and they really don't understand what working in industry is like. The way they misuse their resources, again, they don't know what it's like to have a commitment to resources.

A printing and publishing firm:

> I don't think the universities take sufficient trouble (and industry can equally be held to blame) to find out what we in industry are looking for and prefer to present us with a number of graduates and say: if you find what you need, all well and good: take it or leave it.

An electronic engineering firm:

> I get the impression that when the economy is good they (the academics) are not terribly responsive. When the economy is bad (a) they need financing, and (b) by definition they need to be able to place their students. But I get the impression that when things are going well they prefer to be a law unto themselves.

A banking firm:

> (It is all related) to the security of tenure... there are many professors running around departments that would adapt their syllabi... make them more multi-disciplinary... there are others who would not... but they have security of tenure that cannot be bettered.

A building and civil engineering contractor:

> I've been disappointed whilst I've been in industry to see how few
> graduates there are working in industry outside the fields of engineering
> and business studies and business management.
>   (Q: Do you think this is because of graduates' attitude to industry or
> industry's attitude to graduates?) I think it's the first, the attitude of arts
> and humanities graduates to industry, and I think this is an underlying
> fault in the country generally. There are very bright people on that side
> who could make a contribution in industry.... They're going into the
> professions or the civil service, some of them occasionally come through if
> they go through an accountancy qualification or something like that, but I
> think there's an awful lot of brain power being lost to British industry in
> the non-engineering fields through a lack of perception of opportunities
> in industry by graduates themselves, or wrong perceptions of what
> industry is about. You know, British industry doesn't get a particularly
> good press and I think there's a feeling either the challenge isn't there or
> the environment is a little bit wrong.

LINKS BETWEEN EMPLOYERS AND HIGHER EDUCATION

A substantial number of comments urge closer links between industry and
higher education institutions; a need for more educational planning for
industry's needs; and, in particular, more emphasis in course work on the
values of the free enterprise system. A large number mention the need for
industry and commerce to have a 'better press' among very able graduates,
and the need to take some of the requirements of industry inside universities
and polytechnics by changing course content.

A large good retailing chain:

> On the whole, if I could do anything in terms of education generally, it
> would be in polys rather than universities. The standard of teaching
> business studies is poor because the people who teach it either have never
> been in business, never worked in industry or commerce, or, equally, have
> been out of it too long.

A large textile and fibre manufacturer:

> It is important to develop contact between industry and the university
> system but recognizing that they are two almost irreconcilable establish-
> ments. You have to work away at local and small-scale things and you will
> not get Sir Keith or the DES to achieve it from on high.

A merchant bank:

> A great many very good people are going into the service sector,
> including the financial side. More *should* perhaps go into industry, but the
> main fault lies with industry, who don't offer the chances of rapid
> promotion and responsibility that graduates can find in merchant banks,
> and generally don't sell themselves well enough.

An engineering firm:

> I think the Germans have got it much better. It would be unthinkable in a firm like us in Germany not to have someone who was a professor on the board, it would be unthinkable to have a professor who did not have an engineering directorship with some significant company. But you can't legislate for that, you have to create the conditions in which it comes about, so I give him the problem but not the solution, he's got to bring about much closer contact between industry and commerce.

Other employers saw higher education as sequestering young people from the 'real' world and thus creating a 'shortage' of social skills.
A clothing manufacturer:

> Graduates should be more prepared to get their hands dirty before they take positions of command.... When they are in managerial positions they should be able to deal socially with customers, staff, etc.

A diversified manufacturer and retailer:

> Somehow we have (created a system) that allows a person to go to school and on to university without getting to see how the world works.

Not surprisingly, many employers wanted students to understand the value of the free enterprise system and how it operates in practical terms. An example follows from a senior recruiter in a large computer manufacturing firm:

> I think that there are serious problems in the British educational system that prevent, or that put the blinkers on, kids. If I can put it this way, when I was at school — I went to the local grammar school, and I was in the science stream, and when I was 15 years old they brought us on very quickly.... We were doing quite advanced maths when we were 15. And they said to us: if you do well and you work really hard, you might be able to sit your A levels when you're 16 or 17, a year earlier. And then if you get really good marks you might sit scholarship papers, you might get an Oxbridge scholarship. And if you get a really good degree you might be able to get a job in the civil service! That was their approach. Not once did anybody say to us you might be able to start your own engineering business. There is a cultural problem at school — and it's not at university, it's in school. The kids are taught by people who don't understand what's involved in starting one. And these kids grow up and they're 35 or 40 years old before the idea gets into their head that they might be able to start a business. Now, I work a lot in America and kids there when they're students are starting businesses. I mean you've got 'Apple' and things like that which are businesses started by quite young people. Students, while they are students, have their own businesses. I mean they might only be washing shirts or delivering newspapers, but they have a business. Whereas in England there's a cultural void created by schools, and to a certain extent in engineering by university staff. It's mainly at school level.

And a third point, this is the other thing, that people who go to university – and we had the same problem when we started this business – don't understand the very basics of business. When I left university I didn't understand what the word 'profit' meant. I didn't understand how profit and loss was computed. I didn't understand the difference between a profit and loss account, and a balance sheet. I mean, these are three important things – the basics of business are a balance sheet, your profit and loss account and your cash flow account. But nobody ever – and it would have been very easy to put on a short course – nobody ever teaches the really basic facts of business.... You get people who've got the most weird ideas about how a company has to generate its money.... If you make a machine and the materials cost £100 and the direct assembly labour costs you about £50, so the direct labour and materials are about £150, some of these characters think you can sell it for £200. You know, we are not making our goods in a tent, in the middle of Oldham Road. We have overheads and they don't understand that. They don't understand that, for instance, inventory is included in profit. They think that, if you declare a profit of £100,000 you've got £100,000 cash in the bank. They don't understand how it's computed. And it's dangerous. Not only is it dangerous for people who are starting businesses not to know these things, it's dangerous because it causes a lot of unnecessary bad feeling.

A large food retailing chain:

Now a lot of the girls who go through university meet a special segment in society and they don't meet the randy 16-year-old in the back of the warehouse, etc., and I think that not enough is explained whilst they are going through the learning process about working life. Certainly on the retailing side, it consists of pressure, of demands, of working unsocial hours, working at weekends, etc. These people could be prepared for this as they are prepared for everything else in life....

A marine engineering firm:

Make the experiences provided more relevant to the outside world. A 21-year-old graduate is far more naive in many ways and less prepared for the outside world than a 21-year-old who has spent three to five years in the world of work. I don't think we should be protecting graduates from the outside world.

Some employers were specific about the skills needed.
    A manufacturer of home products:

I don't see university as a preparation for career in industry.... Some graduates recruited here will say to me after being in the organization for six months – 'I wish I'd known 18 months ago what I now know about how to run a meeting, or make a presentation or write a document. If I'd known that then I'd have progressed quicker.'

These general remarks on the need for closer working relationships between educational institutions and industry did not typically take the form of urging more 'manpower planning'. But several employers did feel that the system could better reflect the needs of industry, although the processes for accomplishing this were not specified.

A large holding company:

> I think there has to be a very much closer future matching of the options provided in the large proportion of higher education courses in relation to the job requirements of the country's economy. We've managed to get away with the old idea of saying it really doesn't matter how wide our course portfolio should be because the real object of life is enrichment. We cannot afford to ignore the country's economic needs in terms of what's going on − in the competitiveness of the country's industrial world markets and the preparation that education makes towards the supply of expertise and skill in these areas.... I think one of the big problems we face generally right from graduation stage, people become academics or businessmen and there is very little cross-pollenization.

A public sector employer:

> I don't believe it possible, for reasons of time-lag etc., to run the universities on the basis of forecast and required type of discipline. It's too complex, although I believe we should go half way there. I believe there should be a guide, employer-oriented rather than the Robbins idea of student-oriented. The emphasis should be on engineers, etc., and I believe the emphasis is very wrong at the moment.

A few employers argued that industry needed to make its requirements clearer. One, an automobile manufacturer, stressed the importance of trying to have links with institutions of higher education that are personal and not too broadly based:

> I think we get the products from the institutions that we deserve. If we arrive once a year (in departments and institutions) expecting to be welcomed with open arms, and expect our precise needs to be met − in that case we're in for a rude shock. If we are to get the product we want from institutions, we have to collaborate with them. It is a two-way process. If an organization like (name of company) is dealing with a mass of institutions, then the likely impact that one can have on courses is minimal. The impact one can have is if one collaborates across a broad front within an institution, that is the way to go.

There are several themes running through the words of the small group of employers who are more or less disgruntled with higher education. They feel that students are sheltered too much from the 'real world' of work and do not acquire habits of hard work, skills of communication, or knowledge of the financial facts of life; nevertheless, when they graduate their expectations are too high. They, and their teachers, are seen as protected from economic disciplines, and enjoying immunity from the pressures and risks the business community has to endure. They are sometimes seen as positively inculcating anti-business attitudes – and the private sector employers sometimes seem to associate them in this particularly with the civil service and the professions. Along with these negative attitudes go complaints that educators do not take the trouble to find out what employers need from graduates, though there is some readiness to accept that the fault here may lie also with industry itself. Remedies suggested are staff exchanges, recruiting part-time teachers from industry, and of course, practical work experience as a part of the course. There is some irritation at reported failures by institutions to co-operate in such schemes.

HOW MUCH HIGHER EDUCATION AND WHAT KIND?

On the overall scale or provision, employers had much to say. Their comments covered evaluations of two decades of expansion of higher education, the system that had resulted and the rise in expectations which they felt there had been among young graduates. Among the relatively few employers who were critical of the system as a whole, a typical example is a large manufacturer:

> I think higher education is a wasteful process. Some degree of concentration is necessary. They must face up to the fact that they are not cost-effective in all subjects. We would like to see chemistry concentrated at half the number of schools and if funds were allocated accordingly they would turn out a better product – exactly the same in biochemistry and pharmacology.

At the other extreme, few argued that more money should be spent on higher education, as did a representative of a nationalized industry:

> Basically, I think more money should be spent on education, and there should not be too many constraints on the availability of higher education....

Employers who offered criticisms of the overall level of provision often did so in rather vague terms – expressing a general unease with its planning and structure, often touching on a number of related issues. One, a representative of a diversified publishing and paper products company, is reported at length below. He discusses the problems of increased access to higher education and the benefits of a break between schooling and higher education, and develops a strong argument about public schools and their relation to Oxbridge.

> My basic premise is that there are far too many people going to university and many of them are the wrong types, not just that some of them can't keep up with the academic work but they don't get out of it what they should get out of it. They don't get education and experience, they just get sausage machine knowledge. I actually get sometimes desolate at the number of people I interview who never should have gone at all... who struggle with the thing (because) they have probably gone into the wrong thing.... You can talk to graduates and... it becomes fairly apparent that there are a number of them who feel they have been subjected to pressure

both by school and from parents. They have streamed them through into university courses which frankly, with hindsight, they are not even sure they wanted. My view is that people who have got most out of university were the people who do their national service first. I did it afterwards. I regret it in many ways because I believe I would have got more out of it when I was 20 than I did at 18. I think a pre-university year might be a good thing or a university course that included in it some kind of compulsory pieces of experience. I don't know if it could be VSO or even something in the community which got them to contribute in an area outside themselves, with no evident gain for themselves. I don't know whether it would work but I am a strong supporter of the Government's ideas in new training for 16 to 18-year-olds and maybe they would do something similar to that. I think that is very true of the non-residential universities. I think when you meet people who continue to live at home and attend a university course, they do lack an awful lot. I did that but I did have two years in the Army afterwards. (One other point) I was horrified to find... my son is at a well known school, supposed to be one of the best in the country... that when one of the boys there, who is a very able lad, decided to go to Bath, his brother went to Oxford; this boy went to Bath and obtained a degree in technology and the school dropped all interest in him and treated him like an outcast. It was quite appalling and this was when my son had only been there a short time and I wasn't able to leap about with hot malt... they just lost interest in him because it may be a notch on the back of their cane but it is not in the right place for (public school name) which has to be respectable 'Red Brick'. A fuss needs to come through the schools and through the parents and I fancy it comes through the school primarily, through the headmasters.... This is a terrible thing to say, but I wish that Oxbridge and Cambridge would cease to exist for ten years − it would have a very beneficial effect on things.

A number of employers argued that the problem with the level and adequacy of provision stemmed from poor planning during the period of expansion. Some question whether students of modest academic achievement benefit from higher education.

A detergent manufacturer:

Higher education has expanded too far... the polys originally started as specialized areas of learning and gradually increased their scope. In most polys now you can take a degree in history for example.... I wonder whether this is necessary.

A manufacturer of fibres and textiles:

We expanded our university population without taking steps (to ensure that the school population was prepared), we didn't think through the total system... we just said we will have more of our university arrangements which were possibly not vocational....
We have certainly spent too much time since the Robbins explosion in trying to push people through university... with a far poorer overall result than if they had gone through some other route, and got an HND or

HNC. We have robbed ourselves in some ways, of people with practical skills.

One employer, however, felt that, although not all students benefited from a higher education, he would not want to see a significant cutback.
A medium-sized bank:

> Refreshing development in the last few years — but it raises a question as to whether an ever-increasing amount can be spent on higher education. We all come across cases where people have gone into higher education with flimsy evidence for it and haven't benefited to a significant degree from it. I welcome this slightly more pragmatic approach — 'should we be more selective?' At the same time, I wouldn't want to see a significant cut back in opportunities for people who go into further education. We are competing with a world where higher education is growing and we have to keep up our share of talent. We are a country which lives on its wits and ingenuity. We have to keep up our expenditure in general terms.

A number of employers mentioned the problem of matching provision to the attendant rise in expectations which graduates have.
A clothing manufacturer:

> Far be it from me to restrict the opportunities of youngsters but I feel it creates expectations... beyond their ability to achieve... they have ability by working hard to get a degree, but often they don't have the drive and initiative to hold down a management post.

A large manufacturer:

> Too many people are being encouraged by schools to take degrees and consequently given false expectations. People with good A levels should go into employment.

A public broadcasting company:

> (Graduates must be made) aware of the fact that because they have a degree this is not the key to everything.

An urban transportation company:

> Graduates are beginning to get the message. A few years ago if they had come out with a degree they thought they would go to the top. Now they are more realistic.... They may have difficulty in settling into a job because going to university has created a higher aspiration than can be filled. I am against élitism but it does have its advantages.

Few such comments included clear policy recommendations. The two exceptions cited below reflect a somewhat more sophisticated view of higher education issues than most. The first proposal, from a senior recruiter with a large accounting firm who has had wide experience of the higher education system, would reorganize the system of granting degrees altogether. All subjects, including technical, would be taught in universities, and only universities would grant degrees.

> I would ask him (Keith Joseph) to redefine for the public at large and for the education world what he means by getting a degree and, having done that, to define the institutions in which that level should be aspired towards and cultivated. I think that the polytechnic/university business has got very stale and it's not going to be made less stale with the current cuts by saying polys have got something unique to offer. In terms of strategic planning, we would do better to go back to the situation of saying universities do degrees and no one else.... Create a parity of esteem for practical pursuits but differentiate the stage where people pursue them.

A more specific proposal from a larger manufacturer:

> (One further point on the) Co-operative Awards in Science and Engineering between the SRC and industry. These are virtually PhD scholarships jointly funded with the SRC. We are supportive of these. What it means is that we have a proposal coming into us from university departments which has some relevance to our interests. We then see if it is of sufficient value to us. If it is, we will nominate an industrial supervisor − the academic department has an academic supervisor and the student is then funded by the SRC and us. They spend at least two months doing PhD working in our labs. There is constant liaison between the two supervisors. They come down and discuss progress of work. Very good in that it's cost-effective for us, it fosters good relationships between the university and our department and has led to recruitment of a number of very good PhDs who are well aware of how industry works because they have worked alongside people in industry. We'd like to see more money put into that possibly at the expense of the SRC fellowship.

Those employers who felt that expansion had gone too fast, and was badly planned, seemed to base their criticisms on four points − (i) that entry standards had declined; (ii) that too many students had been rail-roaded into higher education and were unmotivated; (iii) that expansion, even in the polytechnics, had not been in the technical, vocational areas where it was needed; and (iv) that it raised unrealistic expectations for many graduates. On the other hand, there was also an acknowledgement that the country needed to spend money on higher education to keep up with our competitors: the criticism was rarely unqualified.

CUTS IN EXPENDITURE
A number of employers specifically mentioned the topic of the 1981 cuts in university expenditure and how they had been administered. Some saw them as a good way to push the system into reorganization. A reorganization which was thought necessary both to get the subject balance right and to allocate educational functions properly between types of institution. The cuts were also thought by some to be a means of restoring diminished standards. There was general concern that engineering and technology and

the institutions that are thought to excel in these areas might suffer. The 'technological universities' were mentioned many times in this connection. For some employers the arts were linked to a more general sense that higher education is producing too many graduates. Some, on the other hand, clearly did not support the cuts and expressed this in terms of the higher rates of access to higher education in countries which are our industrial competitors. Firms represented by these comments include a very large chartered accountancy firm, a spokesman for the armed forces, a large holding company with diverse subsidiaries, a large multinational manufacturer, and an engineering firm. The public sector employers generally had significantly less to say about the cuts than those in the private sector.

A large firm of chartered accountants:

> If we have to assume that money is as short for this area as it is for any other social and worthwhile area, I suppose it would be nice if the cuts were a little less than those now being made, which do seem to have discriminated unfairly in favour of some universities against others. But in the end, allocating through the university grants board, or whatever it's called, the resources and leaving them to get on with their own job is probably the only way it can be done. I certainly would not plead for ploughing money into business studies and accounting courses but this is all part of a highly unproductive sector; engineering is a rather more productive area for the future and the nation. I'm really a bit out of my depth.
>
> Let me be honest about the business of the cuts: I see two advantages. One is that the emphasis is very wrong at the moment. There's a massive over-production of sociologists and the arts side despite the employment difficulties and this is said with my disagreement with Robbins. We've been spending a lot of money on educating characters who are 'permanent' students. There is no doubt at all that certain universities have been accepting extremely low standards for too long. I'm for raising standards which are worsening. The effect of the present cuts − obviously too early to tell − but even raising the standard by loss of numbers I think will help.

A holding company:

> One that instantly comes to mind is that I dearly hope that universities, in making their in-house arrangements to cope with the level of cuts, do not cut out engineering and technology disciplines because they are more expensive per head to run than others.

A manufacturer and distributor of food products:

> I think this has been highlighted by the university grants cuts recently. Certain universities have been less hard hit than others and they are the more academically minded. Bradford's been hit − Salford and Aston − this is worrying. I think it's wrong to have hit them harder than Oxbridge who are differently funded. Aston went too far − they've got weird courses and take in the lesser achievers and I think this is a problem the polys got themselves into. They take in too many lesser achievers.

A nationalized industry:

> The optimum view would be that everybody should develop as far as they can. There are economic realities, but that would be the ideal in so far as you move away from that, you are compromising. Developing as many people as possible is important for the individual, but also benefits the economy in the long run. We're still a bit hidebound in this country. The recent UGC cuts – and where they cut – is an illustration of this. If you look at what industry wants, it is courses at places like Salford, Aston, etc. It seems to be 'the establishment' who decided on the cuts, without seeing what industry wanted.

A contracting engineering firm:

> We were very disappointed to see the cuts, especially when you consider that the number of people going through higher education is lower than with our industrial competitors. I'd like to see a slight change in the balance, perhaps there are too many lawyers and not enough engineers. There may be a tendency to put money into some areas which are not essential to the national wealth to the detriment to some that are.... The present system is wasteful but we do need at least as many really well trained graduates as at present.

CONTENT : THE SUBJECT BALANCE

As we have noted throughout this analysis, employers offered few comments about the specific content of courses. Exceptions were those who commented on the need for more specialization or, alternatively, broader courses and those who commented more generally on the subject balance. With respect to the former question, the following comments were typical.

> The thing that worries me is the fact that this enormous proliferation of disciplines exists. You may study too many subjects, not specializing.... If you have done a modular approach you haven't had time to dig. The brightest graduate in this department has a single degree. I worry about the generalist and that's a worry on the polytechnic side of it.

A plastics manufacturer:

> The only reservation I have about the education system is that in a lot of instances we are not seeking the pure mechanical, electrical or production engineer. There appears to be, in terms of the jobs we want graduates to be involved in, and the disciplines which they study, a slight mismatch. One could foresee greater benefits from moving away from a single subject degree....

A computer manufacturer:

> I think British education – British higher education – is excellent, I do. I think the only small complaint, you can't call it a complaint – small suggestion, would be that the people who intend to go out into engineering industry... they should not be allowed to specialize too much,

because you don't make anything in isolation... when they go to university they shouldn't be allowed – well, it's a bad idea to allow people to study just purely electronics. They should do some structural engineering, some materials engineering, they should do thermo-dynamics, you know, heat engineers and things like that. If they're going to do electronics they should be allowed to do it maybe in their last year.

A large public broadcasting company:

We turned away about 1,000 undergraduates (out of 1,300 candidates in the milk-round) because they didn't know enough. They had spent far too much time on a fairly narrow subject without appreciating the implications of the fundamental theory that they had learnt in the first or second year. This is the fault of the institution, because there are some institutions where this doesn't happen – and it's not just Oxford and Cambridge.

A manufacturer of industrial gases:

At both school and university we want more flexibility, without, if possible, losing the depth of study. At school, it is a matter for concern that some people can go through without any technical subject, and also the scientists do not do much on the artistic side. Thirteen or 14 is too young to make informed choices about subjects which can affect one's whole career. At university there is a lot to be said for the Cambridge Natural Sciences Tripos, when one can do several different sciences, only specializing in the final year. But many of the institutions do not offer this degree of flexibility.

A computer manufacturer:

Perhaps, some form of specialization is appropriate, but widening up to business in general, with a degree in accountancy, so one knows what the business world is all about.

One employer mentioned the bewildering array of courses and the problem of matching people to them, coupled with the problem of trying to discover which graduates, and as a consequence, which courses, to support.
   A manufacturer of industrial gases:

... I also find that the universities and polytechnics have such a wide variety of types of degree courses in engineering – chemical, mechanical, electrical, whatever – it is almost bewildering and maybe they all satisfy their respective professional institutes. However, because they are so different in the amount of time and method of teaching, it is difficult for an employer to judge whether this is the right way of doing it....

One employer noted in this context what is relevant to many others: it is questionable how much the content of the course matters – whether specialized or not – since recruitment in a large proportion of firms takes place on the basis of A levels.

It is perfectly clear that from the retention rates studies and success patterns, that those universities that have high standards of entry produce high quality output. Most companies recruit people before they've taken their final degree. We are not really talking about final degrees – we are talking about a lot of factors before that. A level results, the way they've managed in early exams.

A number of employers mentioned both the need to get the subject balance right and the difficulty of doing to. For most this involved less emphasis on arts and social science and more on engineering and science, which arguments were made not only by companies who see a 'shortage' of graduates with such training. Some employers, it would seem, simply would prefer a system in which the balance is different.
A manufacturer of food products:

> There is a need both for freedom and control of the education system to make provision for pure and applied sciences and prevent a glut of arts and social sciences graduates... the economic situation will create this control.

A manufacturer of engineering products:

> I'm caught between requirements of the company and myself. The way things are going you must gear everything towards industry so everyone will have industrial training and only relevant, direct courses will be available. Is that the purpose of university though? You have to make the balance....

A manufacturer of chemical products:

> Also within the higher education sector, many more courses are on electronics engineering and related topics. But we should avoid too many very specialized courses. Higher education does to some extent respond to shortages of trained people, but after too long a lag, and they often react by introducing new courses in areas where there has been a shortage – but will not necessarily be in the future, especially if most institutions all introduce similar courses at the same time. And there should be more flexibility, with institutions being ready to drop or contract more courses as well as introduce new ones.

A large automobile distributor:

> I'd say that the Government should grasp the nettle of the extreme liberalism of the higher education system to the extent that there should be more positive encouragement for bright young people to take courses with a direct relevance to business. Even to the extent of discouraging or limiting the numbers going in for arts and sociology.... I'm not stipulating that (we should have only) engineering and technical graduates – we have not been concerned to go for engineering graduates. Basically we're a commercial company that's simply after practical people of hopefully high intelligence who are interested and motivated to be businessmen.

A large manufacturer:

> The degrees offered at university should be based on the needs of industry rather than the demands of entrants. We need to move away from the democratic method by which departments allocate funds to universities which bears no relationship to the universities' role in our society. And while universities get grants from society then there should be strings attached in terms of meeting society's needs. When and if they become totally independent of the need for grants then they are entitled to the democracy they now exercise.

A refiner of precious metals:

> You have got to try and ensure that there is a good scientific base. Fashions in degrees, etc. change. A few years ago everyone wanted to go in for banking and finance: now it is all computing and electronics. These are important, but it is also very important to ensure that you get a spread of degree subjects, and that really good people are attracted to the more traditional technical courses of engineering, chemistry, metallurgy, etc., as well as the most fashionable subjects.

The level of provision of higher education in the social sciences was a sensitive issue to some. While the question of finding the appropriate discipline balance was discussed in a number of interviews, a specific concern with contraction of the social sciences was raised in only a few.

A clothing manufacurer:

> More courses should be vocationally oriented. To what end do people study the social sciences?

A clothing manufacturer and distributor:

> If there are cuts to be made I must say I would protect technology and business studies and economics and take the pain in the social sciences maybe.

A nationalized industry:

> I don't like social sciences but of course I'm old-fashioned. (Q: You were an arts graduate?) Yes.

Some employers argued for more fundamental changes in the nature of courses.
An engineering consultancy firm:

> I think that more attention should be given to the four-year course in technical subjects, three years does not seem quite long enough. I do think that a lot of the courses are crammed. I'm not suggesting that the universities should have a compulsory choice of psycho-analysis, renaiss-

ance art, economic theories of stone age development, and subjects like that which all civil engineers should have to attend. You can't ram broader ideas down people's throats and it's a terrible mistake to think that you can. You can open doors. People would just not turn up for the lectures, but I believe that you could incorporate more project work into university courses. I believe that you could assess people, build into the assessment procedures more projects. This will get people thinking more in terms of the real world. We really do have to teach quite a lot of people coming out of universities how to get their ideas down on paper, not in a report form but in a drawing form; when they join us we have to teach a lot of them to draw and I don't think we should have to do that. I think the university system should produce the people who are capable of beginning work relatively competently and have got all the necessary basic skills.

A large firm of shipbuilders:

Some universities extend courses to four years to meet the needs of undergraduates. If this is being introduced at the expense of industrial placements then we have to ask if the result justifies the means. One will have to wait the results of the four-year course. I think project work is very useful in industrial training compared with the university work. This is difficult to offer in a recession and also financially inadvisable.

Other employers saw a need for increasing course length but with some industrial training.
A small accountancy firm:

I would say I believe a number of university courses could be increased in length, particularly in engineering. There is great merit from my own observations in letting a graduate do a relatively short course — three years say — then industry, then back for a one-year MSc course. He's then a much more mature student, motivated and gets benefits from that.

So we find employers' opinions about the broad issues of the subject content and length of course in higher education widely divided. The arguments are balanced: some want a four-year degree because they do not see it as their job to train recruits, while others want three because the sooner they can get hold of people the better. Some like specialized courses as 'mind developers'; others want broader courses so that graduates can have acquired some familiarity with a range of disciplines, either technical or more broadly educational. Some express scepticism about the 'liberal' or 'democratic' freedom of institutions to determine their own course content, but these are not at all specific about what to put in its place. All in all, these do not seem to be issues which engage the interest of employers very actively, and the views expressed seem to be almost as much matters of personal taste as considered opinions about the needs of their respective organizations.

CAREERS ADVICE
Some employers saw a problem for the system in the adequacy or otherwise

of careers advice. It is linked by some employers with the perceived lack of mutual understanding between industry and education.

A holding company for a diversified manufacturing group:

> Certainly we would go out of our way as an employer to maintain and foster good contact with careers advisers initially... but sometimes it extends beyond that. I wonder to what extent the educational process has any flow as far as the young person is concerned, it seems to me that they're parcelled up, they're missing something, there's no master mind, the feeling of assurance that somebody or some unit or some part of the local authority, anyone at all is interested in them. Whether that influences attitudes or fails to influence attitudes I don't know. Certainly there is a lack of awareness of what is likely to happen at the next stage... and they really don't seem to have much idea of what is going to happen at sixth form college.

A detergent manufacturer:

> I certainly don't want to be categorized as one who thinks university is a preparation for industry, that everyone should be an engineer or business studies graduate. I think people should do as they want to do but it would be very helpful if the attractions of some of the less popular functions – either at university or industry, could be more thoughtfully explained.

An engineering firm:

> One has to try and affect the climate of opinion. Perhaps the University Careers Service could do more, perhaps you need a special body to encourage and promote the idea of industrial management as a career. And there should be more schemes for management trainees – at the moment these exist mainly in nationalized industries and very large companies.

A manufacturer of domestic appliances:

> I have to be specific; general principles still apply if you think of the early graduate turnover – it is very high in the first couple of years here and career direction changes are very high. That must mean something is going very wrong early on.

A large holding company:

> Schools don't have professional vocational guidance staff, they are people who're obliged to take on the business of careers advice without much experience. On the side of industry, some way has to be found to provide a link... with the academic field.

It is conspicuous that no employer went out of his way to express admiration for the higher education advisory functions, though many play an active part in them. The evidence is thin, but again supports the view, however reluctantly expressed, that higher education — indeed, all education — should be somehow more in touch with 'life', and particularly more closely related with employment, and that there is a bewildering disconnection between the experiences of young people as students and their subsequent lives as employees.

SCHOOLS

A number of employers argued that the major problems in educating skilled and well trained manpower begin in the schools. Some saw this as being less closely related to the higher education system than to provision for 16 to 19-year-olds; some argued that the syllabi were too restricted; others that the emphasis on numeracy was insufficient. One employer felt that the subject matter in schools could be better attuned to the needs of industry. One comment saw the expansion of the higher education system as having disrupted, rather than enhanced, the training of apprentices and skilled craftsmen.

A manufacturer and retailer of footwear:

> Rather than having more higher education there should be an increase in training between normal schooling and work. I think it should be a joint effort between manufacturers and the educational authorities and I think the Manpower Services Commission and Industrial Boards have done themselves a grave disservice.... My real worry about education in this country is this: one of my activities is president of (an international footwear group). We've been researching into improving technical training in the European shoe industry. What has come home to me very forcibly is just how vastly superior training is in a number of continental countries. Very poignantly brought home in the present situation with unemployment/internal business problems. My main concern about the educational system of this country lies in the way we take people who finish their education, who will not go on to a great academic career, and somehow prepare them to be good, adaptable, intelligent working people — that's our great failure — it's in the gap there that our problems lie. I don't think our problems lie within higher education.

A fibre and textile manufacturer:

> You are back down into your schools actually, and I believe our school syllabi are too restricted in many ways.... We expanded our university population without taking steps to make sure the school population was well prepared for it.... We didn't think through the total expansion... we just said we will have more of our university arrangements which were probably not right and probably not vocational.

A clothing manufacturer:

> We need a centre where boys and girls could train in the clothing industry. This would be a tremendous help, give insight into the problems (we are facing)... illustrate what the Far East is producing. I think it would do so much good to teach young people going into industry what they are

up against. After a couple of years' practical experience they could go into industry confidently knowing the problems with competition.

A holding company for a diversified manufacturing group:

> I start earlier than higher education. I think the future must lie in the preparation of people for employment – not specifically for jobs, but there's a gulf between the outside world and what people are taught at school – parents think it's nice that they're at university but the students don't know why they are there; the teachers at school and many of the academics never experience working life in the sense of being in industry. Going back to my school days, I wasn't given job information – we were not at school to prepare for working life. Latin and scripture developed your mind. If you learned a language – I read a letter in *The Economist* saying we are still teaching French via Racine or something – when they try to bring the language into industry the vocabulary is totally unsuitable.

A large public broadcasting company:

> The education system is very segregated. You have got local authority school A, school B, sixth form college, university and poly. There doesn't seem to be much interchange between them. They parcel them up and pass them on to the next one and seem not to be related. (I think) we employers have closer links with universities than some of the sixth form colleges do.

A local authority:

> Perhaps it goes back into the schools. I was talking today about Russian teachers. We would assume that Russian is an asset for people in years ahead: how many kids take Russian at university? They tend to go and find the university course which comprises subjects they have been good at at school. The careers guidance people say this is the sort of course you ought to be going for; I haven't a high opinion of careers guidance at schools.

A widely diversified manufacturer and retailer:

> I think that we had it right when your initial schooling was enabling people to leave at 14 and 15 with the right sort of background to enter into the industrial field – where that was based upon craft apprenticeship, technician, technological, normal development. We have the situation now where the people who traditionally would have entered upon a craft apprenticeship at the age of 15 to 16 are now encouraged to stay at school in the hopes that further education and higher education will be able to use them.... So the boy or girl who would normally go into industry where they could be taken up by individual training schemes available for them are now persuaded: 'You might just get an O level....' Traditionally they would have done very well as craft apprenticeships maybe getting on to technician courses, ONC and HNCs. But now they

come on to the market as a failed A level, as a failed O level candidate; not enough to get to university or any other further education and they are not interested in craft apprenticeships. (These people)... are now coming onto the labour market at the ages of 17 and 18 as failed A level stream and failed O level stream, with the same educational competence which they would have had at 15 or 16 originally. But, at the new age of 17 or 18 they are not going to do a four-year apprenticeship course, and wait four years.

The same now applies to the graduate, that in some ways we have devalued the graduate, so the graduate, instead of being looked at as someone who is special with somewhere to go, he is now just the normal equivalent, say, of the old matriculation lad who didn't take the degree.

One employer argued that too many people are getting higher education and that money should be diverted into early childhood and primary education.
A nationalized industry:

The problem starts at primary school. Better calibre teachers are needed (quality of teaching is more important than size of class.) The qualifications are too low — with better teachers, pupils would not emerge illiterate.

Relatively few employers, however, took the opportunity to comment upon schools. Those that did so tended to stress the need for more practical, industry- and skills-related training, and to express nostalgia for the good old days of the early-leaver apprentice craftsman. The feeling is expressed that perhaps the expansion of higher education has produced an excessively 'academic' orientation in schools. Now that there is more emphasis on academic achievement, there is, paradoxically, more stigma to academic failure.

SUMMARY
In some ways, the evidence presented in this chapter is more interesting for what it does not say than for what it does. With a few articulate and opinionated exceptions — illustrated here — employers were not very interested in taking the chance given them to express views on higher education as a *system*. For the most part they do not think in those terms at all. They are aware of a variety of institutions, a few of which they may know well from contacts either now or in their past experience. They know very little about differences of function or funding; some do not know which institutions belong to which 'sector'. Again with a few exceptions, they are not closely acquainted with the gross quantities involved — student numbers in different subject and institutions; the arts/science split; the numbers of postgraduates; the actual proportions of students with different A level grades; the rate of growth. Still less do they take note of comparisons between such dimensions and those of overseas 'systems'. Such comments as they do make seem very often to be reactions to received opinions from contemporary press stories — for example, the interviews took place just

about the time when there was much press comment on the effects of the UGC cuts on the 'technological universities', and these were frequently named in the course of the interviews.

On the other hand, we see, against a background of general lack of criticism, sharp notes of frustration or irritation with institutions that seem to consume public money but nevertheless fail to produce graduates who understand what a tough job the creation of the nation's wealth has become. There were few signs of identification with the tasks of education, research and scholarship − even among those who were content to let them go their own way − and some of alienation and resentment. The issues of curriculum innovation and the education of mature students, which concern educators and their administrators, seem to leave employers cold. This is, on the whole, not their world, and they do not see why they should have to worry about it. They are happy to talk about the problems related to education in their own organizations, but would rather leave wider issues to others.

7 Conclusion

In this last chapter we move away from differentiation and particularization. No summary is intended however, for the evidence is not of a kind that can be usefully summarized. Nor do we go over all the general arguments that have been put forward. Here we make some general remarks about the project; analyse the evidence against some explanations relevant to the evidence; and comment on the prospects for policy analysis and policy-making, given the highly differentiated perceptions of employers which have been presented throughout.

The balance of the evidence shows that the time has passed when graduates ignored industry, when higher education institutions were reluctant to consider the problems of industry, and when employers could survive without large numbers of highly qualified graduates. The general view from the higher education side is summed up by Lord Boyle in a 1978 statement,[1] and from the employers' side by the CBI in 1981:[2]

> ... we in the universities see no inconsistency between a strong commit-ment to academic disciplines and, at the same time, a recognition of the need to think also about the educational requirements of those who are going to enter industry or the professions.

> Graduates in industry have been the subject of continuing dialogue for several years. To some extent the benefits of this are reflected in the fact that more graduates have been going into industry in recent years and that many of the myths which industrialists have held about universities have been dispelled.

Employers are most at ease and most knowledgeable when giving their perceptions and experiences of their organization's current relationship with higher education institutions. This was also the experience of the Schools and Industry Project as Jamieson and Lightfoot note:[3]

> In general, the strategy of trying to involve industry in a *general discussion* about the nature of education as it related to industry did not prove to be successful, and was rapidly dropped by the project co-ordinators in favour of a focus on more specific issues. There are a number of important

points that can be made about this early change of tactics that will illuminate the whole schools-industry debate. First, one should note that the very term 'debate' is one that is much more at home in the world of education than that of industry. The vast majority of industrialists are not used to 'debating', they pride themselves on being 'men of action', 'doers', rather than talkers.

When discussing such matters as recruitment, work experience, or the value of a degree for their organization, employers were at their most specific and most detailed. In part, as the Schools and Industry Project records, this is because employing organizations tend to field their recruiters as the spokesmen closest to and most knowledgeable about educational issues. For most organizations recruitment is their most permanent relationship with higher education institutions and is the best 'window' onto their experiences and perceptions of higher education.

EDUCATIONALISTS' INTERESTS AND EMPLOYERS' PERCEPTIONS
Future research may benefit from noting some of the variables and relationships which might have been expected to be significant but were shown not to be. Among them is the apparent lack of concern with what is taught in degree courses. As has been reported in Chapters 3 and 6, a large number of employers mentioned general skills that they would definitely expect to find in all higher education courses, such as numeracy, group work, report-writing. Relatively few mentioned the length of the courses, except for some limited discussion of enhanced engineering. Employers differed in respect of preference for specialized as compared to more general degrees. They differed, as well, in the extent to which they anticipated 'topping-up' a graduate's training. Existing training opportunities within an organization and the timing of the onset of productive work after recruitment have a substantial effect on an organization's interest in what the graduate had taught. Small engineering firms, for example, will often expect a new recruit to begin productive work immediately. They will therefore want any previous training to have been more relevant to the work at hand than would be the case, say, in a large accountancy firm giving long training to new recruits. In most cases, firms which want a graduate whose training is immediately relevant will choose a course to recruit from which as nearly as possible delivers this training, rather than work on the development of an appropriate curriculum.

Employers are not always knowledgeable about what their employees may need to know in the long run. Few of our interviewees talked about career patterns and few mentioned the kind of knowledge that a graduate might require if the firm was making a long-term investment. Although in many organizations graduates are hired with the intention of keeping them for the whole of their working life, there is not often any explicit view held about the education thought appropriate for the future. An exception is the minority which valued a course in terms of 'learning to learn'.

Many employers are unaware of the degree of career mobility both between types of jobs and between organizations. A recent large survey of the early careers of 1970 graduates suggests substantial movement between employment sectors and occupations.[4] There is also considerable evidence of change in type of work. Engineers, for example, frequently move into management early in their career. It may be that employers find current courses adequate training for these changes in career pattern; alternatively, it may be the case that employers have not given sufficient thought to this as a problem for their organizations.

Employers, in interviews like these, may be responding to questions in terms of graduates in jobs they now hold, without sufficient regard to the patterns of mobility of their employees or their own long-range goals for them.

A number of other educational issues received scant attention from employers in the interviews. Noteworthy is the relative absence of comment on the intrinsic value of higher education as compared to its market value. Additionally, most employers showed little concern about the 'equalization of life chances' as an educational issue; or with maximizing the 'efficiency' of the national system in allocating manpower. Their preoccupation is most often with finding the best qualified recruits at the least cost to the organization. The value of education as a stabilizing force in developed societies; the exposure of students to differing values and styles of life; the role of higher education institutions in promoting economic development and growth; these were considerations mentioned by very few. Few spoke about the role of higher education in social change or about it being any powerful force for social mobility; few mentioned the opportunities for a 'second chance' education, or the importance of continuing education, or the education of mature students and of ethnic minorities.

BARRIERS TO POLICY-MAKING
The method we have used and the way we have treated the evidence can bring diverse views and complex information to multiple audiences. Civil servants and economists alike can review employers' perceptions of shortages by reading the employers' own arguments. The idiom is presented not only to preserve authenticity but as an historical record. The evidence provides a rich and accessible record of employers' perceptions and experiences. As against this, our method makes considerable demands on the reader and perhaps even more considerable demands on the policy maker. It may illustrate the point that it is easier to operate in a world where we know too little than one in which we know too much.

In the best of all possible worlds for policy analysts and policy makers, the facts about any social problem would be clear and agreed on by those to whom the problem is relevant, while the level of variability in perception of the facts would be low. This survey suggests that the agreed-on 'facts' related to employer expectations of higher education are few; the variability in perceptions on most issues is high.

A number of factors related to employers' perceptions affect the extent to which the evidence can be used to support theory, which might lead to policy formulations. As we have seen, there is considerable variability in employers' views in most problem areas. Large employers tend to have views about higher education that are more highly developed than those of many small employers. In part, this reflects the greater staff resources available for policy analysis. However, small employers employ (collectively) considerably more people than large employers and have different views and priorities from large employers. An employer's views are likely to be weighted more heavily if they are articulately expressed and are expressed in a manner which maps onto the policy maker's or policy analyst's own views. Large employers are more likely to do this. Thus the evidence may be weighted differently by different analysts. Additionally, employers, large and small, do not usually have at hand the information and statistics needed to correlate perceptions with experience, and in many cases they feel they do not need it. Further, it is by no means clear that many of the concepts used by analysts or policy makers correspond to those of employers. Graduate status, for example, loses its force in many employing organizations over time. Such organizations, when they keep records, are unlikely to distinguish graduate status except at recruitment.

Moreover, employers, when they are interviewed, have their own agendas in respect of the interview and higher education policy. Aspects of organizational structure and recruiting practice may be hidden by or unknown to the interviewee. Few, for example, were prepared to go on record indicating precisely which institutions and courses they recruit from and which specifically they prefer. In some cases, as we have seen, employers simply do not know enough about the educational system to comment usefully on it as a whole, preferring to restrict their attentions to that part they do know. This was also found to be the case in the Schools and Industry Project:[5]

This (problem employers have with analysing the issues) was in large part due to their relative ignorance of the school system. In discussing 'what was wrong with the schools', representatives of local industry would frequently fail to understand certain key terms like 'banding' or 'streaming' or get confused about the different pupil exams, like the difference between CSE and GCE, or display a lack of knowledge about the contents of subjects or who controlled education.[6]

EXPLANATION AND EVIDENCE

Conceptually, the study was descriptive rather than theoretical. However, much of the evidence is relevant to a number of analytical and theoretical problems in higher education. We briefly discuss three of these in order to demonstrate the variability in employer expectations of higher education, the difficulty that this variability creates in constructing general theories, and the policies which might derive from them.

The Graduate Labour Market

The 'graduate labour market' is one conceptual framework often used to discuss expectations of higher education. Most often it is shorthand for a number of relationships that are either not known or not specified. However, if its workings could be better understood, it would form an important element in the knowledge base useful for policy debate. This study represents a 'demand-side' discussion of the graduate labour market. (It should be noted, however, that the evidence presented does not constitute the economists' notion of demand but lies closer to an expression of employer 'wants', which would form but one element of 'demand'.)

We shall look at a number of simplifying assumptions often made by economists about the workings of the graduate labour market to see how these hold up in the light of our evidence. At the outset, we note that any explanation of the operation of the labour market which is going to contribute significantly to planning must make strong *ceteris paribus* assumptions if it is to hold true over a long enough period of time to allow for programme development on the supply side. As the evidence shows, however, other things are almost never equal and things do not appear to stay unequal in the same way over time. As an example, we recall the effects of the recent economic recession on graduate recruitment.

The early 1980s have been characterized both by an overall reduction in employer demand and by a slight increase in the number of graduates entering the market. This has shifted the balance away from employers fighting to get graduates towards graduates fighting to get jobs. The evidence presented here would suggest that the present market situation has allowed employers to recruit graduates who come closer to their expressed requirements. In general, this has maintained and reinforced the advantage of university graduates in competing for employment. Changes in supply and demand have also created a buyers' market, which affects perceptions of the value of a degree as well as of recruitment practices. For our immediate purposes, what is significant is (i), except in gross characteristics, these changes would have been unpredictable seven years ago; and (ii) the changes do not affect employing organizations in a systematic and predictable way.

Some large employing organizations have used the experience of the economic downturn of the early seventies as a guide to recruitment in the current recession. They realize the importance of staying in the graduate labour market even if they can only marginally afford it. However, some firms have had to severely cut back their recruitment while others have chosen to recruit no one whom they cannot fully and profitably employ in the short run. Employer response has been unpredictable. What is, perhaps, more predictable, but nevertheless unquantifiable, is the effect of these changes on the opportunity structure of graduates from different courses and institutions. We have seen a general university advantage in recruitment, which is intensified in the recession, and an apparently favoured position for graduates in certain subjects.

Also affected by the recession is the very complex process of substitution. Very few employers argued that they simply wanted to see more civil engineers or more computer programmers. Employers are operating with multi-factor equations which define demand and with the knowledge that substituting one factor for another is necessary and often preferable. Degree discipline is but one element among others which make up these equations. Others are type of institution attended, type of course (full-time, sandwich, etc.), non-academic attainments, and personality characteristics. The different weighting given to these elements, and the different qualities looked for by employers relating to each element create the perception of which graduates are substitutable for others. This, as we have seen, varies as between organizations and as between jobs within organizations. The analysis presented in this study shows that a simple push towards generating more graduates in any particular discipline would not be an appropriate response to what employers say they want. The numbers of graduates in the market clearly represent a base line for employers. However, it is the of characteristics which employers individually define as 'quality' that effects the translation from graduate applicant to graduate recruit. These employer equations for substitution change in response to the economy, the organization's performance, changes in government, or changes in the management of the organization.

Under any definition of labour markets and for any explanations of their operation, there are problems in defining boundaries. As Clark Kerr argued in an early paper on labour markets:[6]

> Labour markets are more often talked about than seen, for their dimensions most frequently are seen by the unknown, and perhaps mystical ideas in people's minds.... (However) unless it is said that each worker has his own market area and each employer has his, there must be some adding of worker and employer preferences to get designated markets.

The process by which these designated markets develop and the differences in employer knowledge and perceptions about boundaries are relatively unmeasured for the graduate labour markets. In Chapter 4 it was shown that many individual employers had relatively clear perceptions of the characteristics of university and polytechnic graduates. However, for employers, the graduate labour market involves many dimensions, of which the type of institution is only one. In this context, the evidence as a whole suggests a high degree of differentiation along variables such as type of institution and course, area of the country, previous course/institutional links from which the boundaries of the 'graduate labour market' are created, but they are by no means clear-cut boundaries.

Clearly, employers, in their demand for labour, may operate in a number of different markets in order to satisfy their requirements, a view developed in notions of dual and segmented labour markets: for example by Doeninger and Priore[7] and Killingworth[8]. These discrete markets are often organized 'hierarchically' in such a way that those workers who can gain access to the 'top' market place will have the opportunities for competing for the 'best' jobs in terms of pay, promotion prospects and job security. From our evidence it could be argued that a large majority of graduates are indeed competing in a different labour market from non-graduates; and some graduates are competing for élite jobs in a market separate from other graduates; technical and non-technical graduates often compete in different markets. Whilst it may be useful to conceive of the graduate labour markets as several parts of a segmented system, the conceptual scheme does not perfectly map on to the evidence. 'Balkanization' and segmentation of labour markets would suggest discrete markets but this evidence suggests considerable blurring of the boundaries. That is, while many employers reruit only graduates to particular jobs, it was discovered that graduates and 18-year-olds competed for some jobs while graduates and (for example) HNC students competed for others. Further, among graduates there is considerable substitution.

Another problem in defining boundaries is created by the fact that employers' conceptions of the graduate labour market do not necessarily coincide with those of educationalists. For example, the great majority of employers included in this study indicated that they do not consider college of higher education graduates for their graduate jobs. In terms of a demand-side description of the boundaries of the graduate labour market, college graduates tend to be excluded, while for educationalists, college graduates are definitely included. Another example is found in the differentiation of job categories. In a recent essay by Lawrence Hunter the case is made that for 'vocational/professional jobs' 'the employer will need to be satisfied as to the appropriateness of the degree education as a base for further training and the build-up of practical know how'.[9] If we look at the evidence we find that the concept of what is 'vocational' is poorly developed by employers, in describing either jobs or courses, although it is extremely important to educators. 'Vocational' can mean to employers anything from a training factor which contributes to someone getting a job to a particular specialized technical course. On the whole, however, it is not very widely used by employers, even though it defines very important functions in the educators' conceptions both of higher education and of the labour market.

With this as background, let us turn to two specific assumptions made by economists about labour markets and see whether they can be supported by our evidence. The neo-classical economist's view of the market relies upon a conception of demand in which (i) employers have a full and perfect knowledge of the labour market; (ii) employers are rational and attempt to maximize profits; (iii) no employer represents a large enough part of the total demand for labour to affect wages; and (iv) employers act individually.

These assumptions allow us to explore two different problems: (i) how do analysts (especially economists) *know* how employers operate within particular labour markets given the paucity of evidence; and (ii) what knowledge of the labour market do employers appear to operate on. As examples we will investigate the assumptions 'perfect knowledge' and 'maximization of profit.'

Few markets are likely to be fully manifest to those who operate in them. We can take this assumption of full and perfect knowledge as an extreme assumption and assess the kind and degree of knowledge employers do have of the graduate labour market. The evidence from the study suggests that employers' understandings are usually partial, reflecting, amongst other things, the limited number of institutions and courses from which they have recruited. Not only do employers have relatively incomplete knowledge about the graduate labour market per se, but this is not apparently important to most of them. The dominant value for most employers is to find the greatest number of satisfactory candidates for the least expenditure of time and money – arguments about wanting 'the best' notwithstanding. Employers typically do not talk about the labour market in terms of the stock and flow of manpower; most do not seem to be aware of or concerned with the first destinations of graduates.

Employers express market pressures and market values in recruiting graduates. This does not, however, mean that they have 'hard' data within their organizations with which to analyse the relationship between the 'state of the market' characteristics of graduates recruited and subsequent performance. Most organizations do not have these data at hand, or at all. Most do not know, for example, what proportion of their employees in different jobs of different ages are graduates. Nor does this apparently matter to many of them; graduate status loses its importance to the organization soon after entry.

Blaug, Peston and Ziderman wrote two decades ago from an academic perspective:[10]

> We have found that most firms have not explicitly recognized the need for a policy of conscious manpower planning over time.... Firms do not keep appropriate records of their labour force, and they make insufficient use of those they do collect. At the same time, the personnel function tends to be undervalued compared with other functions such as design, production, sales or finance.

The evidence presented here would confirm that employers, in fact, feel no compulsion to develop and maintain a thorough and complete analysis of the status of graduates recruited to their organization, their competitors', or other organizations.

While it can thus be argued that employers do not operate with anything like full knowledge of the market, it can equally well be said that such knowledge is in any case an impossible goal because key elements are unmeasurable. Measurement problems arise because (i) it is unlikely that firms will have and/or offer full information on which to aggregate data; (ii) adequate aggregation depends on some knowledge of the population from which a sample of firms would need to be drawn; (iii) theories which might usefully simplify measurement are either themselves excessively complicated or make simplifying assumptions which are likely to be unsupportable in data.

We have seen that employers do not typically keep significant amounts of statistical information on their firms. What they do keep they are often reluctant to disclose. This too was found nearly two decades ago by Blaug et al.:[11]

> We were forcefully reminded at various stages of the pilot work, of what has for long constituted the main obstacle to research at the firm level: the extreme reluctance of firms to disclose economic information relating to the firm as a whole, despite our undertaking to keep secret the identity of individual firms. Despite favourable assurances at earlier stages, only one of the five pilot firms studied provided us with the full range of economic data requested. Unfortunately, there is no outside source for this economic data.
>
> The pilot studies showed that firms generally do not keep their personnel records, and particularly information on the educational background of the labour force, in a form that would enable them to provide us with the sort of information we require. Furthermore, individual firms differ markedly in the availability and accessibility of their personnel data. A few firms have computerized their personnel records, but most firms do not keep their personnel data in one central place, and even when they do, they do not always classify them on a uniform basis, or keep them up-to-date.

In our view, the reasons why firms do not keep this kind of information are because it is not important to them; it is expensive to gather; it is not clear how it would be used; and it would require an enormous co-ordination of co-ordination of effort to ensure comparability. As one employer's representative said: 'We get over a hundred requests for information a year, for the most part from government.' Many of these requests require similar information but in different forms.

A reasonably complete picture of how the graduate labour market operates might theoretically be built up from an adequate sample of employing organizations, but nothing like a full list of firms which draw on highly qualified manpower exists. While there are a number of lists which (probably) cover a large proportion of the firms recruiting graduates each year, these are generally biased in favour of large firms. If there were such a list, a very large number of firms would be needed to provide a satistically reliable sample and the list, to be fully useful, would need to be stratified according to the dimensions thought to be important analytically, or these dimensions would have to be assumed to be randomly distributed amongst firms.

A reasonably complete analysis would want to look at a very large number of factors known to be important in the graduate labour market: eg size of organization, prestige, type of graduates recruited. However, even the differentiation and stratification of firms by size is difficult. In order to distinguish size we can use such diverse measures as (a) share capital; (b) total number of employees; (c) number of highly qualified employees; (d) number of graduates recruited. Further, as we have seen in Chapter 2, some very large organizations operate as a number of smaller units for recruiting, while others operate as a single unit in much the same way as smaller organizations do. An adequate stratification system would also need to take into account the age and status of each firm in the business community, international reputation, and current economic performance. More subtly, organizations have different images, reputations and statuses, and have different rankings among careers advisors, students and other members of the higher education community.

The problem of stratification and differentiation is not confined to firm-level variables but also includes the characteristics of jobs to which graduates are recruited. These can be differentiated and stratified by function, status within the organization, knowledge requirements, difficulty in filling, urgency in filling. Along these dimensions there may or may not be agreement within or between organizations about the characterization of a job. One firm may want a chemist as a recruit for general management and may be relatively unconcerned with his knowledge of chemistry; another firm may want the same graduate chemist because he brings to the firm a specific technical skill which the firm does not have. Within a firm, managers and recruiters may disagree as to whether a generalist, a generalist with specialist knowledge or a specialist is needed to fill a particular job. Institutions and courses can be differentiated and stratified by factors as different as the mathematical content of the course and the quality of the rugby team. Courses differ in intake at A level, and apparently similar courses differ in focus and content.

A number of other factors increase the complexity of the task of obtaining a picture of the graduate labour market. Important among these are time-lags – both on the demand and the supply side. An explanation of the operation of the graduate market must include an explanation of the ways in which its messages are received by participants. The implications of those signals for market performance are only realized at some later stage. As Hunter argues:[12]

> The market does adjust... but rather sluggishly and imperfectly. The inherent lags in training and professional formation to the point of first employment must be influential in this regard. But the tendency of many employers to vary graduate recruitment in line with short-term economic conditions rather than adopt a steady hiring strategy against long-term requirements must be... a contributory element which adds not only to a volatility of demand, but to the uncertainties faced by entrants to higher education and to their advisers.

Similarly, on the supply side, as Bosworth argues:[13]

> Students graduating at the present time will tend to reflect the market positions three, four or more years ago, rather than the current situation.

Neo-classical economic theory not only assumes full knowledge, but also that employers recruit employees so as to maximize profits for the organization. In practice, however, they do not know which graduates are likely to maximize profits or whether they will do so at all. Large employers operate with a number of different short and long-term strategies to increase the possibility of profitable recruitment. Many recruitment decisions have to be taken with a good deal of uncertainty about profitability. Moreover, given the uncertainty of future manpower requirements employers frequently take a short-term view of profitability in relation to recruitment, and choose to make the recruitment process less expensive by limiting the pool of prospective candidates. Finally, of course, the very concept of profit maximization may be one which is in fact far from the minds of those in the organization actually responsible for decisions at the point of recruitment. A number of large recruiters of graduates argued the importance of maintaining a position in the graduate labour market even if it was immediately unprofitable to do so, in order to keep the expectations of careers advisors, academic advisors and students steady over time.

What then is the relationship between analysis at the level of the market, and analysis which looks at the behaviour of individual organizations within that market? The evidence here can be used to inform discussions about markets – for example, we have noted the general preference amongst employers for university graduates. However, we would argue that analysis at the level of the market usually belies the complex actions and expectations of the employers who operate in the market. It is only by putting aside 'macro'-level interpretations that we gain access to the complexity and ambiguity which creates a full picture of the graduate labour market. Current analyses of the operation of the market rely upon a number of simplifying assumptions which are either unsupported or are based on little or no evidence at all. We have reviewed some of these assumptions and have seen that they are not consistent with the ways employers actually express their expectations and requirements; and indeed may over-simplify and over-rationalize the complex set of interactions which constitute graduate recruitment.

The Graduate Credential

In this section we examine one component of much of the discussion surrounding higher education and employment: how employers value the graduate credential. The particularizing analysis presented in Chapter 3 offers a detailed portrait at the level of the individual employer of the value of the degree, and we suggest that a full understanding can only be approached by examining these evaluations against the model of the stratified labour market we have just discussed. Our contention here is that explanations which try to account for increased demand for 'credentialling' or the 'qualification spiral' also rely upon an over-simplified conceptualization both of the character of the 'graduate labour market' and of the nature of employer evaluations of the value of a degree.

Our evidence would suggest a much more complicated historical process leading to the inflation of qualifications than that suggested, for example, by Dore:[14]

> In Britain there is evidence that the spread (of qualifications) though sometimes supply led... is in part demand led. That is to say that competitive bidding for the pool of ability between professions can lead to anticipatory raising of entrance standards and a demand for say, A level leavers, greater than the numbers who would anyway have gone on to A level.

Aggregate evidence does, indeed, show a rise in educational attainment in the working population and very substantially larger numbers with higher education over the past decades. For some professions – for example librarianship, engineering and accountancy – qualifications have risen to the point where graduate entry is now the norm. However, this type of demand-led 'qualification spiral' must be separated from the consequences of the increased supply of graduates from higher education over the past two decades. Although there is considerable evidence that a large proportion of students see a 'vocational' advantage in getting a first degree, there is little evidence that this is the only, or even the most important, motivation for seeking higher education. For most students who are relatively able academically, higher education has simply become a fact of social and economic life. This in itself has led to a substantial increase in the proportion of the population which is 'highly qualified.'

If there is any evidence of what might be called 'vulgar' credentialling on the employers' part, it is in the emphasis on A level passes and grades. From the employers' perspective both A levels (and a later degree) are ways of distinguishing potential ability in a sea of possible candidates. Employers do not necessarily need the A levels or the degree, nor in many cases are they competing for them. What they need is a way of limiting the recruitment exercise. Employers do not necessarily need the A levels or the degree, nor in many cases are they competing for them. What they need is a way of limiting the recruitment exercise. Employers do not appear to value the first degree simply as a 'piece of paper'; as we have shown in Chapter 3, their perceptions of its value are much richer and more varied. Some employers expressed dissatisfaction with the inflation of qualifications which has occurred over the past two or three decades. Some wistfully speak about the men and women with 'good A levels' whom they could recruit directly into their organizations in the past. For these employers the argument is:

> If good A level students go on to higher education we (the employers)
> must wait for them to come out the other side. We might well have taken
> them on without a degree. We will take them on with a degree. The
> maturity, experience and knowledge is worth something to us, as long as
> the expectations of graduates about the work they will be given to do are
> not too high.

The issue of raised expectations of future employees is a serious one
mentioned by many employers. For some, the work they have to offer
graduates is not different from that which the school-leaver with A levels
would have done in the past. The three years in higher education are not
seen as irrelevant; individuals and organizations gain from the enhanced
knowledge, skills and maturity. However, for a good number of jobs the
degree is not in itself necessary. The critical factor is that the academically
able students do go on to higher education, a fact of economic life which the
employers do not feel responsible for but have to accept.

As against this, it must be argued that, for many employers, the
'knowledge explosion' has involved a change in perception about what is
required for a job. In some fields of study it is acknowledged that it is
difficult to get the necessary work into even the three years of the usual
degree programme.

We get a fuller picture of how the degree is valued by placing the
arguments about it against the general setting in which they are used. This is
a similar process as, say, setting Julius Caesar or Timon of Athens in modern
dress and against a contemporary background. The words take on new and
more subtle meanings set against different backgrounds.

The statements which describe the value of the degree need to be in an
appropriate economic and social context. An organization's competitive
position in the graduate labour market or the perceptions firms have of the
stratification of the market provide the context against which the evidence
can be analysed; and this context changes over time. The arguments which
employers use to describe the value of the degree at each point in time need
to be set against the employers' prospects in the labour market. In some
cases, we see 'top' employing organizations which have never had a problem
with graduate recruitment looking for such esoteric qualities as 'captain of
boats'. In others we see firms struggling to regain their place in the graduate
labour market: 'We are not really a household word' or 'On the whole we
have not been an attractive company to the outside world.'

The value of a degree will be assessed according to how and where the
firm places itself and its jobs relative to other firms. An indirect indication of
how an organization sees itself is given by where it recruits its graduates and
the reasons it gives for doing so. There are, to take an example, employing
organizations which recruit largely from what are perceived to be the top
universities − Oxbridge, Imperial College, several of the old civics. There
are some which take quite a number of their recruits from these 'top'
institutions but a quantity from a number of others. There are some who
never visit Oxbridge. It is not sufficient to understand the mix of
characteristics which employers have in mind when selecting between

candidates; we must also take into account the 'pool' from which candidates are selected.

As an example, the argument often put forward that 'the degree is not everything, personality is the essential factor' is, when used by a large and prestigious firm which recruits primarily from Oxbridge, a different argument from that used by a charity which recruits from a local polytechnic. Similarly the argument 'We are only interested in the knowledge a graduate has acquired' may take on a different meaning if the firm visits only one or two of the institutions offering a certain course rather than all the institutions offering the same. The real value of the degree may be evaluated as 'the completion of a course at an institution near the firm.' To this might be added, 'if we cannot find an HND first' or 'provided he gets at least a 2.1.'

Employing organizations change and refine their perceptions of which 'pool' is appropriate for which jobs. As we have seen, the key factors are that the pool includes a large proportion of candidates which they require *and* that drawing from the pool is as simple and cost-effective as possible. Evaluating the degree as part of the process of delineating the appropriate pool is a process which is firm-specific. The effect at the aggregate level may appear to be a spiralling demand for qualifications. If this is the case, it is based on a very large number of separate decisions taken by employing organizations which may create an effect, at the level of the firm, both unintended and, in some cases, unwanted; it may, in part, result from the fact that signals between employing organizations and higher education in the past, as now, have been rather weakly given and received.

We see, then, an interesting and complex picture of the demand for degrees – a picture considerably more complicated than that of employers steadily pushing up qualifications or encouraging students into education they do not want or need. For some jobs, employers would *prefer* but cannot find a non-graduate with good A levels. For some jobs a degree is acceptable but not necessarily highly valued, and there are employer concerns about excessive graduate expectations. In other jobs the degree is both necessary and highly valued. Assessing the value of – and hence the demand for – a degree depends not only on looking at the arguments that are offered by employers but also on setting these arguments against the organization's actual recruitment strategy. Employers surely mean what they say but they may not mean only what they say.

Graduate Selection
The importance of non-academic characteristics in the assessment and selection of graduates can hardly be exaggerated. Ashton and McGuire[15] in their work on school-leavers develop five selection strategies which employers use which take account of non-academic characteristics:

1 Employer stipulates a minimum level of academic qualifications but, in practice, takes those with the highest qualifications.
2 Academic qualifications are used in pre-selection and perform a screening function. However, the final decision about which of the candidates... to employ is then made on the basis of non-academic criteria.

3 Academic qualifications perform a focusing function, directing the recruitment at students with a given level of ability. If the candidate has non-academic qualities which the employer wants, these will override the academic qualifications.

4 All emphasis is placed on non-academic criteria. This strategy is embodied in the expression, 'You don't need O levels to be a good craftsman.'

5 Educational qualifications perform a negative function.

These strategies are used to differing extents by employers in recruiting school-leavers, some considerably more than others. Most of the employers in our study would fall into Category 2. However, all categories are represented. The conclusion of Ashton and McGuire is one which needs elaboration when considering graduates:

> Success for the pupil in the educational system is dependent on the number and quality of the certificates obtained; the difference between a grade C and a grade D at A level can mean the difference between success and failure in obtaining access to a university place. But for employers using a different selection strategy, educational qualifications perform different functions... employers are not concerned about whether the young person has one additional A level, or whether the pass is at grade C or D. What they are far more concerned with is that the applicant has the right type of personality and motivation.

As we reported in Chapters 3 and 4, employers differ considerably in respect of the *mix* they require of personality characteristics, motivation and involvement in extra-curricular activities and academic qualifications. Employers also differ in the weightings they give to these factors in recruiting into different jobs. Further, the strategies outlined by Ashton and McGuire have to be coupled with knowledge of the 'pool' of graduates to whom the recruitment strategy is applied. Thus there are three elements in the process of assessment of graduates: the mix of qualities and factors; the weight attached to different factors; and the choice of pool of candidates.

The selection of the 'pool' may itself involve a weighting of factors. If, as the evidence suggests, communication skills, modes of dress, confidence, and 'well-roundedness' play an important part in the selection process of organizations, these are partially selected for by choosing particular institutions and courses. Such a process of selection is an iterative one in that organizations may pre-select their pool to select for desired qualities, and then select again at the level of selecting the individual. There can be considerable blurring between strategies 1, 2 and 3 above which is not always made clear by employers in describing the relative weights put on academic and non-academic criteria. A large and prestigious employer may go to considerable lengths to explain the importance of leadership as measured by being 'captain of boats' or curiosity as measured by travel. This employer, however, may visit only a very small number of select higher education institutions. In this case, the non-academic qualities used in selection are only employed after strategic choices have been made about preferred institutions.

We have considered in other chapters the range of non-academic factors that are considered by employers. Here we consider several that are noteworthy by their absence from the evidence, given the important part they have played in the formation of educational policy in past decades. Employers rarely mention or discuss secondary school, social class or family background as factors to be considered in recruitment. But there are a number of factors which may perhaps stand as proxy for these, such as 'communication skills', 'dress', 'social skills', 'confidence at interview', choice of extra-curricular activities, opportunities for outside experiences such as travel. We are not asserting here that employers *do* select by family background and perceptions of social status but that the evidence suggests that they *may do* so. Some of the important non-meritocratic factors which are sought will have a strong association with family background and social status. Selection of the 'pool' of candidates to interview may have an implicit class and social bias because of an over-representation of middle and upper-class students in particular institutions and courses. This is largely because non-academic and academic characteristics interact throughout the academic career. Middle and upper middle-class children do better than working-class children in every educational transition and it would be surprising indeed if these factors ceased to operate directly or indirectly in the transition from higher education to work.

As Halsey[16] has shown, there is a 'persistent class difference in survival rates.... A service-class boy in our sample was four times as likely as his working-class peer to be found at school at the age of 16, eight times as likely at the age of 17, ten times more likely at the age of 18 and 11 times more likely to enter a university.' However, for those who survived long enough to achieve one A level or a Higher School Certificate, the survival rates began to converge. Of those similarly qualified, 63% of the men and women from the service class went on to university compared to 53% of those from the working class. Less than one in forty of the working class in the present study reached this level of qualification as compared with one in four from the service class. When we look at graduates, we are already looking at a selective sub-set of the age cohort. However, our evidence suggests that the effects of class background do not continue to play as strong a part in determining life changes once an individual gets to the top of the academic ladder.

The weight given to class background and other status factors in the transition from higher education to work is difficult to assess because of the interaction of academic and non-academic characteristics. At one level of argument, it can be said that Oxbridge students are highly sought after because of sheer academic ability. This would ignore the fact that nearly half of these students will have been to independent schools, contrasted with about 5% of the cohort generally and just over 25% of all university entrants – and considerably more middle and upper-middle class students attend independent schools. It can be argued that many employers see Oxbridge graduates as more likely to combine the academic and non-academic qualities looked for and that it is cost-effective to look there first. It can equally well be argued that employers who want the qualities which attend an upper-middle class upbringing and selective schooling for their top jobs recruit from particular institutions independent of the high level of academic achievement.

While such variables as class background may be important in recruitment and while there is a significant degree of stratification within the labour market, we do not argue that the stratification is based primarily on such factors as social class, family or secondary school background, but that differentiation and stratification of the labour market is linked to these variables in a complicated set of relationships. In so far as the social class background of students is associated with type of course or institution, employers who recruit from particular courses or institutions which have disproportionate numbers of students from one class or another will promote a stratification of labour markets which has a class component. The degree to which recruitment to course and institution is associated with social class is not discussed by employers. The extent to which internal stratification of the labour market is linked to social class is difficult to measure and, in fact, may not be measurable at all. Employers are not likely even to divulge their recruitment practices with respect to the full range of courses, institutions, and characteristics of applicants. They would be the first to argue that this would violate their own norms of confidentiality. Further, as we argued, the interaction between academic and non-academic factors would create a measurement problem even if we had better evidence.

We can see from the evidence that Oxbridge graduates and those from other leading universities have a very much better chance at 'top jobs' than others. Selective recruitment to higher education institutions is more easily measured. The survey of undergraduates done for the Expectations of Higher Education Project shows no dramatic differences in the social backgrounds of undergraduates in different types of institutions. University undergraduates were somewhat more likely to come from higher professional families (28%) than public sector undergraduates (polytechnics 20%; colleges 21%). Oxbridge had the highest proportion of fathers in higher professions. These findings reflect the positive connection between A level scores and social background. Seventy-two per cent of the undergraduates from the higher professional families had nine or more A level points compared to 42% of the students from families in semi- or un-skilled occupations. Oxbridge undergraduates, who as we have seen are greatly favoured by many employers, are more likely to have attended independent schools than undergraduates in other institutions and also have relatively higher A level scores. Employer preference for Oxbridge graduates may be a preference both for high academic achievement and for social attainment gained within the family and in selective education. In interviews, less emphasis is typically placed on the latter qualities than on the former.

What we do see from this evidence is that graduates and non-graduates are, by and large, competing for different jobs; university candidates tend to be preferred for the majority of graduate jobs, but by no means all; Oxbridge graduates are still viewed as the cream. We also know, however, that 'on the day' the right non-academic qualifications will override A levels, course and institution for very many jobs and that for another substantial proportion of jobs, knowledge and skills are the most important factors.

Of considerable importance is the fact that employers differ in their perceptions of 'goodness of fit' between the job and the graduate. One well known employer seeks graduates with a reasonable academic record but requires a passion for rebuilding bikes and cars; another wants graduates but those whose physical build matches other workers in the construction industry; other employers will simply require only an excellent academic record. Further, the weighing up of academic and non-academic qualities is not static. Organizations decide on one set of criteria at one point in time and change these as the organization changes or as their perception of the appropriate balance changes.

If we consider together the arguments put forward in the last three sections about the labour market, the value of the degree, and the weighting of non-academic and academic factors in recruitment, we see that a highly complicated model would be needed to account for the number of variables and the degree of variation they exhibit in any attempt to explain such processes as the 'qualification spiral', the screening functions of higher education, and the role of higher education in determining life chances. Existing discussions and models of the operation of the graduate labour market are based upon assumptions which ignore the diverse and complex character of employer evaluations of graduates, as revealed in our evidence.

EVIDENCE AND POLICY

In the last three sections, we have discussed our evidence in relation to three theoretical issues describing the relationships between higher education and employment. These examples highlight several 'findings' from the study.

1 Employers do not speak with a single voice. Nor do they speak with a small number of aggregated voices in chorus, such as 'public sector employers' or 'engineering firms'. This becomes a problem for policy makers when it becomes apparent that they neither define questions in the same way, nor advocate similar strategies with respect to graduates.

2 From our evidence it is impossible to suggest key explanatory variables which might be used to reduce this variation in responses. Size of firm; relative technological orientation; public/private sector; recruitment procedures and strategies — these explain *some* of the variation in most problem areas. But there is almost as much variation within each of these categories as between them.

3 Employers are usually careful to speak only about their own organizations in most problem areas. They do not typically generalize their perceptions to their competitors or their sector of the economy. This means that policy proposals cannot emerge simply from the aggregation of the responses of individual firms.

4 Employers show a decidedly pragmatic approach to educational issues. The continued reliance on GCE A levels in selecting individuals is likely to be a source of considerable grief to educators who, for many years, have tried to broaden perspectives on learning and promote acceptance of the value of other kinds of knowledge and skills. The majority of employers acknowledge the importance of other forms of knowledge and non-academic qualities while at the same time relying on A levels because they are the simplest measure for setting a base line for the recruitment process. As resources for recruitment decline, simplicity in the process of recruitment appears to become even more important.

5 Employers make few specific policy proposals themselves. Some would

like to see more emphasis on engineering and science, but offer few suggestions as to how to bring it about; in any case, there are few signs that it is related to perceived current manpower shortages. Perhaps one exception is the desire to increase the level of numeracy, which has become an issue that many employers can agree on, perhaps because it has been so widely discussed. Numeracy is valuable, they say, and should be encouraged. But there is by no means wide agreement about just what it is.

6 There are, however, a few notably common responses, none of which should be taken out of context as summing up the expectations of 'the employers'. (Again, it is important for the reader to note that we should not read too much into 'many' and 'most' employers. These are approximate and relative in a study of this kind.)

  a University graduates are generally preferred to those from the public sector.
  b College of higher education graduates have not yet made an impact on the graduate labour market in general.
  c Employers generally advocate more contact between higher education and industry.
  d Many employers value graduate work experience — whether this comes in the form of a sandwich course or some employment before or during higher education.
  e Most employers do not advocate manpower planning in any form.
  f Most employers are relatively satisfied with the higher education system as it operates.
  g A substantial proportion would like to see a more numerate graduate population, with better writing skills.
  h Almost all employers are currently able to meet their manpower recruitment needs using one strategy or another.

Does all this apparent caution, vagueness and complexity mean that the evidence from a study such as this cannot contribute usefully to policy debate? We would argue that the answer is firmly no. We can observe in these pages the range and differentiation of opinion. We can see whether claims in respect of any particular policy made 'on behalf of' employers are legitimate or not, in so far as they are alleged to be based on evidence. We can see that there are a great many issues related to employers' expectations about which we have *or can have* little hard data. Further, a study of this kind helps us to distinguish the extent to which a proposed policy is based on agreed or demonstrated social 'facts' or on the values of policy makers.

In the light of these considerations, let us review again, briefly, the evidence as it relates to one example of a currently topical issue — 'shortages,' which was discussed extensively in Chaper 5 and elsewhere. We are suggesting that it is important to distinguish the different (though both important) components of fact and value in policy decisions; that changing a policy would have to be pragmatic in employers' eyes to have an effect; that what is perceived by some as good for the society as a whole might not be seen as good by each employer or even by employers in the aggregate. Most important, we suggest that policy makers may have to operate from an extremely poor knowledge base. Where does this leave us with an issue as important as shortages?

A number of employers, especially those engaged in technical and scientific work, would like to see higher education move towards producing larger numbers of technically qualified graduates. In most cases this is not related to an actual shortage of such graduates in any particular field, but to the perception by some employers that they have greater 'substitutability'. However, within this context, very few employers argue for aggregate manpower planning. While all firms do some forward planning it is clear both from direct responses and from reviewing last year's and this year's recruitment figures that firms need to retain a high degree of flexibility in respect of the future. Most employers have met their needs for qualified manpower by one method or another. However, should economic conditions brighten and the rate of growth in the economy increase, it is clear that some employers would like to see a bigger share of the 'stock' of qualified manpower technically qualified.

Although we suggest that there appear to be few actual shortages of qualified manpower, some employers have had to use a variety of strategies to overcome what they sometimes label as a shortage. This takes us back to what the concept means to them. They may talk of shortage when, in the short run, a non-qualified graduate, someone within the firm, or a technically qualified non-graduate takes a position intended for a graduate with a particular qualification. In the long run, they may for this purpose sponsor or encourage sandwich programmes or develop in-house training. In the course of the survey, however, we heard of no work that was unable to be completed because of shortages of qualified graduates. This does not mean, of course, that employers would not have *preferred* to have an engineer with training, say, in electronics when one with another degree was recruited instead, and therefore speak of a shortage of electronics graduates. The larger question is whether these problems are solvable at the aggregate level. Can the educational system predict the specific requirements of employers four to six years on? The evidence suggests not – not because educators or employers are unwilling, but because employers are unable to specify requirements with enough lead time for appropriate courses to be organized. Further, and of considerable importance, the need for a greater stock of specifically qualified manpower at a single point in time does not necessarily mean that a continued increase in the stock year after year is required. Educational institutions cannot easily respond to the need for particular qualifications required by particular organizations at a particular time.

As we have argued in Chapter 5 much of the discussion of shortages is related to the quality of graduates rather than their quantity. This perception is often embodied in 'the one that got away'. The fishing analogy is one that is frequently used by employers. There are a limited 'number of fish' and there are an even more limited number of 'big ones'. This is a consequence of characteristics of the population as much as characteristics of the individual fish. Every fisherman would like to catch the biggest fish just as every employer would like the 'best' graduate. There was not much indication in this survey that the qualities of 'best', however, were those which the educational system can develop. 'Best' is defined in terms of a combination of academic and non-academic characteristics, and it is not defined in the same way by different employing organizations. Most important, it is seen in relative and not absolute terms, ie as good as or better than the next firm gets; as good as or better than the one that got away; as good as or better than the best one recently recruited. The notion of 'sufficient' good graduate recruits is a 'positional' good, of which one classic example is country cottages. If everyone had a country cottage to get away to, the whole of the population would simply shift at the weekend and holidays; there would be no getting away. Such a good is not achievable by the whole of the population. In this sense, manpower shortages must always be experienced, since a firm only has enough if it has more than its competitors.

Faced with that kind of evidence, where do policy makers move – not just in respect of shortages, but more generally? Firstly, it is necessary to accept the uncertainties of the outcomes of any attempt to make policy in this field: uncertainties that are an inevitable consequence of the necessarily limited knowledge base; the enormous effects of the unpredictable performance of the economy; and the almost equally unpredictable effects of changing technology. Unpredictable, that is, over the relatively long time-scale over which *educational* policy can become effective. Fulton, Gordon and Williams[17] have analysed the primary factors accounting for the uncertainty. These include:

> ... the long time horizon necessary; the certainty of unpredictable technological change in any growing economy; the difficulty of establishing an educational system which can provide in detail all the thousands of specific skills that high-level workers require; the limitations on an individual's freedom of occupational choice which can arise if young people are trained for one and only one specific job; and the problem of ensuring a smooth path of development for higher education, while at the same time overcoming specific high-level manpower shortages as quickly as possible.

The factors are used to support a proposal to increase emphasis on 'recurrent' education. Whatever the other difficulties about such a policy, it would indeed have the advantage of beginning by accepting uncertainty as an important component of educational planning.

A second implication for policy makers is that the high ratio of value to fact in policy should be accepted in this area. We have seen that to 'model' the transition from higher education to work would require a great deal more information than is currently at hand. It would also require information from employers that we are unlikely to get. Nevertheless, policy makers *might* quite legitimately conclude – as a value judgment – that it is desirable to attempt to prevent or mitigate stratification and stultification of the graduate recruitment process and, in the interests of more efficient and equitable distribution of human resources, encourage wider access to the pool of candidates from which graduates are selected. It might be argued, with some support from our evidence, that this would be helped by a modest subsidy to some employers for an extended milk-round and perhaps some special provision for careers advice, and courses in job application, in the less traditionally favoured institutions. Our evidence cannot, of course, demonstrate that this *would* be an effective way of promoting the objective, even if that were desired, but it does suggest its plausibility. And it is less expensive to try out some such options than to do research and evaluation over time to consider their full impact and effectiveness as well as the impact and effectiveness of all the other policies which might be tried in order to maximize one value or another. The evaluation and development of a programme might do rather well on the basis of informed guesswork given the limited data base and variability in employer perceptions.

Employers themselves offer good examples of this. Firms make micro-policies in respect of shortages — eg they decide to sponsor certain students. The 'policy' works; they continue to sponsor until they feel that it is no longer necessary. They do not typically mount a research programme to determine if it is the most cost-effective strategy, the only strategy or the certain strategy.

In our view a part of the problem may lie with those social scientists who appear to be offering the prospect of certain and relatively complete knowledge. Some examples: in our view, Fulton, Gordon and Williams, whom we have already cited, make a valuable contribution to the problems which we have analysed here, but their closing argument contradicts much that they themselves say and that we have argued in this study. 'What is needed in both types of economy (planned and market) is a model of the higher education system and the interactions between it and the rest of the society which enables the outcomes of a variety of different policies to be tested.[18] While such a model might, in theory, be useful, it is unlikely to be a reasonable goal for research. Many important variables are difficult or impossible to measure; if they could be measured, the exercise would be vastly expensive and take so long that it would be of only historical interest upon completion.

In a similar vein, in a recent article, Richard Pearson[19] argues:

At present unemployment is affecting all types of graduates although demand for electronics and computing specialists is holding up. Any upturn in the economy will affect these groups first and, with output static or falling, we will quickly return to the cries of shortages heard by the recruiters in the late 1970s, when it was estimated that there were two vacancies for every graduate in electronics.

Public policy needs to clarify its priorities and practice in accounting for the 'economic' dimension within higher education planning. We do not need to relate higher education to employment prospects for the full range of subjects. For many, indeed the majority of jobs, the subject taught is not important to employers. However, within key vocational areas the discipline is critical. Surely within a higher education system which produces over 80,000 graduates per annum we should not be underproducing in key disciplines such as electronics and computing graduates.

In the same article we read that in the past two years the graduates of maintained sector institutions represented an increase of 30% in such fields

as electronics/electronic engineering and a substantial increase in computing. Since these are relatively new industry/recruitment areas, many
graduates in the subjects are not yet replacing retiring employees but filling
new posts. We do not know (i) much about the demand for the current stock,
(ii) the demand for the current stock plus that which will come through in
the next few years or (iii) how to 'model' the flow over time. In short, we do
not, and cannot, know whether, in any significant sense that relates to the
professional life-span of those concerned, we are in fact 'underproducing' in
'key disciplines.'

Another example is to be found in the evidence from the Institute of
Manpower Studies to the Select Committee on Education, Science and the
Arts, in March 1980.[20] It refers to a need for a 'total approach to an
assessment of future manpower needs' which would include (i) 'a description
of the current manpower systems', in terms of, inter alia, 'the extent of
current manpower imbalances', and 'factors affecting deployment and
utilization'; (ii) economic, social and technological factors likely to affect
future manpower needs; and (iii) knowing how the stock of manpower will
change, through development, mobility, retirement, recruitment. It is
argued that 'relating likely changes in the stock and new entrants to the
possible future demand scenarios will help us to identify any critical
imbalances, particularly shortages. Against these possible imbalances,
policies for the output of first degree graduates can be adjusted.' Our work
reinforces us in the view that imbalances cannot be identified nor shortages
ascertained, that the scenarios for future demand are unpredictable, and
that there would in any case be very great difficulty in a brisk adjustment of
policies for the output of first degree graduates.

A third and final implication of our evidence for policy makers − after
accepting uncertainty, and accepting the inevitability of a high value-fact
ratio, is that more might be achieved at the individual firm/institution level
than by attempts to make policy for a whole higher education 'system' which,
for the most part, employers do not recognize. The point was vigorously
expressed by the chairman of a large manufacturing group − the last of our
employers whom we will quote:

> I think that here at the moment they are placing too much emphasis on
> our ability to produce change in industry through the redirection of
> educational resources. Simply by observation we know that if you are
> going to redirect education it will not have an effect within ten years and it
> may have an effect within thirty. The second thing you know is that
> governments always make the same mistake; they look at things as they
> are and not things as they should be − we are supposed to be short of
> engineers, which we're not − and we're supposed to be short of all sorts of
> things and by the time the government has drawn up that list it would
> have altered.... Much more likely that the people running the technical
> college/ polytechnic/ university, if put under enough pressure will
> respond to market changes: that's likely. What is quite unlikely is this: if
> you place a group of people in the Department of Education and Science
> (into a position of responsibility) it is quite unlikely that they will respond
> to market changes: their jobs are not affected. They just will not respond.
> So you have got to get back to all these people that you are paying for

anyway. The whole educational establishment is cross-centre; you should force all the problems back onto it and make it work for what it's paid for. Not take the decisions for it. They are all highly educated, they are all capable of assessing priorities — let them do it.... If they are not correct there is going to be so much champing at the bit that there will be a reassessment of priorities fairly smartly. Market forces will (obtain). The big assumption in the academic world is that everything stays as it is. In everyday life everything alters every day. I don't know what the hell my competitors are doing today, but they are altering my future for me and I have to react to that. I'm quite happy to react to it — I will have to order my priorities. The educational establishments are quite capable of doing the same.

Many of our protagonists feel similarly. The Committee of Vice-Chancellors and Principals, in its evidence to the Select Committee, wrote on behalf of the universities:[21]

The needs of society must always be foremost among the concerns of those who make university decisions, although it must be recognised that defining those needs is often the major problem. But in matters of higher education they are unlikely, in most cases, to be best discerned centrally by Government agencies. Forty-five universities, each making its own informed interpretation of national needs, may well, between them, arrive at several valid versions of the best long-term pattern of research and teaching while the inevitable mistakes will not be on the grand scale of Government miscalculations. We consider it highly desirable, in the national interest, that the present pluralistic system of decision-making in higher education be preserved.

Appendix A
The Sample of Employing Organizations

Limited project resources, the variety of higher education institutions, the numbers and variety of employing organizations, and the number of links between higher education institutions and employing organizations precluded a probability sample of employing organizations. Alternative means had to be devised for the selection of our target of 150 employing organizations to interview. Our aim was to cover the range of different relationships with higher education which employers might have, especially in terms of their recruitment of graduates. Employers were grouped as:

1 Regular recruiters of graduates
2 Recruiters of graduates on an irregular basis
3 Non-recruiters of graduates
4 Employers concentrated in two regions
5 Small recruiters of professionals
6 Recruiters of 'arts' graduates

The selection strategy adopted for each group is described below.

REGULAR RECRUITERS OF GRADUATES
This was by far the largest group, comprising 80 of the 150 organizations set as the target sample. Their selection was the most systematic. We needed an up-to-date list of all the organizations which might be eligible, a list which would ideally have included information on each organization's industrial base, size, location, recruitment record. No such single list was available but the following data sources combined to produce the required stratification of firms into sampling categories:

1 The 1981 *Register of Graduate Employment and Training* (Roget) containing 1,257 employers of graduates giving details of:
   a type of work offered
   b type of organization
   c degree disciplines preferred and/or required
   d geographical location.
2 The Institute of Manpower Studies (IMS) booklet *Education and Employment 1980*, containing details of polytechnic graduate recruitment into employment.

3 *The First Destinations of University Graduates 1978/79* published by the Universities Statistical Record, giving details of university graduate recruitment into employment.

Sources 2 and 3 above were used to describe the demography of graduates' employment and to give classifications of employers of graduates in broad outline.

4 The list of members of the Standing Conference of Employers of Graduates (SCOEG), together with details of the size of graduate recruitment undertaken by member organizations in the past. Our classification of data supplied by SCOEG was according to the following criteria:
   Group A: 0 − 10 graduates recruited
   Group B: 10 − 30 graduates recruited
   Group C: 30 − 100 graduates recruited
   Group D: 100 − 300 graduates recruited
   Group E: Over 300 graduates recruited

The target population was then stratified according to two different criteria: occupational group and size of graduate recruitment.

Occupational Group
The first destination statistics and the IMS study helped to provide a division into fourteen employer categories to reach our target population:

The Civil and Diplomatic Services
HM Forces
Local Government
Oil, Chemical and Allied Industries
Engineering and Allied Industries
Other Manufacturing Industries
Building Contractors, Civil Engineers and Architects
Public Utilities
Accountancy
Banking and Insurance
Other Commerce
Private Practice
Publishers, Cultural and Entertainment Organizations
All Others

Within each category we could find the number of university and polytechnic graduates recruited in a year. For the study as a whole, eighty employer organizations in this group were to be selected. The distribution of firms was done on the basis of the number of new graduates recruited within particular industrial categories as a proportion of all those entering permanent home employment. Thus within banking and insurance 1,300 graduates were recruited in 1978/79, which constituted about 5% of all graduates entering permanent home employment. Broadly speaking, then, 5% of the employer organizations selected by these criteria should be banking and insurance companies. In sampling terms, we selected firms in proportion to the number of graduates recruited in a particular sector.

Size of Graduate Recruitment

Within the employer categories we wanted to be particularly sensitive to variation in the number of graduates they recruited. To this end we distributed the employers in our target population within the employer categories and laid the individual recruitment figures obtained from SCOEG onto the target population. Within each industrial category we had the appropriate members of our target population along with more detailed information (from SCOEG members) on a number of organizations. We randomly chose SCOEG organizations by size of graduate recruitment. However, SCOEG membership was not evenly spread across all the employer categories and in those with weak representation (for example, central and local government, the armed services, building and construction) an alternative strategy had to be adopted. Here we used employers' own descriptions of the number of their graduate *vacancies* (reproduced in Roget) as an indication of the size of actual graduate *recruitment*. A random sample was then taken within each cell to obtain the eighty organizations to be included within the group.

NON-REGULAR RECRUITERS OF GRADUATES

After consultations with the CBI's Small Firm Council and Higher Education Panel, it was decided to include fifteen small firms. In terms of employing organizations in the UK, these are only relatively small, but then often quite variable. The list was supplied to us by the CBI.

NON-RECRUITERS OF GRADUATES

A substantial number of large and important organizations do not routinely recruit graduates; twelve of these were included in the sample. Taking the 500 largest employers (in terms of numbers employed) in the UK from *The Times' 1000* (which lists the 1,000 largest employers in the UK), and omitting those with entries in Roget (ie those having a regular graduate recruitment exercise), a set of non-regular recruiters of graduates was established. The twelve to be included within our sample were then randomly drawn.

EMPLOYERS CONCENTRATED IN TWO REGIONS

Much of the discussion surrounding graduate recruitment focuses upon the way graduates are recruited locally from higher education into employment. Our main sample had a large number of organizations with headquarters in the South East of England so to produce more of a regional element in the study it was decided to select some employers from East Anglia and Cleveland. From lists of local employers in East Anglia and Cleveland (produced by the University of East Anglia Careers Service and Newcastle Polytechnic Careers Service respectively) sixteen employing organizations were randomly drawn. In the event, these had a high rate of non-response.

SMALL RECRUITERS OF 'PROFESSIONALS'

One of the main areas of graduate recruitment which we felt should be covered was that into small 'professional' organizations. To this end, a number of firms of architects, solicitors and accountants were included within the study.

RECRUITMENT OF 'ARTS' GRADUATES

One area of graduate recruitment which had not been fully covered elsewhere was from predominantly arts-based courses. Consequently, a group of ten employers was selected that included an orchestra, a museum, two theatre companies and a registered charity.

Appendix B
The Interviews

It was intended that we should conduct two interviews within each organization. However, it was impossible strictly to adhere to this plan. Some organizations were so big and complex that more than two interviews were conducted to try to capture the variety of views; some were so small that only one interview was appropriate. In addition, several organizations agreed to participate only on the understanding that a single member of staff would be interviewed.

The number of employing organizations eventually included in the study, and the number of interviews conducted are given in the table below. One hundred and sixty-six employing organizations were asked to take part. Twenty-seven declined (16%), a group disproportionately made up of non-recruiters of graduates. Two hundred and one interviews were conducted in the remaining 138 organizations.

	Number of Employing Organizations	Number of Interviews Conducted
NATIONALIZED INDUSTRY	10	26
CENTRAL/LOCAL GOVERNMENT/		
GOVERNMENT AGENCIES	7	18
PRIVATE EMPLOYERS*		
Accountancy	11	14
Engineering	29	48
Computing	9	17
Other	72	78
Total	121	157
TOTAL	138	201

* Nearly a third of these employers are in whole or in part manufacturers.

The goal of all the interviews was to cover a common series of problem areas and also allow maximum freedom to the interviewee to explain and describe his views. However, the sequence of questions could not be predefined without detracting from the flow and continuity of the interview. It was necessary to develop a procedure by which the interviewer could cover the problem areas identified in advance, while allowing the flexibility to order the questions in whichever sequence appeared most appropriate to maintain the continuity and flow of the interview.

For this purpose a 'map' of questions was developed. The map comprised all the problems areas, divided into groups of questions related to particular areas of discussion (for example: new graduate recruitment; value of postgraduate degrees; etc.). The groups of questions were listed on a single sheet so that the interviewer could have a list of the question areas to be covered.

The way in which data of this sort is recorded is clearly vital. If the aim of the study is to allow respondents to discuss particular problems in their own words, and analytically to use these responses to build up repertoires of employers' responses to particular problems, then it is important to develop a system of data collection which is both sensitive enough to catch these differential interpretations and accessible to the analyst. We decided to tape-record all interviews but not to transcribe fully all interviews. A procedure was developed for reconstructing the interview for analysis in a manner accessible to the analyst. This is described in the full report.

Two forms of schedules of problem areas were developed, one for the managing director interview and one for the personnel director interview. In each of these 'problem series' the predefined problem areas to be covered during the interview were laid out on a separate page, with the problem areas numbered from (1) to (n). For both 'problem series' there was also one sheet which contained all the predefined problems for the appropriate problem series (a problem 'map') together with the page and problem numbers. The problem areas for the personnel directors schedule follow:

INTERVIEW CHECKLIST
1 About how many (first degree) graduates did your firm recruit this year?
2 How many were recruited last year? (Include other years if mentioned.)
3 For what kinds of jobs does your firm recruit graduates?
   Probe: Arts/social sciences, sciences, technical?
        Proportions of each?
4 Can you tell me a little about how recruiting is carried out here?
   Probe: Who is responsible for new graduate recruitment?
        Who is responsible for graduates from other firms?
        Style of recruiting: centralized/decentralized?
        How about recruitment of jobs that are occasionally filled by graduates?

If applicable
5 Could you talk a bit about the extent to which you concentrate your recruitment on different areas of the country?
   Probe: How far do you expect your graduate recruits to be geographically mobile?
6 To what extent do the international branches of your company influence your policy, especially with reference to graduate recruitment?
   Probe: Are graduates able to work outside the UK with other sections of the firm?
        Are new graduates recruited specifically for work abroad?

7 Have there been any significant changes in recruitment practices in response to the economic downturn?
  Probe: Changes in numbers hired?
          Changes in recruiting practices?

7a There has been a lot of talk and writing in recent years about shortages of qualified manpower. Could you say a word about whether this has been a problem in your firm and how it has?
  Probe: Meaning of shortages and examples?
          ('Capable', 'experienced' manpower.)
  Dimensions to probe:
          Positions not filled vs had to take less qualified recruits.
          Not enough top graduates.
          Not enough of a speciality.
          Training inappropriate.
          Retention: want to leave the north; leave too quickly after coming on with us.

8 Which methods/channels of recruitment do you use? Use most often? Are there any of these you never use?
          Agencies
          Careers Service
          Send Literature
          Conduct Milk-round
          CSU Vacancy List
          Local Newspaper
          National Newspaper
          Personal Contacts
          Commercial Directories
          (DOH, GO, GET)
          Direct Applications
          Other (specify)

If not covered

9 What about direct applications?
  Probe: Do you ever take people's direct applications?
          How do you evaluate direct applications?
          Examples of recent recruits?

10 Do you have personal contacts with careers advisers in institutions of higher education?
  Probe: Which institutions specifically?

11 What about other academic contacts?
  Probe: Which institutions/departments specifically?

12 Is there a particular group of institutions you always contact for recruitment?
  Where appropriate: Which institutions do you visit on your milk-round?

13 Could you generalize about the institutions you prefer to recruit from?
          Mostly polytechnics?
          Mostly universities?
          Mostly colleges?

14 Do you take sandwich students on placement? For what jobs?

15 Does your firm/organization sponsor students?
  Probe: Numbers sponsored?
        Which courses?
        Changes in sponsorship programmes in recent years?
        Why sponsor?
16 For what proportion of jobs do you take only what might be called specialists?
  (Examples — only recruit for a textile chemistry job those trained in textile chemistry, or only electrical engineers for certain computing jobs.)
  Probe: It has been suggested that there is a dual market for graduates: technical specialist manpower versus non-specialist future managers. Comment?
  Probe: Value of degrees such as business in polys as compared with, for example, history at Oxford in training future managers?
17 Generally, in recruiting for jobs in your firm/organization, what is the value of the degree perceived to be?
  Probe: (For example) Degree represents what candidate has learned — validation of knowledge/training?
        Maturation over the three years?
        Useful system of pre-selecting good potential recruits for the firm?
        What skills/attitudes to you expect higher education to give graduates?
18 With respect to this issue (value of the degree) would you contrast technical/scientific jobs with your non-technical recruitment? Do you look at the value of the degree somewhat differently for the two types of graduates?
19 It has been suggested that degrees differ in value in the labour market — sometimes this is due to the status of the institution giving the degree, sometimes because a particular course is thought to be good. Could you comment on this, keeping in mind your firm's recruiting practices?

If not covered fully in Questions 10, 11, 12 and 13

20 Which ones?
  For which jobs?
  Probe: Why particular institutions/courses? Keep in mind Question 17.
21 Do you recruit from the polytechnics? Which ones? For which jobs?
  Probe: Why particular institutions/courses? Keep in mind Question 17.
        What special jobs do polytechnics do?
22 Do you recruit from the colleges of higher education? Which ones? For which jobs?
23 If candidates from a university and from a polytechnic applied for the same job, would one have an advantage over the other, other things being equal?
  Probe: For differences in perception of work done at university as compared to polytechnics?
        What about management jobs?
        Scientific jobs?
        Technical jobs?

24 We would like to ask you a few specific questions about recruitment. Could we take as an example the last two (first degree) graduates you have recruited (or two graduates you have recruited recently)? How were they recruited: for example, milk-round, direct application?
   Probe: Is that usual?
25 Which institutions were they from?
   Probe: Are these institutions you usually visit?
          Are they institutions from which you frequently recruit?
26 Which courses/degree programmes were they doing?
   Probe: Have you had much experience with these courses?
          Evaluate generally.
27 What factors – apart from educational background – do you take into account in selecting recruits for these particular positions: for example, personality, extra-curricular activities at university, experience?
   (Would you provide us with your evaluation form used in interviewing?)
28 Why did you recruit graduates for these positions?
   Probe: What about non-degree technical training or in-house training?
          What are the 'added values' that a graduate brings to these jobs?

Where appropriate

29 Do you find differences between the work done in the polytechnics and the universities in training:
          .... job mentioned for person 1?
          .... job mentioned for person 2?
   (Or, where appropriate: do you find differences in the work done in different universities, etc.?)
30 At what level of education or career stage do you prefer to take graduates – straight out of higher education or after they have had some experience?
   Probe: In science/technology?
          In arts/social sciences?
31 What about graduates with work experience – do you recruit any of these?
   Probe: How does the firm see itself on this issue – 'poachers', 'training ground'?
          To what jobs? Same as new graduates or different?
32 How do you generally recruit graduates with experience? Here we are primarily interested in graduates with experience who are under 30.
   Probe: From which companies?
33 How do you evaluate these graduates? To what degree and how do you evaluate the academic experience of graduates coming from other firms?
34 What graduates do they bring to the firm?
35 What value do you place on new recruits having a higher degree – a Masters degree or PhD?
   Probe: Do you discriminate against those with a higher degree?
          In science/technology?
          In arts/social sciences?
36 For what jobs do you recruit those with higher degrees? Why people with higher degrees for these jobs?

37 Some employers have said that in the short run those with higher degrees may not be very useful on some jobs — over-qualified, perhaps? — but that their training makes them adaptable in the long run. What is your experience?

38 Do you expect to continue the training of the graduates you recruit — or in some cases to retrain them? Could you give examples?

   Probe: In each example: Is this the sort of training you might expect the institutions that educate your .... to be doing?

   New graduates as well as graduates with work experience?

39 Are there any categories of employment for which graduates are not systematically recruited but which nevertheless attract some graduate applicants: for example, secretaries, technicians? How are they recruited?

40 Why might graduates be chosen (be preferred) for these jobs?

41 Do you find that when graduates are hired for typically non-graduate jobs that the definition of the job changes: for example, the job becomes upgraded?

42 Are there any problems in hiring graduates for these jobs?

43 Do you recruit non-graduates for any of the major job categories for which you generally recruit graduates?

   Probe: Especially for technical jobs?

44 How are they usually recruited: for example, internally or from outside?

45 What special qualities do non-graduates bring to these jobs?

46 How do these perform when compared to graduates? Are there differences in their attitudes to work?

47 I'd like to take the questioning in a slightly different direction now — but refer back to some questions we have already talked out. Your firm recruits a fair number of .... (job category to be decided with Brunel team). Do you try to recruit new graduates for these jobs?

   Probe: Do you recruit only graduates for these jobs?

48 Why graduates for these jobs?

   Probe: Value of degree?

           (Where appropriate)

           What about those with some technical training or experience but without a degree?

49 Which degree disciplines do you usually recruit these .... from?

If not covered

50 Could you tell me a bit about why you prefer these disciplines (or why that sort of person)?

51 If you are not able to recruit enough new graduates in these disciplines, which other disciplines would you recruit from?

   Or

   If you aren't able to get someone specifically trained in this area from what associated fields do you recruit?

52 What is your preferred method/channel of recruiting for this job?

53 From which higher education institutions do you recruit for this job?

   Probe: Polytechnics, universities, colleges?

           Why these institutions?

           Which type of institutions and which particular institutions do you prefer?

54 Do you find differences between the work done in the polytechnics and universities in training..........?

55 If you could choose three courses and three institutions to recruit your .... from, what would they be? Why?
Probe: Curriculum, personal contacts, past successes, etc.?

56 Do you recruit from the colleges of higher education?

57 Can you give examples of skills that your firm would have liked graduates, generally, to have that you felt they lacked?
In so far as graduates are deficient in specific skills, what sort of skills are these?
>Arts graduates?
>Maths/science graduates?

58 What proportion of the jobs you recruit for need a fairly high level of numeracy?

59 It has been suggested that many graduates lack confidence in their ability to use figures and some of them are positively afraid of numbers. Do you have examples of this in your firm?

60 How do you evaluate numeracy in your firm?

61 Given the increasing number of applicants for most jobs, do your recruiters sometimes feel themselves in a position where they need to use numeracy as an indication of diligence or hard work? Could you comment on this?

62 In your view, what is the most serious recruiting problem your firm currently has? Has had in the past few years?
Probe: Shortages?
>Evaluation of higher education system with respect to problems mentioned.

63 Careers advisers have a role to play in the transition between education and work − could you suggest ways in which their job might be done better or how it could be more useful to you?

64 What general advice would you give a secondary school student about his or her higher education − advice about choice of course and institution to attend?
Probe: Specifically?
>Why?

65 In a recent letter in *The Times*, a leading writer on manpower problems argued that the organization of secondary schooling around examinations may lead students to lose their curiosity and interest in using their minds. It was further argued that employers may not be interested in identifying curiosity or eagerness to master new skills and that this may affect the state of British industry. Could you comment on this?

Notes and References

CHAPTER 1

1 A two-year research project commissioned by the Department of Education and Science and directed by Professor Maurice Kogan, Sir Norman Lindop and Dr Harold Silver. It had three main components: a survey of employers, a survey of final-year undergraduates, and a study of three institutions: a college of higher education, a polytechnic, and a university. In addition, a survey of careers advisors was carried out.

One part of the policy brief, in particular, emphasized some of the policy preoccupations which led to funding the research:

> It has often been said that the higher education system should seek to meet 'the country's needs'. If, as seems likely, this will be heard with increasing frequency, it is important to take steps now to give the formula some definition and focus so that it can properly inform the necessary policy analysis and formulation. In this context the 'country's needs' are often equated with the 'country's economic needs' and even 'the employers' needs' for highly qualified manpower. Certainly it seems likely that employers' attitudes towards and expectations of the education system as a whole are going to be increasingly influential, and this makes it essential that those in higher education, both students and providers, should be as clear as possible in their perceptions and expectations. Similarly, it is important to weight these 'external' expectations alongside those of the students and providers themselves. It is the Department's belief that a better understanding of the expectations which society and different elements of society hold of higher education will allow these to be more precisely articulated than hitherto and will thus promote a more informed debate on what, as a nation, we can legitimately expect of higher education and on how those expectations might best be fulfilled.

2 Fulton, O., Gordon, A., and Williams, G. (1980) Higher education and manpower planning: A comparison of planned and market economies *Education Policy Bulletin* 8 (1) Spring.
3 Catto, G., Goodchild, A., and Hughes, P. (1981) *Higher Education and the Employment of Graduates* Research Paper No. 19, Department of Employment.

4   Select Committee on Education, Science and Arts (1980) *The Funding and Organization of Higher Education* HMSO.
5   Tarsh, J. (1980) The labour market for new graduates *Employment Gazette*
6   Silver, H. and Silver, P. (1981) *Expectations of Higher Education: Some Historical Pointers* (mimeo) Brunel University
7   Reid, E. (1980) Young people and employment (1); Employers use of educational qualifications *Education Policy Bulletin* 8 (1) Spring.
8   Institute of Personnel Management (1980) *Selecting Managers; How British Industry Recruits* Information Report No. 34, IPM.
9   Dainton, F.S. (Chairman) (1965 and 1966) *The Enquiry into the Flow of Candidates in Science and Technology into Higher Education* Cmnd 2893 (Interim) and Cmnd 3541 (Final), HMSO.
10 Finniston, M. (Chairman) (1980) *Engineering Our Future, Report of the Committee of Inquiry into the Engineering Profession* Cmnd 7794, HMSO.
11 Ormrod, J. (Chairman) (1971) *Report of the Committee on Legal Education* Cmnd 4595, HMSO.
12 Barlow, A. (Chairman) (1946) *Scientific Manpower: Report of the Committee* Cmnd 6824, HMSO.
13 Zuckerman, S. (Chairman) (1956) *Scientific and Engineering Manpower in Britain* Joint publication of the Ministry of Labour and National Service and the Lord President of the Council (36-227), HMSO.
14 Zuckerman, S. (Chairman) (1959) *Scientific and Engineering Manpower in Great Britain* Cmnd 902, HMSO.
15 Zuckerman, S. (Chairman) (1962) *Scientific and Technological Manpower in Great Britain* Cmnd 2146, HMSO.
16 Swann, M. (Chairman) (1968) *The Flow of Scientists, Engineers and Technologists* Cmnd 3760, HMSO.
17 Dainton (1965 and 1966) *op.cit.*
18 The Royal Institute of Chemistry (1970) *The Relationship Between University Courses in Chemistry and the Needs of Industry*
19 Catto, Goodchild and Hughes (1981) *op.cit.*
20 Mace, J. (1975) The shortage of engineers *Higher Education Review* 10 (2).
21 Bulmer, M. (1979) Concepts in the analysis of qualitative data *Sociological Review* 27 (4).
22 Bulmer (1979) *op.cit.*
23 Stenhouse, L. (1979) The problem of standards in illuminative research *Scottish Educational Review* 11 January
24 Stenhouse, L. (1978) Case study and case records: Towards a contemporary history of education *British Educational Research Journal* 4(2).
25 See Stenhouse, L. et al. (1982) *Teaching About Race Relations* Routledge & Kegan Paul.
26 Roizen, J. and Jepson, M. (1984) *Expectations of Higher Education: the Employers' Perspective* (Mimeo) Brunel University.

CHAPTER 2
1   How big is British business? *Employment Gazette* January 1978.
2   *op.cit.* Note 1 above.
3   See, for example, Universities Statistical Record (1982) *The First Destinations of University Graduates 1980-81*.
4   Harris, John (1984) *Some Views of an Ex-Employer/Recruiter* Paper 10, The

Expectations of Higher Education Project, Dept. of Government, Brunel University.

5 The 1982 DES-sponsored report, *The Provision of Sandwich Courses in Higher Education*, based primarily on a survey of placement officers, argues: 'What has actually happened in the institutional supply has outstripped industrial demand. In 1960 there were just 9,000 sandwich students.... By 1970 there were 50,000.'

6 *The Financial Times* 17 June 1982.

CHAPTER 3

1 Withey, S.B. et al. (1971) *A Degree and What Else: Correlates and Consequences of a College Education* New York: McGraw Hill.

CHAPTER 4

1 Cited in Robinson, E. (1968) *The New Polytechnics* Penguin.
2 Robinson (1968) *op.cit.*
3 Universities Statistical Record (1980) *The First Destinations of University Graduates 1978-79*; Polytechnic Careers Advisors Statistics Working Party (1980) *The First Destinations of Polytechnic Graduates Qualifying in 1980.*
4 Becher, T. and Kogan, M. (1980) *Process and Structure in Higher Education* Heinemann.
5 Silver and Silver (1981) *op.cit.* Note 6 in Chapter 1 above.
6 Universities Statistical Record (1980) *op.cit.*
7 Universities Statistical Record (1980) *The First Destinations of University and Polytechnic Graduates 1980.*
8 Universities Statistical Record (1980) *op.cit.* Notes 3 and 7 above.
9 Gordon, Alan (1983) Attitudes of employers to the recruitment of graduates *Educational Studies* 9 (1).
10 Kirkland, J. and Jepson, M. (1984) *The Role of the Careers Advisor* Paper 8, The Expectations of Higher Education Project, Dept. of Government, Brunel University.
11 Boys, C.J. (1984) *A Survey of Students' Attitudes* Paper 9, The Expectations of Higher Education Project, Dept. of Government, Brunel University.

CHAPTER 5

1 Williams, G. (1980) Evidence to Select Committee on Education, Science and Arts (1980) *op.cit.* Note 4 in Chapter 1 above.
2 *The Times* 25 September 1981.
3 Finniston (1980) *op.cit.* Note 10 in Chapter 1 above.
4 Sleigh et al. (1980) *The Manpower Implications of Micro-Electronics* Department of Employment.
5 *The Times op.cit.*
6 Mace, J.D. and Taylor, S.M. (1975) The demand for engineers in British industry. Some implications for manpower forecasting *British Journal of Industrial Relations* 13 (2).
7 Fulton, Gordon and Williams (1980) *op.cit.* Note 2 in Chapter 1 above.
8 Finniston (1980) *op.cit.*
9 NEDC, Quoted in Mace and Taylor (1975) *op.cit.*
10 Mace and Taylor (1975) *op.cit.*
11 Mace and Taylor (1975) *op.cit.*
12 Powell, Anthony (1951) *A Question of Upbringing* London: Heinemann.

CHAPTER 7

1 Boule, Lord (1978) Universities and Britain's future *Association of University Teachers* and *Times Higher Education Supplement*

2 *Graduates in Industry* (1981) (mimeo) Confederation of British Industries.

3 Jamieson, I. and Lightfoot, M. (1982) *Schools and Industry* Schools Council Working Paper 73, Methuen.

4 Williamson, P. (1981) *Early Careers of 1970 Graduates* Research Paper No. 26, Department of Employment.

5 Jamieson and Lightfoot (1982) *op.cit.*

6 Kerr, Clark (1977) The Balkanization of labour markets. In *Labour Markets and Wage Determination* University of California Press.

7 Doeringer, P.B. and Piore, M.J. (1971) *Internal Labour Markets and Manpower Analysis* Heath.

8 Killingworth, C. (1968) *Jobs and Incomes for Negroes* Butterworth.

9 Hunter, L.C. (1981) In Lindley, R. (Ed.) *Higher Education and the Labour Market* Guildford: Society for Research into Higher Education.

10 Blaug, M., Peston, M. and Ziderman A. (1969) *The Utilization of Educated Manpower* Oliver & Boyd.

11 Blaug, Peston and Ziderman (1969) *op.cit.*

12 Hunter (1981) *op.cit.*

13 Bosworth, D. (1981) In Lindley, R. (Ed.) (1981) *op.cit.*

14 Dore, R. (1976) *The Diploma Disease* Allen & Unwin.

15 Ashton, D.N. and Maguire, M.J. (1980) The function of academic and non-academic criteria in employers' selection strategies *British Journal of Guidance and Counselling* 8 (2).

16 Halsey, A.H., Heath, A.F. and Ridge, J.M. (1980) *Origins and Destinations* Clarendon Press.

17 Fulton, Gordon and Williams (1980) *op.cit.* Note 2 in Chapter 1 above.

18 Fulton, Gordon and Williams (1980) *op.cit.* Note 2 in Chapter 1 above.

19 Pearson, R. (1983) Output after the cuts *Times Higher Education Supplement* 25 March.

20 Institute of Manpower Studies (1980) Evidence to Select Committee on Education, Science and Arts (1980) *op.cit.* Note 4 in Chapter 1 above.

21 Committee of Vice-Chancellors and Principals (1980) Evidence to Select Committee on Education, Science and Arts (1980) *op.cit.* Note 4 in Chapter 1 above.

The Society for Research into Higher Education

The Society for Research into Higher Education exists to encourage and co-ordinate research and development in all aspects of higher education. It thus draws to public attention both the need for research and development and the needs of the research community. Its income is derived from subscriptions, and from research or other specific grants. It is wholly independent. Its corporate members are universities, polytechnics, institutes of higher education, research institutions and professional and governmental bodies. Its individual members are teachers and researchers, administrators and students. Members are found in all parts of the world and the Society regards its international work as amongst its most important activities.

The Society discusses and comments on policy, organizes conferences and sponsors research. Under the imprint SRHE & NFER-NELSON it is a specialist publisher of research, having over 30 titles in print. It also publishes Studies in Higher Education *(three times a year),* Higher Education Abstracts *(three times a year),* International Newsletter *(twice a year), a* Bulletin *(six times a year), and jointly with the Committee for Research into Teacher Education (CRITE)* Evaluation Newsletter *(twice a year).*

The Society's committees, study groups and local branches are run by members, with help from a small secretariat, and aim to provide a forum for discussion. Some of the groups, at present the Teacher Education Study Group and the Staff Development Group, have their own subscriptions and organization, as do some Regional Branches. The Governing Council, elected by members, comments on current issues and discusses policies with leading figures in politics and education. The Society organizes seminars on current research for officials of the DES and other ministries, and is in touch with bodies in Britain such as the CNAA, NAB, CVCP, UGC and the British Council; and with sister-bodies overseas. Its current research projects include one on the relationship between entry qualifications and degree results, directed by Prof. W.D. Furneaux (Brunel) and one on 'Questions of Quality' directed by Prof. G.C. Moodie (York).

The Society's annual conferences take up central themes, viz. 'Education for the Professions' (1984, with the help and support of DTI, UNESCO and many professional bodies), 'Continuing Education' (1985, organized in collaboration with Goldsmiths' College, the Open University and the University of Surrey, with advice from the DES and the CBI), 'Standards and criteria in HE' (1986). Joint conferences are held, viz. 'Cognitive Processes' (1985, with the Cognitive Psychology Section of the BPS), on the DES 'Green Paper' (1985, with The Times Higher Education Supplement*) and on 'Information Technology' (1986, with the Council for Educational Technology). For some of the Society's conferences, special studies are commissioned in advance, as 'Precedings'.*

Members receive free of charge the Society's Abstracts, *annual conference proceedings (or 'Precedings'), and* Bulletin *and* International Newsletter, *and may buy SRHE & NFER-NELSON books at booksellers' discount. Corporate members receive the Society's journal* Studies in Higher Education *free, individuals at a heavy discount. They may also obtain* Evaluation Newsletter *and certain other journals at discount, including the NFER* Register of Educational Research.

Further information may be obtained from the Society for Research into Higher Education, At the University, Guildford GU2 5XH, UK.